Studio Thinking 3

The Real Benefits of Visual Arts Education

Kimberly M. Sheridan, Shirley Veenema,
Ellen Winner, and Lois Hetland

Foreword to the Third Edition by Mario R. Rossero
Foreword to the First Edition by David N. Perkins

TEACHERS COLLEGE PRESS

TEACHERS COLLEGE | COLUMBIA UNIVERSITY
NEW YORK AND LONDON

Published by Teachers College Press,® 1234 Amsterdam Avenue, New York, NY 10027

Cover images: Rachel Barglow (top left and bottom right), Danielle Devellis (top right), Rosemary Raughley (bottom left), and Hiliana Aquilo (Nikes).

Library of Congress Cataloging-in-Publication Data
Names: Sheridan, Kimberly M., author. | Veenema, Shirley A. author. | Winner, Ellen, author. | Hetland, Lois, 1953– author.
Title: Studio thinking 3 : the real benefits of visual arts education / Kimberly M. Sheridan, Shirley Veenema, Ellen Winner, and Lois Hetland.
Other titles: Studio thinking three
Description: New York : Teachers College Press, 2023. | Includes bibliographical references and index.
Identifiers: LCCN 2022011134 (print) | LCCN 2022011135 (ebook) | ISBN 9780807766514 (hardcover) | ISBN 9780807766507 (paperback) | ISBN 9780807780800 (ebook)
Subjects: LCSH: Art—Study and teaching—United States. | Team learning approach in education—United States.
Classification: LCC N353 .S78 2023 (print) | LCC N353 (ebook) | DDC 707.1—dc23/eng/20220418
LC record available at https://lccn.loc.gov/2022011134
LC ebook record available at https://lccn.loc.gov/2022011135

ISBN 978-0-8077-6650-7 (paper)
ISBN 978-0-8077-6651-4 (hardcover)
ISBN 978-0-8077-8080-0 (ebook)

Printed on acid-free paper
Manufactured in the United States of America

For Elliot Eisner and Mihalyi Csikszentmihalyi, who blazed the trail, and for Maestro Mateo Hazelwood, who championed the translation of Studio Thinking to music education.

Contents

**PART II. INTRODUCING THE STUDIO HABITS OF MIND:
A DISPOSITIONAL VIEW OF *WHAT* THE ARTS TEACH**

PART III: INTEGRATING STUDIO STRUCTURES OF LEARNING WITH THE STUDIO HABITS OF MIND

Foreword to the Third Edition

Reading this third edition of *Studio Thinking*, I am reminded of the power behind the original concepts, and I am eager to see the impact of the updates and additions. Considering these ideas at this current moment in time, 2 years into the ups and downs of the COVID-19 pandemic, they strike me as more essential than ever. I am excited about a number of the core ideas that resonate for the field of visual arts, design, and media arts education—legitimizing and making arts teaching and learning visible; uplifting student voice, agency, and autonomy; and further describing and making the case for visual arts education.

Speaking from the classroom outward, I am reminded of a unit that emerged in my middle school classroom toward the latter half of my teaching career, circa 1999. I borrowed artwork from four uniquely different artists in our Pittsburgh-area community for my students to dissect in our classroom. As a classroom community we analyzed each work, looking for themes, patterns, messages, and techniques. A collection of small ceramic vessels yielded parameters for one of our projects for the quarter: how students could create a family of interconnected clay objects that were united through common texture, color, and shape. From these constraints, students worked in small groups to produce their own ceramic families with the most interesting narratives behind their work. I mention this story because, although I was able to construct and design this unit successfully, I was still struggling to develop the language to communicate most effectively *how* and *what* students were learning in my classroom externally to administrators, peers, and students' families.

My students' ability to envision and express the concepts derived from a classroom critique of a living contemporary artist's work was not something invisible and mysterious. Like many of the accounts included in this edition, there was a rigorous process that I employed to aid my students in thinking like an artist and employing artistic techniques and processes to achieve an answer, a response, to the collective prompt that we developed. As art educators, we require the ability to name the components of our practice, in order to make arts teaching and learning visible to our students, but also visible to key decision-makers, such as administrators conducting observations, peers struggling to see another approach, and families who want to be welcomed into their students' creative experiences.

Always, but especially at a time like the present in 2022, creating space for student voice, agency, and autonomy is critical in order to best prepare students for future success as contributing citizens of the world. As art educators we take steps every day to support student ownership of learning, and this begins with establishing a conducive environment. As our authors note, teachers create a studio culture in classrooms by designing the social climate there. By forging these creatively safe spaces for experimentation and critique, teachers also provide a space for students' social–emotional learning and expression. The art room/studio has historically been known for a cacophony of activity, but how are we deconstructing that "noise" to show what's truly taking place? Learners are guided and encouraged through the Studio Structures as well as throughout the Habits, with educators' demo-lectures, individual coaching, and that oh-so-valuable instinct to question and push, the Stretch and Exploration.

You'll often hear me championing the notion that leadership skills are intrinsically embedded within the role of the art educator and artist–teacher: resource navigation, expert time management, collaboration, problem-solving, and community convening. I would also argue that leadership skills are intrinsically embedded in the role of student artist: the planning, weighing of choices, prioritizing of media, defense of ideas, and rallying of collaborators. These attributes grow out of and from the Studio Habits and processes that learners glean from a robust art education experience that tackles challenging problems and big questions.

The *Boston Globe* piece reprinted in the book is a healthy reminder of our collective duty to lock arms and continually make the case for the value of art education. First and foremost, we must define the impact and effect of a visual arts, design, and media arts education through arts-based outcomes. Rather than accepting the square peg/round hole of defining arts learning outcomes solely through art's impact on other subjects, more than a century of scholarly work makes our field well-prepared to articulate the arts-based benefits of art education, and the Studio Habits give us language, a framework, and a voice to this end. We can see these arts-based outcomes emerge when we look at the practitioners' work within the text.

With the addition of the chapter about assessment, we see real-life examples of utilizing the Habits as a means for authentic measurement of arts learning that includes the student's voice as well. The lessons learned in the art room/studio have broader application and reach: *How do I successfully work in a resource-constrained environment? How do I effectively communicate a difficult idea to an audience? How do I create plans that have defined boundaries, yet allow for creativity/flexibility?* By Understanding Art Worlds, students can amplify their own voices and assess the impact as well. We have such a rich artistic history, and whether we consider the impact of Picasso's *Guernica* or Hank Willis Thomas's For Freedoms projects, we know that our artistic tools can create work that is in service to society.

As we are all on this journey of continual growth and development, I am happy to see this work evolve and grow. I believe that by employing the ideas outlined herein, we can also ensure that the art room/studio and our practice is designed for inclusivity and equity for our learners and communities. It's a true honor to welcome folks into this new edition, and Kimberly, Shirley, Ellen, and Lois have my utmost gratitude for their contributions to the field. I also would like to acknowledge the many practitioners whose work is the backbone behind these ideas, and who do the heroic and necessary work of championing art education every day.

Mario R. Rossero
Executive Director
National Art Education Association (NAEA)

Foreword to the First Edition

You do not have to read very far into *Studio Thinking* to feel that, like Lewis Carroll's Alice, you have stepped through the looking glass into a fantasy world where the colors are brighter, the scenes richer, and the adventure altogether more engaging than what you recall about school. You are likely to find rather drab not only many of your memories of studying mathematics or history, but also many of your school arts experiences. Certainly I do. It's not that my arts teachers lacked the knack; I actually think they were rather good. It's just that not enough time was staked out for the patterns of learning we read about here.

So, having stepped through the looking glass into this strange world of studio learning, how do we make sense of it all? Here the pathways branch. Maybe the visual arts are a special sort of undertaking, some might say. Or maybe these are very special teachers and very special students. Or maybe this is the sort of messing around we can afford when we're not dealing with high-stakes core subject matters.

But what if none of these answers leads anywhere worthwhile? What if, far from a fantasy world, studio learning turns out to be much more realistic regarding the way learning really works than most typical classroom settings?

Toward vetting these possibilities, let's get a little clearer about that studio world on the other side of the looking glass. Exactly what is so very exotic about it, compared to typical patterns of educational practice? My longtime colleagues Lois Hetland, Ellen Winner, Shirley Veenema, and Kim Sheridan do a fine job of portraying the world they have studied, the rhythm and the drama and sometimes the comedy of the studio classroom. For one thing, as the name "studio thinking" suggests, students spend most of their time developing works of art, instead of reading books or listening to ideas from their arts instructors or doing highly targeted technical exercises. We discover that all these traditional elements have a presence, but with distinctive proportion and placement. We learn that receiving information in the form of Demonstration–Lectures is a strong part of the pattern, but information is immediately applied as the studio work proceeds. It's not just for next week or the year after, it's for today—this canvas, this pot, this sculpture. We also learn that the studio work is spiced with a surprising amount of reflection. The

studio teachers we meet are constantly circulating among the learners, prodding them to think about what they are doing and why they are doing it, as well as conducting critical reflective sessions where the group stands back and contemplates the enterprise, its significance, its progress, its shortfalls, and its lessons for the future.

This quick picture of events on the other side of the looking glass leads toward a big generalization. Most educational practice reflects what might be called an *export paradigm*. What learners do today focuses on exporting knowledge for use in a range of envisioned futures. The math in the textbook is for application somewhere, sometime, in some supermarket or on some income tax form or during possible careers in business, engineering, or science. The history acquired might someday help to make sense of an election and to cast a vote more wisely. The specific activities—problem sets for honing skills, answering questions toward understanding principles, memorizing information toward quizzes—are blatantly exercises that target much later payoffs.

What is so very odd about studio learning is its *import paradigm*. It's about using knowledge right now in a serious way for a complex and significant endeavor. Learners deploy what their instructors explain and demonstrate to produce meaningful and engaging works of art. Of course, it's not just about now, it's about later too. The world of later is well served by the kinds of projects addressed and the reflective discourse around them.

Studio learning is not the only pattern of pedagogy that attempts this import paradigm. Many teachers of the core disciplines find ways to engage learners in problem-based learning, project-based learning, case study approaches to learning, and community participation activities, to mention a few. Although such endeavors (like studio learning) can vary enormously in their quality, they display a common deep structure: Students learn for later by importing knowledge into rich undertakings now.

Back to the looking glass question: Where is the fantasy and where is the reality for learning? Well, speaking of looking glasses, it's worth remembering that the whole point of education is to function as a mirror of the future—not a flat mirror, presenting to the learner an anticipated future in all its messy, complicated, and upsetting details, but a convex mirror that renders the future in a substantially reduced and more tractable but still multidimensional form. Learning is likely to be successful to the extent that what learners do today mirrors the future. So the basic point here is pretty simple: An import paradigm in general is a better mirror of the future than an export paradigm, even though, paradoxically, the export paradigm seems to shoot for the future more directly.

Why is the import paradigm a better mirror? Turning to studio thinking specifically, studio activities are fully developed junior versions of what we would like learners to get better at and do more of later. Good studio activities capture the full motivational, technical, and creative dynamic of creating works of art as a professional artist or a serious amateur might do later in life. There are challenges of craft and of expression. There are experiments, failures, and successes. There are demands for reflection and self-discipline. Without the authors' sensitive profile, one might imagine studio work as mostly a matter of developing technical skills. Nothing of the sort. While this is part of the game, the learners' struggles with their challenges cultivate a number of studio habits of mind, for example: persistence, envisioning possibilities, expressing, observing, reflecting, and stretching beyond the immediate and familiar.

The export paradigm does not score so well as a mirror of the future. For one thing, the mirror is often broken into a hundred shards, reflecting only bits and pieces of what will come. The export paradigm suffers from what I like to call "elementitis." We teach the elements now, with the idea that they will coalesce later. We teach component skills, vocabulary, principles, theories, core examples, and when a student asks, "But what is it all for?" the answer promises that it will all come together next year, or in high school, or in college. Mind you, this is not a caution against spending some serious time on technical elements that need targeted development. We see plenty of that in studio work. It's a caution against the endless deferral of large-scale meaningful undertakings.

The export paradigm also tends to suffer from "aboutitis." The export paradigm tries to approach future complexities by talking about them rather than engaging in them. Thus, students typically learn information *about* history—often rather intricate stories about what happened and how others interpreted it—rather than engaging in historical reasoning or interpreting current events through an historical lens. The analogy in the world of art would be learning a lot about artistic creative processes without actually doing much of it. Aboutitis, like elementitis, makes education less of a mirror of the future.

There is a natural reservation about all this. However stimulating our journey through the looking glass of studio learning, perhaps like Lewis Carroll's fantasy worlds it speaks to real life only indirectly and suggestively. Perhaps bits and pieces of studio thinking and other import approaches might fruitfully come into the teaching of the core disciplines, but that's about it. Perhaps those disciplines do not for the most part accommodate so well the rich full-scale endeavors of the studio.

Such a reservation is, I fear, more a failure of ingenuity and imagination than anything else. Indeed, one does not even have to imagine. What amount to studio learning versions of study in the core disciplines already exist in thousands of classrooms, facilitated by thousands of dedicated teachers—various incarnations of strategies mentioned before, such as problem-based learning, project-based learning, case study approaches, community participation, and so on. No fantasies, these are realities today.

And it's no fantasy that, for both logical and psychological reasons, the import paradigm is a better bet. Importing knowledge into complex meaningful endeavors now, with the future in view, is a stronger model of learning than warehousing knowledge for the future. It's the Humpty Dumpty of the export model that's the fragile one. And that's not Jabberwocky! So let's step through the looking glass into *Studio Thinking* and join Lois, Ellen, Shirley, Kim, and a number of art teachers and students for a vision not only of learning in the arts but what could be learning most anywhere.

—David N. Perkins, Professor Emeritus,
Harvard Graduate School of Education

Preface to the Third Edition

It's 10:32 a.m., and your art students have just left for their next class. You race into the faculty room for coffee before your next group arrives, only to find visitors from another school who've been looking for you. They want to hear about your classes. How do you teach art? they want to know.

You try to collect your thoughts while attempting to look composed. How can you adequately describe your responsive, intense, multifaceted classroom? There are the students, of course—each one of them is different. And there's the curriculum, your current project, the schedule, and how you keep records. There are materials, how you acquire them, store them, maintain them, set up access to them—that's a conversation all by itself. Not to mention dealing with technology, the administrators ("Are you covering the standards?"), your fellow art teachers, the partner organizations, the social workers, and the school psychologist. Then there's the school principal, always wondering whether time dedicated to the arts might be better used for math or reading. There's what you do about assessment and reporting, and how you deal with teachers in other subjects, and field trips, and homework, and absences. . . .

You ask your visitors, "How much time did you say you had?"

When we began our study of rigorous teaching of visual arts at the high school level, we knew we were entering a complex landscape, and we meant to find language to help teachers and researchers describe it. We were not looking for a prescription that dictated what *should* be done and what was *best*. Rather, we wanted to map visual arts teaching in ways that would allow teachers and researchers to see that territory more clearly, to convey more easily what they knew about classrooms and teaching, to ponder alternate routes they might take, and to learn more readily from other experienced travelers. From the start, we were quite sure that visual arts teaching involves more than instruction in merely art techniques, and we sought to uncover the full spectrum of what really is taught and how that's accomplished. Our goal was to understand the kinds of thinking that teachers help students develop in visual arts classes and the supports they use to do that.

We have written this book to introduce that descriptive language and to offer practical examples of these two types of concepts—*how* teachers plan and carry out instruction, which we call the *Studio Structures* (see Part I) and *what* is taught in visual arts classes, which we call the *Studio Habits of Mind* (see Part II). The many examples given of art projects are taken from the teachers who graciously invited us into their classes to observe them and their students in action and from teachers who agreed to speak with us in interviews. We provide images, quotations, and examples to ground the concepts in real classrooms within the real opportunities and limits of schools.

We have chosen not to follow the development of each art project from start to finish. Rather, we draw on parts of a project pertinent to our discussion. The projects are labeled with numbers indicating their chapter and location within a chapter, and for readers who may want to focus on the development of individual projects, we have provided cross-references throughout our discussions. In Appendix A we include a table listing all the projects referred to in the book and their locations in the chapters.

Our focus in this book is primarily on the decisions teachers make, but in several places we also show how students respond to these decisions in their work, talk, and behavior. As you read, pay attention to the many different ways teachers describe what they intend students to learn, and the many adaptations each teacher uses of the four organizational Studio Structures (see Part III). Our aim is to provide strong evidence that the real curriculum in the visual arts extends far beyond the teaching of technique and to demonstrate that such teaching engenders the development of serious thinking dispositions that are valued both within and beyond the arts.

NEW IN THE THIRD EDITION

Our third edition, *Studio Thinking 3*, capitalizes on what we have learned since publication of the first edition in 2007 and second edition in 2013. Through observations, interviews, and conversations with educators in diverse contexts, reading other researchers' uses of our framework, and reflecting on our own research and practice, we have deepened and broadened our understanding of what Studio Thinking is and how it can be used. We have made updates throughout the book that reflect this learning.

Studio Thinking 3 is expanded in the following ways:

Students as Contemporary Artists: Building Agency in the Studio (Part III, Chapter 16)

We have added a chapter discussing our recent research revisiting our original data set with a new focus on how studio teaching supports learner agency. Chapter 16 highlights how studio teachers support learners' autonomy and how these strategies work to develop learners' artistic agency, which we define as their capacity to engage in creative processes where they *find* problems, form and refine *their* ideas, and learn to use techniques, tools, and materials to create increasingly self-directed artworks.

Part IV: Studio Thinking in Contemporary Practice (Chapters 17, 18, 19)

We have added a new Part IV that looks at how the Studio Thinking Framework has been used in varied contemporary contexts.

In Chapter 17, *Artist-Teachers*, we look at how artistic practices and teaching practices intertwine and how the Studio Thinking Framework can nurture the relationship between them. We focus on the stories of seven artist-teachers working in different geographical and educational contexts and how they have used the Studio Thinking Framework in their artistic and teaching practices.

In Chapter 18, *Assessment is a Conversation*, we address the topic of assessment in the arts. We draw on the practices of four teachers who have thought deeply about assessment and consider how the Studio Thinking Framework informs assessment in the arts.

In Chapter 19, *Studio Thinking*, we discuss how the Studio Thinking Framework has informed teaching and research in visual arts, theater, dance, music, arts integration, STEAM, and other contexts. We consider how these uses inform our thinking about the Studio Thinking Framework and envision its continuing use. We hope to hear from anyone who is using the framework. Please write to us at sheridan.kim@gmail.com.

Acknowledgments

First and importantly, we thank John Bryant and Patricia Bauman of the Bauman Family Foundation for their generous support of our work in arts education over the years. Indeed, without their support of Ellen Winner's and Lois Hetland's analyses of the relationship between arts education and academic performance, the Studio Thinking Project would not have been carried out.

The original research for Studio Thinking, begun over two decades ago, was funded by the J. Paul Getty Trust, and we gratefully acknowledge the administration at that time: Barry Munitz, Jack Meyers, Sir Kenneth Robinson, and Deborah Marrow. Drs. Linda Nathan and Stephanie Perrin welcomed us into their schools in the year 2000. The original research was carried out in collaboration with five inspiring visual arts teachers in 2001–2003: Beth Balliro, Kathleen Marsh, Guy Michel Telemaque, Jason Green, and Jim Woodside. Harvard Project Zero sponsored the work, David Perkins wrote the foreword for the first edition, and Patricia Palmer helped with filming, interviewing, coding, data analysis, and project coordination. We thank them all.

Carol Fromboluti at the U.S. Department of Education funded an extension of our initial work in Alameda County, California (2003–2010). Louise Music (who wrote the foreword for the second edition) and Ann Wettrich worked closely with us in Alameda County, as did many teachers, artists, and administrators. Our gratitude goes to them all. Mónika Aldarondo worked with us on the second edition, and we thank her along with those who worked with us on this third edition: David Ardito, Kimberley D'Adamo, Danielle DeVellis, Natalia Dominguez, JoE Douillette, Todd Elkin, Diane Jaquith, Bryce Johnson, Trena Noval, and Jaimee Taborda. We also thank the students who allowed us to photograph their work and video them. It is an honor to have Mario Rossero, Executive Director of the National Art Education Association, author the foreword for our third edition.

Below we list the many educators and artists who have contributed to our thinking and/or have used the Studio Thinking Framework over the years. There are many others whose names we do not know, and we thank you all. You give the research life by using it. We are eager to hear news at any time from you. Please write to us at sheridan.kim@gmail.com.

David Alexander, Lim Kok Boon, Mark Borchelt, Candace Brooks, Ray Cagan, Sharron DeAnjolis, India Clark, Kevin Clark, Guy Claxton, Judith Contrucci, Kitty Conde, Barbara Cox, Mark Cross, John Crowe, Lucinda Daly, Matt Dealy, David Donahue, Shawna Flanigan, Cally Flox, Heather Francis, Joe Fusaro, Karol Gates, Elise Gallinot, Lynn Goldsmith, Jessica Hamlin, Evan Hastings, Matthew Hazelwood, Stephanie Heriger, Lois Hetland's colleagues and students at the Massachusetts College of Art and Design, Aline Hill-Ries, Jim JerDon, Faith Johnson, Tana Johnson, Gunta Kaza, Jaime Knight, Cleopatra Knight-Wilkins, Robert Leyen, Chris Lim, Steve Locke, Bill Lucas, Peter Lutkoski, Lynn Yau, Alison Marshall, Julia Marshall, Camilla McComb, Arzu Mistry, Geetha Narayanan, Kimberly Powell, Stephanie Riven, Renee Sandell, Kim Sheridan's colleagues and students at George Mason University, Ricco Siasoco, Marie Smith, Ellen Spencer, Mary Ann Stankiewicz, Miriam Stahl, Connie Stewart, Sara Stillman, Jennifer Stuart, Kate Thomas, Mary Jo Thompson, and Dale Zalmstra.

ONE

Making the Case for the Arts

Arts Education Is Not Just a Luxury.

Arts education has always been in a tenuous position in the United States. All too often the arts have been considered a luxury in our schools—an arena for self-expression, perhaps, but not a necessary part of education. This attitude is revealed in our fixation on mandated standardized tests, which assess arts education badly if at all.

The public's understanding of what is learned in the arts is often vague. Ask someone what students learn in art classes, and you are likely to hear that they learn how to paint, or draw, or throw a pot. That's true, but it only tells us what they *do*, not how they learn to *think*. It is like saying that students learn writing skills in writing class. Of course students learn artistic craft in arts classes. But we must ask what else they learn. Does experience in the arts change students' minds so that they can approach the world as an artist would? Students must be given the opportunity to think like artists, just as they should also be given the opportunity to approach the world mathematically, scientifically, historically, and linguistically. The arts are one way of knowing the world—as important as the other disciplines to our societal health. It is our belief that the most important product of an arts education is the development of students' *artistic minds*—the ways of thinking that guide how they engage in the complex work of artmaking.

To make the case for the value of arts education, we need to learn what the arts actually teach and what art students actually learn. In the pages that follow, we describe what powerful modes of thinking students can discover when they study the visual arts seriously. We chose the visual arts as our laboratory, but we could as well have chosen music, dance, or drama. It is our hope that others will extend this kind of study to the other art forms, and indeed some have already begun to do so (e.g., Alexander, 2010; Alexander & Cassell, 2011; Goldstein, 2021; Goldstein & Thompson, 2019; Goldstein & Young, 2019; Hogan & Winner, 2019). We present the case here that the visual arts teach students not only dispositions that are specific to the visual arts—the craft of the visual arts and an understanding of the art worlds within and outside of the classroom (Efland, 1976, 1983)—but also at least six additional dispositions that appear to us to be very general kinds of habits of mind.

The word *disposition* is one we have taken from the work of David Perkins and his colleagues (Perkins et al., 1993; Tishman et al., 1993; Tishman et al., 1995). Dispositions involve a trio of qualities—dispositions are skills, but the skills are only used when one is *alert* to opportunities and has the *inclination* to use them Our Studio Habits of Mind are dispositions that we saw being taught in studio classrooms. We believe these dispositions are central to artistic thinking and behavior.

THE FRAMEWORK OF STUDIO THINKING

In the study described in these pages, we set out to discover what excellent visual art teachers teach, how they teach, and what students learn in their classes. During the school year of 2001–2002, we looked closely at what goes on in five excellent, but very different, arts classrooms. (The five teachers we studied and the methods we used to conduct our research are described in Appendix B.) Despite the debates and the rhetoric about the importance of the arts in education, surprisingly, no other formal studies had, to our knowledge, directly examined the kinds of teaching and learning that actually occur inside visual arts classrooms. A few pioneering studies have investigated in careful detail what goes on in non-arts classrooms (e.g., Lampert's *Teaching Problems and the Problems of Teaching*, 2003; Stevenson's *The Learning Gap*, 1994; and Stigler & Hiebert's *The Teaching Gap*, 1999), and we have followed in their tradition.

Based on what we found in our initial study, we developed the framework we call *Studio Thinking*. This framework describes two aspects of studio art teaching: (1) four *Studio Structures* (how learning experiences are organized), and (2) eight *Studio Habits of Mind*.

Studio Structures for Learning

The visual art teachers we studied organized their instruction using variations on a few basic patterns of time, space, and interactions. Four of these patterns focus on learning:

Demonstration–Lecture, Students-at-Work, Critique, and Exhibition. An overview of the four learning structures is presented in Figure 1.1; they are discussed in more detail in Chapters 3, 12, 13, 14, and 15.

Studio Habits of Mind

Alongside the four Studio Structures, we also observed eight dispositions; we call them the Studio Habits of Mind and see them as the "hidden curriculum"—really the essential curriculum—in visual arts classes. We concluded that, in addition to two basic arenas of learning—teaching the craft of the visual arts (e.g., techniques, tool use, organizing and maintaining studio spaces), and teaching about the art worlds beyond the classroom (e.g., in art history, visual culture, galleries, curators, critics, collaborations, and all subject matters and modalities addressed by visual artists)—at least six other important kinds of general cognitive and attitudinal dispositions are developed in serious visual arts classes.

The dispositions that emerged from our study bear some striking similarities to those that Elliot Eisner argues the arts teach (e.g., learning to attend to relationships, flexibility, and the ability to shift direction, expression, and imagination); see Eisner's book *The Arts and the Creation of Mind* (2002). The model we present here of visual arts learning is also consistent with the National Core Arts Standards (SEADAE, 2014), with its emphasis on artistic processes and thinking.

In our study we witnessed teachers striving to instill all eight Studio Habits of Mind (or dispositions, see Figure 1.2). We observed that whenever teachers were helping students develop technical skills (part of the habit of mind we refer to as Develop Craft), they were also inculcating one or more of the other seven habits of mind. These habits of mind are dispositions that are used in many academic arenas and in daily life: the dispositions to *Observe, Envision, Reflect, Express,* Stretch and *Explore, Engage and Persist,* and *Understand Art Worlds.*

These habits of mind are important not only for the visual arts but for all the arts disciplines, as well as for many other areas of study. Similar mental habits are deployed in the serious study of dance, music, theater, science, mathematics, history, literature, and writing. For example, students must learn a great deal about tools and materials in a science lab, and this kind of learning is analogous to the art studio habit we call *Develop Craft.* The disposition to *Engage and Persist* is clearly important in any serious endeavor: Students need to learn to find problems of interest and work with them deeply over sustained periods of time. The disposition *Envision* is important in the sciences (e.g., generating hypotheses),

in history (e.g., developing historical imagination), and in mathematics (e.g., imagining how to represent space and time algorithmically). *Express* is important in any kind of writing, even in analytical nonfiction and historical narratives. *Observe*, or its corollaries, *listen* and *attend*, is required across all disciplines. The disposition to *Reflect* (becoming aware of one's decisions and working style, becoming able to assess one's work and that of others) is also important in every discipline. *Stretch and Explore* emphasizes the need to experiment and take risks, regardless of the domain of focus. *Understand Art Worlds* has its parallels in other disciplines, when students are asked to identify links between what they do as *students* in a particular domain and what *professionals* in that domain do, have done, and are doing. Good science, history, English, and mathematics teachers (as well as teachers of any other subject) propose problems to think about that are currently being grappled with by contemporary practitioners and engage their students in understanding how the work, patterns of interaction, and thinking taught in classes operate in the world beyond the classroom.

WHY A FRAME FOR STUDIO TEACHING AND LEARNING?

Making art is often intuitive. Artists typically do not faithfully execute a predetermined, explicit plan for their art; rather, they engage in creative processes that result in evolving bodies of personalized artworks. These creative processes are complex and involve many habits, routines, and modes of thinking. The same is true for artists-teachers. Teachers have a curriculum or plan that they intend to teach, but, as they engage with students, they often rely on tacit knowledge, or in other words their "gut," to respond to students' diverse ways of thinking and making art.

David Perkins has long posed "thinking frames" as tools to guide, reflect on, and sharpen our gut thought processes (Perkins, 1986; Ritchhart & Perkins, 2005). These frames help us represent ideas more clearly to ourselves and others and give insight on how and when to proceed as we find and solve complex problems in the world. Making and teaching art is a varied, complex, and evolving practice. We view the research presented in this book as providing a kind of thinking frame to reflect on these practices. Our work with artists, educators, and researchers using the Studio Thinking Framework since the publication of the first edition of this book has given us insight into the varied ways Studio Thinking can function to frame arts teaching and learning.

Figure 1.1. Four Studio Structures for Learning

Demonstration–Lecture

- Teachers (and others) deliver information about processes and products and set assignments
- Information is immediately useful to students for class work or homework
- Information is conveyed quickly and efficiently to reserve time for work and reflection
- Visual examples are frequent and sometimes extended
- Interaction occurs to varying degrees

Critique

- Central structure for discussion and reflection
- A pause to focus on observation, conversation, and reflection
- Focus on student works
- Works are completed or in progress
- Display is temporary and informal

Students-at-Work

- Students make artworks based on teachers' assignments
- Assignments specify materials, tools, and/or challenges
- Teachers observe and consult with individuals or small groups
- Teachers sometimes talk briefly to the whole class

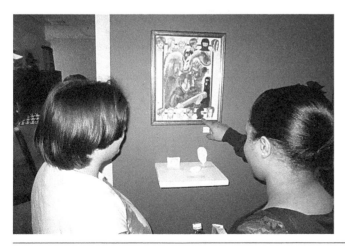

Exhibition

- Selects, organizes, and publicly displays works and/or images and related text
- Can involve any or all of the other three structures
- Takes many forms, whether physical or virtual, installed or performed, ephemeral or permanent, sanctioned or guerrilla, informal or formal, or curated gallery style
- Often occurs outside of class space and time, including in virtual spaces
- Develops in phases: Planning, Installation, Exhibition, and Aftermath

Figure 1.2. Eight Studio Habits of Mind

We present the Habits of Mind in an oval because they are non-hierarchical, so no habit comes first or last. The habits do not operate and should not be taught in a set sequence that privileges any one over others. Instead, one can begin with any habit and follow its generative energy that leads to the others as studio experiences unfold.

Develop Craft

Technique: Learning to use tools (e.g., viewfinders, brushes) and materials (e.g., charcoal, paint); learning artistic conventions (e.g., perspective, color mixing)
Studio Practice: Learning to care for tools, materials, and space

Understand Art Worlds

Domain: Learning about art history and current practice
Communities: Learning to interact as an artist with other artists (i.e., in classrooms, in local arts organizations, and across the art field) and within the broader society

Engage and Persist

Learning to embrace problems of relevance within some art world and/or of personal importance, to develop focus and other mental states conducive to working and persevering at art tasks

Stretch and Explore

Learning to reach beyond one's capacities, to explore playfully without a preconceived plan, and to embrace the opportunity to learn from mistakes and accidents

Envision

Learning to picture mentally what cannot be directly observed and to imagine possible next steps in making a piece

Reflect

Question and Explain: Learning to think and talk with others about an aspect of one's work or working process
Evaluate: Learning to judge one's own work and working process, and the work of others in relation to standards of the field

Express

Learning to create works that convey an idea, a feeling, or a personal meaning

Observe

Learning to attend to visual contexts more closely than ordinary "looking" requires, and thereby to see things that otherwise might not be seen

Frames Provide a Common Language

Artist-teachers use the Studio Thinking Framework to talk with themselves and others—students, fellow teachers, parents, administrators—about learning and teaching in art. The artist-teachers we work with regularly point to how the framework helps them see students' work and artistic processes more clearly, and how it helps students see their own learning as well. The framework's language is rooted in art—it was developed through observation of studio practices and artist-teachers' reflections on those practices—but is framed in terms of habits of mind that are a part of other disciplines and everyday life outside of art. We have seen our framework used as a language that helps provide those unfamiliar with art a greater understanding of art's practices and values. The Studio Thinking Framework helps articulate the value of arts to others.

Frames Focus Attention

Educators use the Studio Thinking Framework as a lens to help bring some aspect of the complexity of artmaking and teaching into clearer focus; for instance, teachers may focus attention on a particular habit of mind, such as Envision, as they plan an assignment or respond to students as they work. Through this selective attention, teachers make the parts of the artistic process more visible to themselves and their students.

But just as the map is not the territory, no framework reflects the full reality of the process. A Studio Habit of Mind like Envision involves complex thought processes and practices, and it is inextricably linked to Observe and other habits of mind. Though the definitions of each Studio Habit of Mind may sound simple and discrete, the processes they represent are bottomless in their depth and blurry at their edges (how do you separate out Envisioning from Observing when our mental models are always filling in what we think we are seeing?). Educators strive to use the Studio Thinking Framework to examine more closely parts of their complex, integrated practice, without reducing artistic practice to eight simple, separate parts.

Frames Guide Assessment

Studio teaching is marked by ongoing formative assessment; the Studio Habits of Mind offer a frame to organize that assessment. In Chapter 18, we discuss how teachers use the frames as a shared language for students, teachers, parents, administrators, and other stakeholders to make clear what is valued in the arts, and on what grounds students' artmaking is evaluated. The Studio Thinking Framework assesses students' thinking, not just their finished products.

Frames Inform Research

The definitions of the Studio Structures and the Studio Habits of Mind taught in art are tools to help art education researchers (including artist-teachers carrying out action research in their own classrooms) organize complex data about the contexts in which students learn. As researchers ask questions, such as how critiques affect student learning, or how observation in science and art connect, they can use the Studio Thinking Framework to help structure their analyses. In Chapter 16, we report on how we revisited our original data with a new inquiry into how studio teaching supports learner agency. In Chapter 19, we identify additional ways researchers have used the Studio Thinking Framework to study learning in varied contexts. While we discuss these examples of research, we also encourage readers to think of their artistic and teaching practice as a potential site for research and imagine ways in which Studio Thinking can help frame their inquiry.

CONCLUSION

The Studio Thinking Framework is not a curriculum. Rather, it is a framework built from the study of the pedagogical practices of studio art teachers. Our study of the enacted practices of studio teachers suggests rich tacit knowledge about student learning in art, a "hidden curriculum" which we have tried to articulate. Art education evolves, and educators have used the Studio Thinking Framework to inform their teaching practices. Thus, we have included a Part IV in this edition of the book, where we focus our attention on how others have used and transformed the framework in the process. In Chapter 17, we explore how seven different contemporary artist-teachers see connections between their artistic and teaching practices and how they use the framework to inform their teaching. In Chapter 18, we take on the topic of assessment in the arts, drawing from the practices of four artist-teachers to show how they engage with students, colleagues, and other stakeholders in conversations about how to assess the quality of students' thinking and artmaking. In our closing chapter, we take a broader view on what we have learned by watching the many ways people have used the framework in visual arts, across the art forms, and outside of studio classrooms.

It is our hope that this book will provide arts educators, advocates, and researchers with the arguments they need to lobby for strengthening the arts in our schools. Arts teachers, those who prepare arts teachers for licensure, and principals and curriculum directors can all use our findings in conversation with one another, with beginning teachers, and with teachers of other disciplines; in this way, the role of the visual arts in teaching disciplinary thinking can become clearer to all educators. Our findings can help arts teachers refine their teaching practices, help arts advocates explain arts education to decisionmakers, and help researchers explain proposed studies to funders. Non-arts teachers have much to learn from how excellent arts teachers personalize instruction, engage in just-in-time interventions as they circle the room while students work, and stimulate students' critical and self-reflective skills during regular critique sessions. Finally, the Studio Thinking Framework lays the foundation for further research on learning and teaching in the arts, including in other art forms besides the visual arts.

In September 2007, at the same time as the first edition of this book appeared, the *Boston Globe* published our thoughts about the importance of arts education. That short piece was widely circulated in the arts education community and republished in the *NAEA Newsletter* (2007) and the *Arts Education Policy Review* (Winner & Hetland, 2007). In it, we argued against a long history of instrumental arguments for the value of the arts in education. As the position of the arts was increasingly weakened in schools, arts advocates claimed that arts improve achievement in academic subjects that "really count," such as reading and mathematics. Believing that educational decision-makers wouldn't accept arguments based on the inherent value of arts learning, these advocates skirted the fundamental question of the core benefits of studying the arts. They relied on instrumental arguments without synthesizing the empirical evidence.

Winner and Hetland (2000) edited a series of meta-analytic studies published in the *Journal of Aesthetic Education* that examined the relationship between arts education and academic achievement. Seven of the 10 studies showed no significant relationship between the study of an art form and one or more academic outcomes. Some results showed an *association* between taking arts courses and doing well in school, but no *experimental* evidence that allowed the conclusion that arts education *caused* stronger academic outcomes. We concluded that the evidence did not support the claim that keeping arts in schools would improve academic achievement. More research of higher quality needed to be conducted. We also wondered why advocates held so fiercely to such claims, which did not emphasize the core values of the arts. The arts teach important modes of thinking. These habits of thinking are important whether or not they transfer to more academic areas of the curriculum. That is the argument we make in this piece, reprinted here in full from *The Boston Globe*.

ART FOR OUR SAKE: SCHOOL ARTS CLASSES MATTER MORE THAN EVER—BUT NOT FOR THE REASONS YOU THINK

Reprinted from Winner, E., & Hetland, L. (2007. September 2).
Art for Our Sake. *Boston Globe*.

Why do we teach the arts in schools?
In an educational system strapped for money and increasingly ruled by standardized tests, arts courses can seem almost a needless extravagance, and the arts are being cut back at schools across the country.

One justification for keeping the arts has now become almost a mantra for parents, arts teachers, and even politicians: arts make you smarter. The notion that arts classes improve children's scores on the SAT, the MCAS, and other tests is practically gospel among arts-advocacy groups. A Gallup poll last year found that 80% of Americans believed that learning a musical instrument would improve math and science skills.

But that claim turns out to be unfounded. It's true that students involved in the arts do better in school and on their SATs than those who are not involved. However, correlation isn't causation, and an analysis we did several years ago showed no evidence that arts training actually causes scores to rise.

There is, however, a very good reason to teach arts in schools, and it's not the one that arts supporters tend to fall back on. In a recent study of several art classes in Boston-area schools, we found that arts programs teach a specific set of thinking skills rarely addressed elsewhere in the curriculum—and that far from being irrelevant in a test-driven education system, arts education is becoming even more important as standardized tests like the MCAS exert a narrowing influence over what schools teach.

The implications are broad, not just for schools but for society. As schools cut time for the arts, they may be losing their ability to produce not just the artistic creators of the future, but innovative leaders who improve the world they inherit. And by continuing to focus on the arts' dubious links to improved test scores, arts advocates are losing their most powerful weapon: a real grasp of what arts bring to education.

It is well established that intelligence and thinking ability are far more complex than what we choose to measure on standardized tests. The high-stakes exams we use in our schools, almost exclusively focused on verbal and quantitative skills, reward children who have a knack for language and math and who can absorb and regurgitate information. They reveal little about a student's intellectual depth or desire to learn, and are poor predictors of eventual success and satisfaction in life.

As schools increasingly shape their classes to produce high test scores, many life skills not measured by tests just don't get taught. It seems plausible to imagine that art classes might help fill the gap by encouraging different kinds of thinking, but there has been remarkably little careful study of what skills and modes of thinking the arts actually teach.

To determine what happens inside arts classes, we spent an academic year studying five visual-arts classrooms in two local Boston-area schools, videotaping and photographing classes, analyzing what we saw, and interviewing teachers and their students.

What we found in our analysis should worry parents and teachers facing cutbacks in school arts programs. While students in art classes learn techniques specific to art, such as how to draw, how to mix paint, or how to center a pot, they're also taught a remarkable array of mental habits not emphasized elsewhere in school.

Such skills include visual-spatial abilities, reflection, self-criticism, and the willingness to experiment and learn from mistakes. All are important to numerous careers, but are widely ignored by today's standardized tests.

In our study, funded by the J. Paul Getty Trust, we worked with classes at the Boston Arts Academy, a public school in the Fenway, and the private Walnut Hill School for the arts in Natick. Students at each school concentrate on visual arts, music, drama, or dance, and spend at least three hours a day working on their art. Their teachers are practicing artists. We restricted ourselves to a small sample of high-quality programs to evaluate what the visual arts could achieve given adequate time and resources.

Although the approach is necessarily subjective, we tried to set the study up to be as evidence-based as possible. We videotaped classes and watched student-teacher interactions repeatedly, identifying specific habits and skills, and coding the segments to count the times each was taught. We compared our provisional analysis with those the teachers gave when we showed them clips of their classes. We also interviewed students and analyzed samples of their work.

In our analysis, we identified eight "studio habits of mind" that arts classes taught, including the development of artistic craft. Each of these stood out from testable skills taught elsewhere in school.

One of these habits was persistence: Students worked on projects over sustained periods of time and were expected to find meaningful problems and persevere through frustration. Another was expression: Students were urged to move beyond technical skill to create works rich in emotion, atmosphere, and their own personal voice or vision. A third was making clear connections between schoolwork and the world outside the classroom: Students were taught to see their projects as part of the larger art world, past and present. In one drawing class at Walnut Hill, Jim Woodside showed students how Edward Hopper captured the drama of light; at the Boston Arts Academy, students studied invitations to contemporary art exhibitions before designing their own. In this way students could see the parallels between their art and professional work.

Each of these habits clearly has a role in life and learning, but we were particularly struck by the potentially broad value of four other kinds of thinking being taught in the art classes we documented: observing, envisioning, innovating through exploration, and reflective self-evaluation. Though far more difficult to quantify on a test than reading comprehension or math computation, each has a high value as a learning tool, both in school and elsewhere in life.

The first thing we noticed was that visual arts students are trained to look, a task far more complex than one might think. Seeing is framed by expectation, and expectation often gets in the way of perceiving the world accurately. To take a simple example: When asked to draw a human face, most people will set the eyes near the top of the head. But this isn't how a face is really proportioned, as students learn: our eyes divide the head nearly at the center line. If asked to draw a whole person, people tend to draw the hands much smaller than the face—again an inaccurate perception. The power of our expectations explains why beginners draw eyes too high and hands too small. Observational drawing requires breaking away from stereotypes and seeing accurately and directly.

We saw students pushed to notice what they might not have seen before. For instance, in Guy Michel Telemaque's first design class of the term at the Boston Arts Academy, 9th-graders practice looking with one eye through a cardboard frame called a viewfinder. "Forget that you're looking at somebody's arm or a table," Telemaque tells his students. "Just think about the shapes, the colors, the lines, and the textures." Over and over we listened to teachers telling their students to look more closely at the model and see it in terms of its essential geometry.

Seeing clearly by looking past one's preconceptions is central to a variety of professions, from medicine to law. Naturalists must be able to tell one species from another; climatologists need to see atmospheric patterns in data as well as in clouds. Writers need keen observational skills too, as do doctors.

Another pattern of thought we saw being cultivated in art classes is envisioning—forming mental images internally and using them to guide actions and solve problems. "How much white space will you be leaving in your self-portrait?" asked Kathleen Marsh at the Boston Arts Academy. "How many other kinds of orange can you imagine?" asked Beth Balliro, also at the Boston Arts Academy, as she nudged her student to move beyond one shade. We noticed art teachers giving students a great deal of practice in this area: What would that look like if you got rid of this form, changed that line, or altered the background? All were questions we heard repeatedly, prompting students to imagine what was not there.

Like observing, envisioning is a skill with payoffs far beyond the art world. Einstein said that he thought in images. The historian has to imagine events and motivations from the past, the novelist an entire setting. Chemists need to envision molecular structures and rotate them. The inventor—the envisioner par excellence—must dream up ideas to be turned into real solutions. Envisioning is important in everyday life as well, whether for remembering faces as they change over time, or for finding our way around a new city, or for assembling children's toys. Visualization is recognized as important in other school subjects: The National Council of Teachers of Mathematics and the National Science Education Standards both see it as essential to problem-solving, but art classes are where this skill is most directly and intensively taught.

We also found innovation to be a central skill in art classes. Art classes place a high value on breaking the mold. Teachers encourage students to innovate through exploration—to experiment, take risks, and just muck around and see what can be learned. In ceramics, for example, capitalizing on error is a major consideration, says Balliro at the Boston Arts Academy. To a student struggling to stick clay together, she says, "There are specific ways to do it, but I want you guys to play around in this first project. Just go with that and see what happens and maybe you'll learn a new technique." Teachers in our study told students not to worry about mistakes, but instead to let mistakes lead to unexpected discoveries.

Finally, many people don't think of art class as a place where reflection is central, but instead as a place where students take a break from thinking. But artmaking is nonverbal thinking, and verbal thinking (often public and spoken) is a focal activity of arts classes. We repeatedly saw art teachers push their students to engage in reflective self-evaluation. They were asked to step back, analyze, judge, and sometimes reconceive their projects entirely.

During class critiques, and one-to-one as students worked, teachers asked students to reflect: Is that working? Is this what I intended to do? Can I make this better? What's next? At Walnut Hill School, Jason Green questioned individual students almost relentlessly as they began a new clay sculpture: "What about this form? Do you want to make the whole thing? Which part of it?" In group critiques, students also learned to evaluate the work of their peers. Making such judgments "in the absence of rule" is a highly sophisticated mental endeavor, says Elliot Eisner, a noted art-education specialist at Stanford University.

Though we both have a long history in arts education, we were startled to find such systematic emphasis on thinking and perception in the art classes we studied. In contrast to the reputation of the arts as mainly about expressive craft, we found that teachers talked about decisions, choices, and understanding far more than they talked about feelings.

By unveiling a powerful thinking culture in the art room, our study suggests ways that we can move beyond the debate over the value of arts, and start using the arts to restore balance and depth to an education system increasingly skewed toward readily testable skills and information.

While arts teachers rightly resist making their classes like "academic" classes, teachers of academic subjects might well benefit from making their classes more like arts classes. Math students, for instance, could post their in-process solutions regularly and discuss them together. If students worked on long-term projects using primary sources in history class, they would learn to work like real historians and their teachers could offer personalized and "just in time" guidance.

Despite the pressures to prepare students for high-stakes tests, some teachers and schools continue to use methods similar to those in the art studio. Ron Berger, a former 5th-grade classroom teacher in a public school in Shutesbury, Mass., provides an inspiring example. He adopted an arts-like approach to all subjects, including math, language arts, science, and social studies. His students engage in long-term investigations rather than one-shot assignments or memorization. Their work is continually assessed publicly in critiques so students develop the ability to reflect and improve. Projects are "real work," not "school work"—work that is original and makes a contribution to knowledge.

For example, students investigated the purity of drinking water in their town wells, working in collaboration with a local college and learning how to analyze the water in a college lab. No one in the town knew whether the well waters were safe, and the students discovered and reported that they were. Deborah Meier, a leading American school reformer and founding principal of the Mission Hill School in Boston, praises Berger's teaching. She worries that "Top-down mandates may actually hinder this kind of culture of high standards."

We don't need the arts in our schools to raise mathematical and verbal skills—we already target these in math and language arts. We need the arts because, in addition to introducing students to aesthetic appreciation, they teach other modes of thinking we value.

For students living in a rapidly changing world, the arts teach vital modes of seeing, imagining, inventing, and thinking. If our primary demand of students is that they recall established facts, the children we educate today will find themselves ill-equipped to deal with problems like global warming, terrorism, and pandemics.

Those who have learned the lessons of the arts, however—how to see new patterns, how to learn from mistakes, and how to envision solutions—are the ones likely to come up with the novel answers needed most for the future.

Part I

STUDIO CLASSROOMS:
THE *HOW* OF STUDIO TEACHING

Walk into a studio art class, and you may feel you have left school. The students look relaxed; sometimes they sit on the floor or music plays softly. After materials are set up, students dig in, not concerned about getting clay on their hands or paint on their jeans. You see the teacher introducing concepts and demonstrating, and then you watch as students become engrossed in their projects. Often their work is part of a much longer project, already begun, extending for weeks. Sometimes a work of art by an established artist is displayed and discussed, because something the artist did relates to today's work. Today we are working on light. Let's see how Edward Hopper used light. Today we are working on portraits. Let's look at Cubist portraits and compare them with more realistic ones to get a feel for the many ways there are to represent the world. Our next unit is about power. Let's look at Kara Walker, Carrie Mae Weems, and Layla Ali.

Students talk among themselves quietly as they begin to work, and the teacher circles around, watching for teachable moments and zeroing in on individual or group of students with a comment, suggestion, question, or critique. At a midpoint or the end of class, critiques often gather students to share and discuss their work, sessions in which critical judgment and metacognition are nurtured.

A studio classroom is much more complicated than it looks at first impression. The students who originally appeared so casual are actually working hard—they are thinking visually, analytically, critically, creatively.

In Chapter 2 we discuss how teachers develop a studio culture—how they design the physical environment and how they create projects that are engaging and focused on developing students' thinking. In Chapter 3 we delve into the three structures of a studio art classroom through which teachers guide student learning in the classroom: Demonstration–Lecture, Students-at-Work, and Critique, followed by a discussion of a fourth structure, Exhibition, that incorporates the other three Studio Structures for learning.

TWO

Elements of Studio Classrooms

On the surface, a studio classroom might appear to require little teacher planning. Teachers usually talk briefly and often quite informally. While students are making art, teachers might appear, to casual observation, to be milling about aimlessly. And when the group looks at students' work and talks about it together, teachers respond in an impromptu way and encourage students to do much of the reflecting. Getting students to clean everything up might appear to be the toughest part of art teaching!

However, this informality belies the careful thinking and artfulness required to make a studio class work. As we observed art teachers, we saw three areas of focus that teachers used to make their art classrooms into places in which students engage rigorously in learning:

- Creating a studio culture
- Focusing thinking with studio assignments
- Teaching through artworks

In what follows, we describe the elements we observed in each of these areas of focus.

CREATING A STUDIO CULTURE

Studio classrooms have a different feel than classrooms in many other disciplines. The space is set up to promote work flow, there is sometimes music playing to create a mood and to sustain or modulate students' energy, and students are usually absorbed by handling (often messy and sometimes complex and even dangerous) materials and tools. The teachers we observed were attentive to a range of elements (e.g., space, time, language, music, and routines) that contributed to creating a studio culture to support the learning they intended.

Designing the Physical Space

The arrangement of space is a powerful factor in helping to accomplish instructional goals. A primary consideration is getting materials and tools into students' hands efficiently. When teachers have the space, they often set up materials stations that students can access from several directions to avoid waiting, and then ask students to collect what they need. Other times, when materials must be put away because space is shared, teachers use student assistants to pass out materials from a central materials center. Teachers sometimes choose to set up the classroom just enough to get students started, and then, throughout the class, bring students new materials for later phases of work.

Wall space is also a potential teaching tool. At the Boston Arts Academy, Kathleen Marsh, Beth Balliro, and Guy Michel Telemaque organized wall spaces to express disciplinary, school, and personal values; models of work; and intentions for learning. Even though the rooms at the Academy are shared, teachers use the walls to display a rich array of professional and student artworks and texts of various types, including instructions for routines, goals, quotations, announcements, and humorous and personal reminders. Similarly, at Walnut Hill, Jason Green and Jim Woodside also use the walls to teach. One wall in Jason's ceramic studio features a large matrix of tiles that reveals how systematic mixing and layering of glazes produce different effects after firing. Jim's classroom walls are usually lined with students' works in progress, from students in the current class and from students in other classes.

The organization and labeling of space to house materials and tools is also an important consideration. Jason has clear plastic drawers labeled and filled with ceramic tools, and he labels shelves with students' names as personal storage areas for works in progress. Jim labels spaces for student portfolios, again, so all student work is accessible to both students and teacher for review and reflection.

Configurations of furniture also impact how classes function. Beth sets up the studio in one way when students use clay and in a totally different arrangement for painting. These adjustments accommodate different social groupings as well as different uses of materials. Jason also reconfigures the classroom space, removing the pottery wheels when the class begins to focus on sculpture. As sculpture begins, he sets up a central table and individual sculpture stools so students can choose how to position themselves relative to their work and their peers. Jim keeps his studio quite open, often with a central object of focus (e.g., a 10-foot diameter still life of variously sized boxes, a splay of crumpled black paper hanging from the ceiling). This spatial choice unifies the class and encourages students to explore several vantage points before committing to a position for drawing. In addition, Jim uses three different "seating" options to allow students to choose their perspective on the still life. Students can observe from a low level (sitting on the floor with a drawing board propped on a brick), from a mid-level (sitting astride drawing horses), or from above (standing at easels). The flexibility to move and to make choices encourages students to observe and to think in new ways about the opportunities for their work. Teachers use space to support their learning intentions.

Designing Classroom Light and Sound

Teachers also create atmospheres with light and sound to help students persist in their work. In several of the classes we observed, teachers used music as background to help students develop a flow in their work, whether to energize or calm them. For example, both Kathleen and Guy Michel sometimes held Open Studio, in which students harness their energy with popular music and a social buzz. In these classes, students joke, talk, and move around a lot as they work. Jim often plays more upbeat music in the late afternoons, to lift the energy during the late hours of long afternoon classes when students are tired. And for cleanup, some teachers use popular music to provide an energetic, upbeat atmosphere and to manage the routine—when the song is over, the class assesses what's left to be cleaned and starts in again as necessary.

Conversely, for projects that require quiet concentration, Kathleen sometimes declares a "Closed Studio." In these sessions, students work silently while calming music plays in the background as an aid to concentration for those who are easily distracted. Jim often used more complex jazz playing quietly in the early hours of classes, when students are making decisions about composition and focusing on new skills. Again, teachers make the choice of music intentionally so that it supports students' learning for particular situations.

Light is another tool teachers use to set atmospheres conducive to learning. In Kathleen's portrait assignment, students each set an individual light source to create the strong values they were emphasizing in their charcoal drawings. Jim frequently changes the lighting for different challenges and even during a single class. He pulls the shades, uses spotlights, turns overhead lights on or off, and occasionally lines the window shades with strings of small white lights. In addition to creating aesthetic interest, such variation emphasizes the strong influence of light on mood and encourages students to use it as an

Figure 2.1. Jim sets up dramatic lighting for a figure drawing class.

element in their artworks to express different meanings with values (Figure 2.1).

Designing the Social Climate

Teachers not only design the physical space, they also design informal and sometimes more formal ways that students interact with one another and with teachers to create a social climate that nurtures learning.

Teacher–Student Interactions. As students make artworks, teachers observe and intervene. Such observation and responsive teaching is critical to student learning. Teachers are also thoughtful, however, about students' needs for privacy at times to develop a relationship with materials, tools, and their own work. For instance, Jim spends the first minutes of class tidying up and organizing, while the students refocus on their works in progress before the class activity starts in earnest. Similarly, we noticed Jason working on his own coil sculpture during a Coil Project. He used his sculpture stool as a perch from which to observe students when they needed time without being distracted. By stepping back, these teachers set an atmosphere of unobserved independence for the students, while remaining close enough to see what is going on and being ready to intervene with questions, suggestions, or demonstrations as the need and opportunity arise.

Studio teachers' use of language models artful talk for students that helps them think about their work in more sophisticated ways. The language also conveys important messages about what is valued and possible in that classroom. The teachers we observed often used such words and phrases as *decisions, planning, think about, what if, you might consider, I wonder if, experiment, it might be because, you could try (x or y or z)*, and so forth, all of which are utterances intended to encourage approaching work or ideas thoughtfully. This kind of talk encourages the studio habits of Reflection ("tell me how you're deciding"), Envision ("see it in your mind"), and Stretch and Explore ("play around"). Students internalize the vocabularies that teachers model for thinking about art. In our observations of classes and our later interviews with students, we frequently heard students use the same language as their teachers when talking about their work.

Peer Interactions. Teachers also need to ensure that students feel safe and respected by each other. For instance, teachers at the Boston Arts Academy explicitly instruct students in how to make constructive criticism rather than hurtful comments in critiques. For the beginning students, they taught peer critique methods such as making a positive comment first and then phrasing suggestions for improvement in neutral terms (e.g., "I wonder what would happen if you," "That makes me think about," and "I had trouble with that . . . and I tried . . . and it worked pretty well").

Teachers also want to create a climate where students are engaged with each other, collaborating and learning to participate in a community of artists. While Jim acknowledges that students are not always as clear and helpful to each other in their advice during critiques as he might be, he encourages them to talk so that they learn to learn from one another:

> If I had them never talking to each other, it could be a sort of a flat atmosphere where not much exchange goes on. At worst, it could be a competitive, threatening atmosphere . . . you're going to have an atmosphere. Something's going to happen, so you may as well take control of it and make it serve your needs, serve the class.

FOCUSING THINKING WITH STUDIO ASSIGNMENTS

Assignments are one of the main ways that teachers guide and nurture students' learning. By constraining a few directions of thinking and emphasizing others, assignments can shape the direction students aim their investigations with materials, tools, and processes.

What Are Studio Assignments?

Teachers create assignments in order to develop one or several kinds of dispositions. Assignments specify or suggest the range of materials and tools to be used, and they pose one or more challenges that are open-ended and can spur a range of responses. Assignments vary in length (from a few minutes to several weeks), can be done in class or as homework, and promote growth for students at a wide range of levels. Studio assignments are designed to support students' developing dispositions.

TEACHING THROUGH ARTWORKS

In many high school classes in non-arts disciplines, connections between work made by professionals and by students are often left to chance. Professional work seems more a source of "true facts" than of evidence for how disciplinary experts think and express that thinking. Nor is student work exploited as a way to foster thinking, or to show the thinking that students have already developed. Instead, work is completed in private, graded in private, and privately stowed (or thrown) away.

In contrast, in the studio classes we observed, work by both professionals and students has a prominent place as evidence of thinking and understanding. Whether as an introduction to an assignment, a quick example while students are making art, or when teachers and students are talking about work in progress or completed, studio teachers seize frequent opportunities to use works of art as sources of information. Because making is at the center of the studio experience, what is made also has an important place. Artwork, both finished and in progress, is made by professionals and made by students, and we saw teachers employ a number of strategies to make the artwork into effective teaching tools.

Among the best strategies are those that engage students in thinking about artists' processes. Video clips produced by several organizations can be used to reveal artists' processes and thinking in their own words. For example, Art21 (art21.org/artists/) offers videos of contemporary artists speaking about their work from their studios. Museums provide digital access to their collections and to the perspectives of artists. For instance, the Tate Channel (www.tate.org.uk/art) features artists and works shown at the Tate Modern in London. Local art organizations and museums also often offer resources for students to connect with artists in their own communities.

Student work is public, and teachers use it as a central tool for learning and reflection. Often, student work from many classes is casually hung or stored in sight around the room. Sometimes the work is merely a background, and other times it becomes a focal example of a problem or solution. Students also see others' work as it is created, hear teachers' comments to peers, and participate directly in commenting on their peers' work in critiques. Student work is visible almost all the time, but we need to be aware of, and take full advantage of, its value as a teaching tool.

Professional work is also used as a teaching tool. It models possibilities for artistic problems and solutions, and teachers use it in a wide variety of ways. For example, at Walnut Hill, Jason and Jim set up a show of their own work as the year began. The show introduced the students to their teachers' aesthetic values, attitudes, and skills and sent a clear message to students: Your teachers are working artists.

Such modeling continued throughout the year. Jason brought in collections of pottery made by his potter friends and exhibition invitations featuring their work, both of which revealed a wide range of variations to consider in the current assignment. He set up a computer in a corner of the clay studio to share digital pictorial sequences of clay-making processes and images of work related to the assignment from other places and eras. Jim brought in stacks of art books and reproductions so he could show students examples as they worked on problems; they provided ready material for profitable browsing, as well. He also used works by professional artists to help students visualize problems, as he did by showing pieces by Hopper and Diebenkorn when introducing the assignment about expressing relationships between figures.

At the Boston Arts Academy, Guy Michel frequently used art magazines to illustrate design principles and challenges. Beth made copies of images of traditional African vessel types. Kathleen gave a slideshow as she introduced the assignment to make self-portraits while wearing constructed-paper hats and vests. In addition, teachers set up contacts with practicing artists and other members of the art world, such as curators, restorers, and designers. Students visited museums and studios and reported back to the class. And artists visited classes and worked with students—e.g., artists from the Institute of Contemporary Art worked with students at Boston Arts Academy on a sculpture project.

Reflecting on Work at Different Stages of Completion

Artwork, and particularly student artwork, is not just looked at and talked about when it is "done." The teachers we observed held critiques on sketches, on works in mid-process, on completed works, and on bodies of work from a semester, year, or from all 4 years of high school. Critiques at different stages have different functions: Critiques of works in progress can help students hold their initial plans more loosely and consider different ways of completing their work. Critiques of finished works or bodies of work can help students think and talk about what they have accomplished and imagine the next challenges they might face.

Figure 2.2. Teacher Beth Balliro keeps the talk grounded in a student's work.

Keeping Talk About Artwork Grounded

The teachers we observed worked to keep talk about artworks firmly grounded on specific pieces (Figure 2.2). As they commented on a piece, the teachers gestured toward aspects of the work that illustrated their words. Jason, for example, often held and encouraged students to touch, rub, hold, and use the ceramic objects in the studio. He also encouraged them to continue to handle and think about earlier works they had taken home. During critiques, students are encouraged to point out parts of the work that interest them or connect to a point they wish to make. As words are connected to visuals, ideas become clearer and more concrete.

Selecting and Arranging Work Intentionally

Teachers select and arrange works to encourage students to draw thoughtful comparisons among them. For example, at the start of the assignment in which students built sculptures from repeating elements ("unit" sculptures), Jason asked students to examine structures that repeated units, such as stacks of plaster molded bottles, a brick wall, and a mud-wasp's nest. As conversations about works progress, teachers focus on works that illustrate a point particularly well, often by physically moving a piece to the center of the temporary display. Every work need not be discussed in every critique. Sometimes the point is to compare and contrast approaches across works; at other times, central ideas can be discussed more cogently and vividly by looking at single works. Of course, it is important for all students to receive regular response to their work, but setting up the expectation that not all pieces will be discussed in *every* conversation makes looking at artwork a more flexible part of the studio routine.

Using the Work to Illustrate Key Concepts

When teachers give an assignment, not all students may understand key concepts. Looking at artwork allows a chance to revisit and illustrate the central ideas. For instance, Jason describes how examining finished student work helps students realize the importance of attending to small details of ceramic craft.

> Things do become, I think, a lot clearer when the work is finished. I may have been talking about

how not to leave a sharp edge on a trimmed foot. And after the pot is fired and it comes out, you can almost cut your hand if they didn't smooth something out. So things like that become amplified, and hopefully [they] recall information that I gave them earlier; it was in the back of their mind—but now it solidifies. And their example's right there in front of them.

Now, with these elements of studio classrooms in mind, we turn our attention to describing the Studio Structures for learning that studio teachers use to organize time, space, and interactions with and among students in efforts to facilitate their learning.

THREE

Studio Structures for Learning

Over the course of a semester, class time can be organized in many different ways to support (or obstruct) student learning. Different goals and projects require their own instructional shapes. The studio arts teachers we studied organized space, time, and interactions in their classes by using variations on three basic Studio Structures: *Demonstration–Lectures, Students-at-Work*, and *Critiques*. We also identified a fourth studio structure, *Exhibition*, which typically occurs outside the classroom but impacts the learning and teaching therein.

These Studio Structures create an atmosphere in which students work as artists with other artists (teachers and peers). Each structure supports specific aspects of student learning. Demonstration–Lectures convey information, so they forecast whatever the assignment is meant to emphasize (e.g., *Express* for an assignment focusing on the emotionally evocative space between figures; *Envision* for an assignment focused on imagining a vessel that would suit a particular ritual purpose). The Students-at-Work structure emphasizes the growth and development of individual students, because it keeps the *making* of art at the center of the learning experience and allows teachers to shift attention flexibly from student to student and to carefully observe students and the evidence of their learning as they work. Thus, we see the Students-at-Work structure as the one that most helps teachers attend to an individual student's "zone of proximal development" (Vygotsky, 1978, 1984)—the range within which an individual can learn when supported by a more competent other. Critiques support a dynamic flow of thinking among teachers and students that connects the *intended* learning in particular assignments with the ongoing *enacted* learning of individual students. While Exhibition usually takes place away from the artmaking space and time, we see it as an authentic practice integral to participation in the art world. Students need to think about their artworks as part of an ongoing public conversation, and engaging in all phases of exhibition helps them to think in this way.

In addition to these *learning* structures, we defined a *management* structure, *Studio Transitions*. Classes always began and ended with Studio Transitions, and sometimes mid-class transitions also occurred (e.g., breaks). The teachers found different ways to minimize the time spent in transitions (e.g., setup and cleanup), which, unless carefully managed, can use up a lot of time that could be spent on learning. The teachers we observed spent a good deal of effort in the beginning of the year establishing management routines to keep transitions from unduly interfering with time for artmaking. Teachers showed students where and how materials and tools are stored, assigned roles for cleaning up the studio, and created individual spaces for students to store their work and materials.

Teachers varied and sequenced the structures they used depending on their goals and projects. The simplest way is to begin with a Demonstration–Lecture, followed by a Students-at-Work segment, and concluding with a Critique. However, teachers often chose a different order, or repeated a structure within a single class. Teachers also made many modifications within each type of structure; for example, within Critiques, they might use written or oral forms, employ them in midprocessor to synthesize learning around finished works, or to refocus a conversation. But all the teaching we observed could be categorized into combinations of these structures.

THE DEMONSTRATION-LECTURE

I'll do demonstrations in throwing—I mean, I try to do it pretty quickly just so they can have a chance to work. Because I mean, that's really why they are there.

—Jason Green

The *Demonstration–Lecture* is a brief, visually rich lecture by the teacher to the class (or to a small group) that conveys information that students will use immediately. Students see authentic art being made, tools being used, or images of work made by others. Demonstration–Lectures, therefore, offer inspiring models. Here are the basic ingredients:

- *Group Focus.* Demonstration–Lectures have a group focus for efficiency. The teacher demonstrates to the whole group, either to give an overview of a project or of several materials, tools, and/or processes students will use that may require further one-on-one or small group follow-up, or to focus on a single, specific technique that can be employed in the assignment.

- *Visual Emphasis.* Information is presented visually so it engages and informs students. Teachers frequently use images and model processes in Demonstration–Lectures.
- *Immediate Relevance.* Demonstration–Lectures relate to work students will be doing soon.
- *Brevity.* Demonstration–Lectures are brief so as to allow enough class time for students to make and reflect on their work.
- *Connection.* Demonstration–Lectures connect ideas. They relate skills, attitudes, and concepts already introduced to those that will be explored and developed in Students-at-Work and Critique structures of current and future classes. Sometimes, teachers use the informal quality of these class segments to build students' appreciation for the ways that peers can serve as resources to each other, suggesting that students who have more experience consult with others.

A Contrast to Traditional Lectures

Art students are encouraged to be visual thinkers. Visual demonstration illuminates complex, multistep thinking that might otherwise be difficult to understand and remember, and it shows students what artistic expertise looks like. The essential difference between Demonstration–Lectures and traditional lectures is the frequent and often extended use that teachers make of visual examples, including objects (e.g., artworks, still life objects, tools), images (e.g., books, photographs, posters, electronic media), and processes (e.g., modeling step-by-step how to use materials or tools to accomplish particular intentions). In Demonstration–Lectures, teachers rarely talk for long without referring to something that can be seen.

A second way in which the Demonstration–Lecture diverges from traditional lectures is that the information presented is intended to be immediately useful for carrying out class work and homework. This motivates students to pay attention and helps them maintain focus. Because of the emphasis on brevity in Demonstration–Lectures, interaction among students and teachers may be brief, although teachers do interact with students to varying degrees during these class structures. Occasionally, Demonstration–Lectures become general class discussions.

Finally, through Demonstration–Lectures, teachers present a wide variety of models for ways to meet and solve visual arts challenges. Through modeling, students learn about the relationships among the materials and tools of a medium, what other artists have done with these materials and tools, and what they themselves might do with them. The information presented is not for the purpose of memorization, but for starting students off in working creatively to make art. Generally, teachers show several approaches or images, so that students use examples as inspiration rather than something to copy. Through modeling, teachers exemplify their beliefs about art and working as artists. In addition to the specific processes and multiple examples introduced in Demonstration–Lectures, the structure exposes students regularly to their teacher as an artist, who is thinking and experimenting purposefully, playfully, autonomously, and collaboratively. The teacher models the methods through which art students as well as mature artists develop artistry.

The Role of Demonstration–Lectures

Through Demonstration–Lectures, teachers introduce what they want students to learn in three general ways:

- Setting tasks (assignments)
- Illustrating concepts
- Modeling processes, approaches, and attitudes

The three examples that follow show how three teachers adapt the Demonstration–Lecture structure to their needs.

SETTING TASKS:
AFRICAN POTTERY PROJECT   (EXAMPLE 3.1)

While introducing ceramics to the 9th grade at Boston Arts Academy, Beth Balliro leads an interactive Demonstration–Lecture for a project in which students are to make pottery inspired by pan-African styles using coil building and surface patterning (see also Example 11.2). She uses the Demonstration–Lecture to introduce the new project and show how it relates to research on Africa that the students are conducting in their humanities course. Later, Beth demonstrates coil-building as a technique. In the part of the Demonstration–Lecture described here, Beth sets a practical, theoretical, and cultural-historical background for the work the students are about to undertake.

As is typical in Demonstration–Lectures, Beth addresses the class as a whole about a project they will start on right away. "We're going to start looking at some context, I guess you could say. Some sort of ideas surrounding the artwork we're about to start making." The

Demonstration–Lecture is brief, to give students time to explore these ideas in their own artwork. "We're going to fly through this. So, don't fall behind. Stay on top of things," Beth tells her students.

Beth starts out by providing some background on African ceramics. She makes it accessible through a story about John Biggers, a contemporary African American artist, and his visual impressions of West African art from a visit to Ghana. Many of her students read below grade level, so Beth structures a shared oral reading from a short text that students would have had difficulty understanding on their own. The reading is supported by reference to many visual images of ceramic vessels, and these ground the interactive Demonstration–Lecture in the concepts she wants her students to understand (i.e., style, definitions of "art," coil-built pottery, and pattern).

The two-page reading is followed by eight pages of images of richly patterned African ceramic vessels made by a coil technique. Through these pictures, Beth engages her students conceptually in identifying and comparing elements of the style she wants them to interpret in the creation of their own vessels. She emphasizes the importance of the concept of *pattern* by pointing to the images and to objects in the room, such as a student's shirt. Then she asks her students to select three images that would inspire the design of their own vessels. The images allow the students to think about style and pattern, and to envision what they could begin to do with those concepts in their own creations.

Finally, the Demonstration–Lecture serves as the vehicle for connecting the skills and concepts required for this project (coil technique, patterned surfaces on ceramic vessels), the context of African culture (i.e., the focus of their humanities course), and the further skills students will explore later in Students-at-Work and Critique sessions (style, form, other hand-building techniques, and the question of what counts as art within different cultural contexts—a recurring theme in Boston Arts Academy art classes). Thus, the atypical features of this Demonstration–Lecture (e.g., we rarely saw as much interaction or reading as is illustrated here, and we often saw examination of actual objects rather than pictures of objects) illustrate how flexible the structure can be in accommodating the goals of the teacher, the constraints of the context, and the needs of the students.

ILLUSTRATING CONCEPTS:
TILE PROJECT   (EXAMPLE 3.2)

At Walnut Hill, Jason Green uses Demonstration–Lectures extensively to introduce assignments, illustrate concepts, and model use of techniques and tools. In the following example, we see him introducing a project that will involve creating tiles as a way to think about texture on the "skin" of a ceramic sculpture (see also Examples 9.2 and 11.5). Conceptually, Jason wants students to understand the "states of the clay"—that is, states like slip, slurry, plastic, leather-hard, bone-dry, bisque-fired, glaze-fired, and all the intermediate "states" that ceramicists use as their raw material for making art with clay. In addition, he wants students to develop the habits of (1) imagining many possible processes and outcomes and adapting their visions as they work with the material, and (2) pushing themselves to create many possibilities by playing purposefully with the material before they commit to a technique for a finished piece.

The students are in the spring term of their year-long course in ceramics when Jason calls them over to introduce the new assignment:

> The next part of the project after we get your form built, the 3D part built, we're going to put some texture on the outside. So, before you do that, you're going to make two flat tiles. One of those tiles is going to use all the states of the clay.

Jason quickly shows the students images of tiles from different cultures and eras, in various styles and shapes, all from photos in a stack of art books he has borrowed from the library. He then demonstrates using a slab roller and a template for sizing the tiles. To help students imagine possibilities, Jason shows them processes using hands and hand tools, including smearing, scratching, cutting against a template, and experimenting with surface textures. As he talks and demonstrates, Jason shows or passes around pieces of clay in different "states": bone-dry, wet or plastic, and slurry. All of this is entirely visual and tactile, whether he's showing the parts of a tool, the steps of a process, or the variation in the material. Jason closes the Demonstration–Lecture with a reminder that he wants students to try things out:

> So, it's just going to be experimental. So, don't worry too much about it, OK? You want to experiment. You can make a pattern. You might smear this on to the tile [*holding a piece of slurry*]. And find a tool to make a texture in it [*pushing it with his fingernail*]. Or you can then maybe put bone-dry pieces in [*sprinkling some chips of hard clay on the slab*].

Jason demonstrates a lot in a single class. His demonstrations give students many options and choices about what they might pursue in their own work. Everything demonstrated is of immediate value in the assigned projects. Finally, everything Jason shows refers back to skills and concepts he has already introduced and developed; in this case, texturing sculptural surfaces refers back to the surfaces of thrown pots from the first semester. What he demonstrates also foreshadows upcoming concepts and skill—in this case, a tile project that uses molds.

While the five elements of Demonstration–Lecture are clearly evident in Jason's classes, his use of the structure is specific to his goals, to the context of his course and school, and to the needs of the students he is teaching, just as was Beth's very different approach to this structure.

MODELING PROCESSES, APPROACHES, AND ATTITUDES: LIGHT AND BOXES PROJECT   (EXAMPLE 3.3)

About 2 months into his drawing class at Walnut Hill, Jim Woodside introduces an assignment that focuses on light. His Demonstration–Lecture offers students information that will be immediately useful to them and is very short—under 10 minutes for this 3-hour class. Brevity and immediacy are prototypical qualities of this structure, as are Jim's use of visual images, emphasis on modeling of processes, and the ways he connects previous work to the new assignment and the new assignment to the future.

Jim uses just a few words to convey the purpose of the assignment to his students ("Light light light light. That's what we're going to work on today"), but he also shows them how it connects to previous work. Students have been drawing from observation all term, and they will do so again today. "All right, what do you notice looking at the still life today?" he asks. This is the same still life that students observed recently when learning perspective drawing—an elaborate collection of variously sized and positioned wooden boxes (see also Example 8.2). This week, to emphasize value drawing, the still life is dramatically lit to reveal strong shadows and highlights. Jim reminds students of previous drawings they have done, suggesting that they use viewfinders as a compositional tool.

> I want you to use the viewfinders like we have in the last couple of weeks—very, very important and helpful in a drawing like this; and using an eraser as a tool is not a new idea. Remember how I had said in the past to you: Using an eraser is not about correcting mistakes, that's what you do with an eraser when you take a math test [*holding up an eraser*]. Using an eraser is just another drawing tool.

In addition, he helps students imagine what finished works might look like by showing drawings that students in other classes have done already for this assignment.

Jim moves quickly through the purpose of the assignment—naming it explicitly, but not dwelling on it at this early stage in the class, because he knows it will make more sense later as students experience challenges and results for themselves; he is careful to model quite deliberately how students should approach their own work. He suggests that the project will be easier if they sit on the floor to work, "because a lot of what goes on with drawing this way is going to have to do with gravity." He shows them how to rub charcoal on their paper surfaces to prepare them and how to use a sheet beneath their drawing sheet to catch the extra charcoal that can then be returned to the jar "so we're not wasting it." He also models drawing while suggesting ways to begin.

> So, if I see a white box up there or a strong white tone on the side of one of those shapes [*pointing to the still-life*], that's where I'll start. I suggest you start with the lightest forms first, OK [*starting to draw a shape with the eraser; then switching erasers*]? You can get a little bit crisper of an edge with this eraser sometimes. All right?

The materials for the project (powdered charcoal, kneaded and gum erasers, newsprint) are common and inexpensive. Jim shows students particular characteristics of each material and tool they'll be using.

> Each of you is going to have a kneaded eraser [*holding up eraser*]—do all of you know how to work a kneaded eraser? . . . it's self-cleaning, so as it gets black like that—which it will right away—as you use it on this [*pulling at eraser*]—you just sort of pull it and then fold it in on itself, and it'll keep working for a while.

He also wants students to be aware that the charcoal is messy and unhealthy to breathe, so he shows them exactly how to avoid making charcoal dust storms. This is important information for using charcoal and also models that artists should be concerned with health and safety issues in the studio.

> We want to try to keep this stuff to a minimum in the air, all right? So, I don't want to see you like doing this and then blowing it [*pretending to blow on sheet*]—I don't want to have like clouds of this stuff in the air. I mean, it's not going to kill you—it's not—but it's, you know, we just want to try to keep it down so you don't start coughing all day.

In addition, Jim is aware that the technical drawing process of "pulling light out of the piece of paper" may be frustrating for his students. "Obviously this is going to be messy. You're not going to get this sort of nice, pristine perfect drawing, but you're going to learn to see this thing [*pointing to still-life*] in terms of shape and light only." He alerts them to common mistakes, such as drawing lines and filling in the shapes, rather than "going right directly to the shape." The drawing tools (erasers) are cruder and more blunt than the tools with which they're most familiar, so he also uses the Demonstration–Lecture to make suggestions for how they might work. He suggests they squint as a way to see the essence of the shapes.

> It gets blurry, and it gets simpler, OK? It's reduced down into real simple forms of light and dark—and that's gonna help you. So here's how we're going to start this. Each of you—to begin with we're going to do an exercise, a small drawing this size on newsprint.

In addition to offering visual information about processes and possibilities, Jim uses the Demonstration–Lecture to set a relaxed, experimental atmosphere about the assignment:

> Maybe we will expand to larger drawings today and maybe we'll stick to this size, but let's just start out doing this. We're going to proceed with it and see how it goes. But let's not worry about that just now.

Once again, this structure accommodates the teacher's intentions and purposes for particular students in a particular context.

STUDENTS-AT-WORK

I just call it teaching.

—Kathleen Marsh

The structure we refer to as *Students-at-Work* forms the heart of an art class. Here students work independently on a project, typically one introduced to them in a Demonstration–Lecture. As the students work, the teacher circles the room, offering timely interventions on an informal basis. In a Students-at-Work session, students' primary means for learning about art is through doing. The teacher provides the resources, the challenge, and the individual guidance.

Here are the major characteristics of the Students-at-Work structure:

- *Focus on Making*. Learning occurs mainly through working with materials.
- *Independent Work*. Students work on their own, but in a shared studio space under the guidance of their teacher.
- *Ongoing Assessment*. Teachers observe and assist students while they are working.
- *Individualized Interventions*. Teachers consult with students individually and tailor the assignment and their comments to each student's needs and goals.

Though students usually work individually during these sessions, they do so under the careful guidance of their teacher and in the community of the studio classroom where their classmates are also working. The Students-at-Work structure allows for both independent work and for a collaborative and informal sharing of information, thinking processes, and understanding.

Personalized Teaching

Students-at-Work sessions offer time for teachers to shift from standing at the center of students' attention to observing students as they work. During these sessions, teachers generally work with individual students, personalizing their comments and suggestions. Teachers watch students' work in progress carefully and consult with students one-on-one. These consults may be quick or extended interactions. Consults promote thoughtful decisions. They might include encouraging remarks, brief demonstrations with the materials, questions that help students reflect on their work in progress, or extended conversations about a student's intentions for a piece or about how a particular piece relates to broader goals in the course and to the student's potential for developing as an artist.

The Role of Students-at-Work

Students-at-Work is the cornerstone of the studio classroom. In the 38 class sessions we observed, the largest percentage of time (typically 60–75%) was spent with students working independently on projects while the teacher observed and consulted with students individually about their work.

In the Students-at-Work sessions, students are deeply involved with the materials of the assigned project—drawing, painting, sketching, or forming objects out of clay; thinking seriously; and making artistic decisions as they work. Students carefully observe their works, envision next steps of their projects, and explore new techniques, materials, and ideas. Students learn to reflect continually on the processes of using and making decisions about materials.

The teacher plays a key diagnostic role, observing the students working and consulting one-on-one to guide them in their work. The Students-at-Work structure has three broad roles in the studio classroom.

- Putting *making* at the center of learning (with perception and reflection growing out of making)
- Assessing work *processes* (not just resulting products)
- *Individualizing* the curriculum

Putting Making at the Center of Learning. Teachers' decisions to devote most of their classroom time to having students make art is what makes an art class a studio class. Students-at-Work sessions give students the time, space, materials, and support they need to create artworks and put into action the ideas that are introduced and discussed during Demonstration–Lectures and Critiques.

Assessing Work Processes. In Students-at-Work sessions, teachers continually assess students in all phases of their working *process*, rather than just evaluating their final *products*. They see students' plans for a piece develop, watch how students start, make decisions, and change directions, and see immediately how students respond to instruction. This observation of students as they work is the fundamental way teachers assess how students' minds are developing as they work and learn, and allows teachers to help students in the moment, often the most effective way to instruct. Students told us that they learned more from their teacher's comments on works in process than from comments on completed works.

Individualizing the Curriculum. In a sense, teachers have two sets of curricula in a studio classroom: one for the whole class, and one for each individual student. This personalized curriculum is developed in response to the specific abilities, needs, and interests of each student. While individualizing is in no way unique to studio art teaching (excellent teachers of all subjects know how to individualize to great advantage), the studio classroom has long used individualization and can provide a model of individualized teaching for the rest of the academic curriculum. As Jim explains, "I do have goals for individual kids . . . each kid is very different. [My studio class] is absolutely equally a class activity and an individual activity." By allowing teachers to gather information about how individual students work and learn, the Students-at-Work sessions enable teachers to define and carry through individualized responses to help each student along a personal path of development. Thus, the Students-at-Work structure supports teachers working effectively with heterogeneous skill levels in one classroom.

THE CRITIQUE

That's why we have these critiques; I try to get them to realize that they need to start looking at their results very carefully. I want them to start looking and getting information and applying that back to what they're going to do next.

—Jason Green

Critiques are central to a studio class—a chance for students and teachers to reflect as a group on their work and working process. In Critiques, artmaking is paused, so that students and teacher can reflect on the work and the process of creation. Here are four ingredients of Critiques:

- *Focus on Artworks.* The students as a group focus their attention on their own and other students' work.
- *Reflective.* Students think about the meanings and expressions conveyed by works of art and think about what is successful, what is not, and why.
- *Verbal.* Students must put their reflections into words as they are asked to describe their working process and products and to explain and evaluate their artworks.
- *Forward-looking.* The discussion aims to guide individual students' future work and help them to envision new possibilities.

Features of Critiques

Critiques do not have a rigid format or single purpose. They are structured in a wide variety of ways, occur at many different points in the working process, and are used to further different ends. However, Critiques have two distinguishing features that earn them a place of honor in the studio classroom. First, they focus attention on students' work and working processes. And second, Critiques are explicitly social. Students share their work with the teacher and other students and get responses from them. Taken together, these two features make Critiques an important forum for helping students develop an understanding of their work and development as artists.

The Work Does the Teaching. By focusing on student work, critiques become a powerful teaching tool. Just looking collectively at a piece of art is useful for both students and teachers. When students see the range of ways their classmates have approached an assignment, they begin to envision possibilities outside their usual habits. A concept that eludes a student may suddenly "click" once seen and discussed in a classmate's work. Critiques are where students learn most genuinely from one another.

Teachers, too, find it informative to see all the work during a Critique. Doing so gives teachers a quick and powerful way to gauge where students are as a group, to see how individuals vary in relation to the group and to expert norms, and how best to help individuals and the group address their current needs in the next project.

A Community of Arts Learners. Students learn in conversation with others. While students often talk about their own work during Critiques, and teachers also generally comment on individual students' work, Critiques involve an explicit shift from individual to group work as the class comes together as a community to discuss one another's works. Critiques involve sharing work and responses with others. Students gain insight about their own artmaking by verbalizing thoughts about their own work and by hearing how others talk about their work. They also learn by looking at others' works and hearing how these works are discussed. A 9th-grade student in Guy Michel Telemaque's design class at the Boston Arts Academy talked about the value of learning from others during critiques:

> After we did art pieces, we'd sit down together and talk about it. And that helps a lot because you get certain opinions or advice from not just the teacher but the students around you better observing your work. And you could take that advice and use it on the next piece.

The Role of Critiques

In Critiques, students and teachers look back on art that is being or has recently been made by the students. The purpose is to understand and evaluate students' work and working process and to look forward as individual students begin to envision possibilities for how to proceed. Critiques can take many forms, and teachers structure them to suit particular students' needs and to address goals for the class as a whole. In the 38 classes we observed, there were 25 Critiques, ranging from a 2.5-minute session to a 2.5-hour-long session with seniors who had been working independently for the previous month. Critiques offer a forum for balancing the learning opportunities of an assignment with the needs and insights of individual students in a dynamic interplay.

Each of the teachers we observed structured Critiques differently. But for all teachers, Critiques played the following key roles in fostering learning in the arts:

Helping Students Connect Their Working Process to the Final Product. In the Critiques we observed, students' artworks are not viewed as static objects to be evaluated, but rather as a record of the students' thinking and making process. A key aim of the Critique is to make explicit and analyze the decisions that went into making a piece.

Critiques often employ a reverse engineering technique in which students and teachers try to understand how something was made; identify the effects of different decisions, marks, and techniques; and imagine how the work could have been made differently. For instance, as Jason's students pick up and examine ceramic pieces, he asks them to notice evidence of the artists' hands on the pieces and think about how the pieces appear to have been made, why they were made that way, and what they would look like had the artist made them differently.

The product is not the only thing that matters in assessment—students are praised for stretching beyond their usual style or habits of working, even if the resulting artwork is not particularly successful. Conversely, a successful piece may be criticized if the student did not venture outside their "comfort zone" to make it. Works are often praised in terms of the thought process behind them: "a smart solution," "a really powerful decision."

Helping Students Learn to Observe, Interpret, Explain, and Evaluate Works. Artworks can seem impenetrable to students. While students can often tell whether or not they like a piece, they have to learn to understand and notice how different aspects of a work contribute to its general effect. Through Critiques, teachers instruct students in how to notice details and patterns in artworks, how to understand what the works communicate and why, how to verbalize what they see, and how to evaluate the effectiveness of works. A key aim of Critiques is to help students explain what they see, think, and feel about work and working.

Teachers push students to notice more dimensions of the work by asking them to focus on specific aspects rather than just the whole. For instance, Kathleen Marsh asks her students to talk about the composition for each self-portrait, and Guy Michel Telemaque asks students to think about how light acts as a subject in each of their photographs. This narrower focus helps students organize their thinking about artworks and pushes them to think beyond the novice response of "I like it."

Teachers model how they want students to look at and think about artworks. They often talk aloud through their thought process as they view a work. They point out details and features that they notice, they describe what the work reminds them of or the feelings it evokes, and they articulate visions of how the piece would look if a part were changed. The aim is not to communicate an authoritative interpretation of a work, but rather to model a process of thinking about it.

Teachers may give general strategies for thinking about and evaluating work. For instance, Jim tells his senior Critique group to ask themselves the question, "What part of a work seems most extraneous? What could be taken away, and the central thrust of the work would remain the same?" He tells them this strategy can be a useful way to push work forward when there's nothing obviously wrong with it—a way to improve a piece that is already successful.

Highlighting Key Concepts in the Assignment or Course.

While the assignments in the classes we observed were open-ended and not prescriptive, they often served as a targeted exploration of an artistic concept or concepts. At the Boston Arts Academy, these key concepts were often formalized in an assignment rubric. At Walnut Hill, they tended to be more informally presented in the teacher's instructions, description, or demonstration of the assignment. Teachers often used Critiques to highlight these concepts in students' work.

In addition, each teacher had key ideas that they touched upon over and over throughout the year. For instance, Jim repeatedly stressed the idea that technique should serve expressive purposes and that expressive, emotional aspects of works arise from the ordinary. On the very first day of class, he helped students see the expressive potential of a still life of a collection of objects painted white, and, in Critiques throughout the year, he repeatedly revisited the relationship between technique and expression. Teachers have a variety of key ideas, such as examining the relationships between form and function, between observation and abstraction, or between the students' artwork and their lives. During Critiques, teachers point to ways in which students' work illustrates aspects of these central ideas and suggest ways students could incorporate or develop them in their work.

Guiding Students' Future Work.

Critiques look back at what has been done to help shape students' work on the current piece-in-progress and on the pieces they will make in the future. Sometimes this guidance is explicit: Students receive specific suggestions, whether for the piece being critiqued or for the next assignment. The guidance may also be implicit: Teachers instill the idea that each project should be reflected on and should inform future work, as Jason said in the lead quotation for this section. Critiques encourage students to push beyond just

looking at the work "as is" and help them develop the habit of envisioning new possibilities for what it could become.

Critiques extend beyond reflections on the work itself, because fundamentally they are reflections by students about themselves as developing artists. Teachers help students see elements that are characteristic of their work and help them identify strengths on which to build. Teachers learn about their students' approaches to work not only by observing the works but also by listening to what their students say. For instance, after a Critique, Jim noted about one student: "I think that she's really finding a way to draw here. Now I know that I know this from talking to her a lot and looking at her other drawings. But she's finding a way to draw that is really smart and really her own." Through Critiques, students develop an understanding of their personal way of working and how this style may differ from that of other students in the class.

VARIATIONS IN USE OF THE STUDIO STRUCTURES

Teachers weave the three basic Studio Structures of Demonstration–Lecture, Students-at-Work, and Critiques together in many different ways.

ABA Shape

In the simplest model, students work in long stretches of unbroken time, sandwiched between an introduction and a conclusion. We refer to this pattern as the ABA shape: whole-group/individual/whole-group.

The class begins with a whole group gathering, such as in a Demonstration–Lecture in which an assignment or working process is explained. Or the class might begin with a brief Critique of work from a previous class that leads into work for the current class. That's the A section of the ABA shape. The class then shifts to an individualized Students-at-Work session for the bulk of the class period (60–75% of the class time)—the B of the shape. The class concludes by returning to whole-group time, with either a Critique of the work made during the class, or a Demonstration–Lecture reviewing what was learned and highlighting what will come in the next class—this is the closing A of the ABA shape.

Although we saw many close variations, we saw no "pure" ABA-structured classes. Sometimes teachers would spread this ABA shape over two classes. For instance, at the Boston Arts Academy, Guy Michel, who had shorter class sessions than some of the other teachers (1.5 hours twice a week compared with 3 hours once a week), sometimes spent one class introducing and getting

Figure 3.1. Time Bar Showing the Punctuated Class Shape

From Jim Woodside's class, session 1, working on the Contour Drawing Project

■ Studio Transition 11%

■ Demo/Lecture 28%

■ Students-at-Work 38%

■ Critique 24%

students started on a project (Demonstration–Lecture followed by Students-at-Work), and then used the next session as an entirely unbroken work session followed only by clean-up (Students-at-Work followed by Studio Transition). This allowed students to enter into their work deeply and lessened the amount of time spent setting up and cleaning up.

Punctuated Shape

The most common approach we observed to shaping class time employs shorter structures layered more frequently and at shorter intervals within a single class. We call this type of sequence a *punctuated shape* (see Figure 3.1). Here we see structures arranged in the following order: Studio Transition; Demonstration–Lecture; Students-at-Work; brief Demonstration–Lecture; brief Students-at-Work; brief Demonstration–Lecture; Studio Transition (break); long Critique; brief Demonstration–Lecture.

Such interspersion gives teachers more opportunities to refocus students on the habits that teachers intend them to learn, to help the group build thinking together about their work, and to introduce new ideas incrementally, rather than with heavy doses of Demonstration–Lecture as class begins.

We cannot claim to know which variations are best. We suspect that there is no "most effective" way, but, rather, many ways that serve different goals and contexts.

A FOURTH OVERARCHING STRUCTURE: EXHIBITION

Exhibition, in all its forms, whether it's in visual arts or science or humanities, is incredibly important to the cycle of the learning process. It's one thing to be working in your sketchbook, another to do research from a prompt that your teacher gives you, another to struggle in the studio, and yet another to go through a critique. But the exhibition is really the final, and an extremely critical, bookend piece that students have to experience—where your work becomes public. It would almost be like rehearsing and never performing. To go through the process is really valuable and to be specific and transparent about what those skills are that go into creating an exhibition really matters.

—Kathleen Marsh

Art is a public discourse.

—Steve Locke, Professor, Pratt Institute, Brooklyn, NY

Exhibition is the structure that comes into play when artists "let work go"—moving it from the private process of creation by its makers to the ongoing, public process of recreation by its viewers. Exhibition can take many forms: physical or virtual, installed or performed, ephemeral or permanent, a sanctioned or guerrilla installation, informal or formal. Whether in a classroom corner display, a hallway, a public outside space, a blog, website, or a dedicated gallery space, an exhibition can reveal the strength of a work, show the process of making work, or—at the lowest level—merely get something on the walls so they aren't bare. Students can be indifferent to what teachers have tacked up and not even see it, or they can be responsible for creating exhibits themselves; perhaps as small groups showing their own work, as curators of peers' work, or by maintaining rotating, ongoing displays of single pieces of their own work, updated weekly. Whatever the form, Exhibition can be a structure that promotes student learning if teachers are alert to that potential and motivated to use exhibitions in this way.

FEATURES OF EXHIBITION

Phases of Exhibition

An exhibition involves far more than a public showing of works and requires multiple phases: planning, installing, showing, and de-installing, as shown in Table 3.1. Each one of these phases involves multiple steps, again as shown in the table below. Students collectively plan, organize, and implement a complex social event to showcase their artwork and communicate their ideas to a broader public. At BAA, students took Exhibition courses as part of their required curriculum each year, and, by their senior year, they were fully responsible for all phases of their final exhibition. In Chapter 15 we give examples of how exhibition was used at both schools.

Studio Structures Are Embedded in the Phases of the Exhibition Process

Though Exhibition is its own structure, the other Studio Structures are embedded in all phases of the Exhibition process. In addition to being classroom formats, the three basic learning structures also operate within the larger Exhibition structure.

In the Demonstration–Lecture, teachers or other students might explain how to set up each component

Table 3.1. Phases of a Gallery-Style Exhibition

I. Planning Phase
Setting a Theme or Focus
Determining Schedule, Timeline, and Roles
Designing Publicity and Invitations
Securing and Designing Space
Selecting and Preparing Works
II. Installation Phase
Preparing Space
Creating Signage and Labels
Setting Up the Display
Setting Up the Lighting
III. Public Phase
Transitioning to an Exhibition
Ensuring Exhibition Is Open as Advertised
Maintaining the Exhibition
Holding Public Exhibition Events
IV. Aftermath Phase
De-Installing the Exhibition
Repairing and Storing Materials and Tools

of the Exhibition, or demonstrate a hanging technique. During Students-at-Work, teachers might help students edit their work, removing pieces of lesser quality that distract viewers and leaving only those that best represent the artist's voice; re-teach a skill such as leveling a work or hammering short pins into hard plaster walls; or reorganize works to balance the display or better convey some thematic meaning. And Critiques, too, can be held profitably in the exhibition space, with students prompted to think about how the works are displayed, what the arrangement communicates. In Exhibition, students may be able to focus more on the quality of the craft, the success of the expression, and how well their intentions are conveyed to a particular audience—and if not well, why not, and what, if anything, to do about that.

WHAT CAN BE LEARNED FROM EXHIBITION

Engaging in Public Discourse

Exhibition is primarily an opportunity for learning how to engage in art as public discourse. Art is an expression of the artist, but it is never made in isolation; rather, it is made in relationship to all the work by others in other places at other times. In schools, it is all too easy for students to see their work solely as a private expression, coming uniquely from themselves and speaking only to themselves. Even when posting images online, students may lack the inclination and alertness to understand how their work communicates to varying audiences in these contexts. Teaching Exhibition well means helping students understand what it means to have their artist voice heard in the public discourse about art.

For Kathleen Marsh, helping students understand the full artistic cycle from creating to sharing art is central:

> We're definitely training all of them to understand the end of the cycle—the putting your own work out there, knowing how to curate and hang and measure and paint walls, putting your work out to the world, and saying, tell me what you think, give me your feedback. The big one is connecting to your audience and owning the entire process.

As students make decisions about the many components of an exhibition (signage, artist statements, organization of show, verbal engagement with the audience, and the artworks themselves), they learn how to present themselves as artists and engage with audiences. Using Exhibition well means providing guidance in how to select, organize, and display images so that they are compelling, and it means helping students think through how works might communicate to audiences. Helping students to understand the exhibition process writ large is particularly important, since it is no longer a hierarchical, mediated practice in visual arts. Rather, children, youth, and adults now engage in public display as a regular part of their lives. Sharing art and other visual representations with wide audiences has become a quotidian experience through social media and other digital outlets (Freedman et al., 2013; Ito et al., 2010; Lenhart & Madden, 2005; Peppler, 2010). Sheridan & Gardner (2012) claim that our models of what constitutes artistic development for all children shift as the artistic practices change—the new collaborative and public forms of youth art highlight different capacities of artistic practice and change how we conceptualize children's and youth's artistic development. When youth share their artworks in digital public spheres, art teachers can help them think more deeply about the meaning and implications of what they display and how.

In addition, Exhibition can be highly motivating for students. Kathleen believes requiring students to exhibit acts against the "tendency to be lazy, the tendency to be sloppy, the tendency to settle for second best, the tendency to over-edit yourself, the tendency to say, None of this is good, so I'm not putting anything in." When she asked her students what was needed to make an exhibition good, they listed "Communication, productivity and rigor, time management, and accountability. A distinguished, rigorous, and productive person takes on tasks that are beyond their own and helps without asking and does jobs in their own time."

Exhibition can also be powerful in developing an art program. It encourages high standards and makes artistic efforts visible, and it can also be a potent form of advocacy, promoting programs to stakeholders. Dave Ardito, Director of Art in the Arlington Public Schools in Massachusetts, describes this process in his school system. Teachers regularly hold exhibition receptions where they converse about their programs with parents. They show student work in the school committee room, and the school board receives printed statements about the exhibitions at each of their meetings that are read aloud and televised. In this way, the board, parents, and the broader public are all informed about art program goals, materials, and exemplars. Exhibition takes students' work and work processes into a broader world.

Part II

INTRODUCING THE STUDIO HABITS OF MIND: A DISPOSITIONAL VIEW OF *WHAT* THE ARTS TEACH

Watch an entire studio art class with the aim of discovering what is being taught in that class. Observers first notice students learning a multitude of techniques—throwing pots on the wheel, mixing pigments, transforming digital images, and so on. Looking a little closer reveals that what is going on is a lot more complex than the teaching of technique; students are learning many other ways of thinking at the same time as they are mastering techniques.

In the classes we observed, we saw eight ways of thinking being taught, and we refer to these as Studio Habits of Mind (often shortened to SHoM). In the chapters that follow in Part II, we describe each one of these habits of mind in alphabetical order.

The SHoM are not hierarchical, as emphasized by the circular arrangement of the habits in Figure 1.2. The habits do not work and should not be taught in a set sequence that privileges any one over another. Instead, one can begin with any habit and follow its generative energy into dynamic, interacting habit clusters as experiences unfold.

Studio Habits as Dispositions. Each studio habit is considered as a *disposition* that includes not only *skills* but also the *inclination* to use these skills and *alertness* to opportunities to deploy particular skills (Perkins et al., 1993). A dispositional perspective is useful for teachers in identifying assignments, lessons, and projects that are truly effective. Of course, no one project has to emphasize all three dispositional elements, just as no one project needs to foster all eight studio habits. The habits and their dispositional elements are aids to support teachers' professional judgments, not substitutes or mandates that replace teacher expertise.

Skill. Each habit has its own core skills, as discussed in the chapters that follow. An assignment works when students at diverse skill levels can use it to develop skill in one or more habits that are just at the edge of their ability. For instance, when Beth Balliro taught color theory, she introduced the color wheel (see Examples 4.1, 6.1, and 12.1). Students copied the wheel and a few notes into their journals. Then they made paintings that required them to use color to express an environment in which an imaginary creature—a creature they had imagined that symbolized aspects of themselves—was born (using complementary colors) and died (using neutral colors). Some students in the class were skilled in the use of color and some had never thought about color theoretically before. But this assignment allowed students to enter from any level of learning and build their skills through exploration and reflection.

Alertness. "Attention, attention, attention," says the Zen master. Where, in the stream of life's experiences, can we recognize opportunities to use abilities to good advantage? Alertness is that recognition. When Beth assigned students to "spy" on their families to see how they used "vessels" at home (Example 13.2), she fostered their alertness to consider the functions of vessels. When Kathleen Marsh assigned a texture collection, to be made by rubbing patterns found outside and in students' homes, as homework (during the self-portrait assignment, see Examples 4.2, 9.3), she fostered their alertness to an aesthetic element she wanted them to begin using more mindfully in their work. When Guy Michel Telemaque asked students to cut thumbnail images from popular magazines so that the images became unrecognizable and were transformed into pure design elements, he fostered alertness to the presence of design in familiar contexts. When Jason Green asked students to drink from their own fired ceramic cups, he fostered an alertness to nonfunctional elements such as sharp lips and awkward handles. All of these assignments help students develop habits of alertness to aesthetic qualities in the world around them.

An assignment succeeds in developing alertness to the extent that it helps students notice connections between their subjective experience and the world around them, guiding them to think about their experiences as visual artists do. Assignments that address central ideas in the field of visual art provide opportunities by offering windows into what experts consider and work with when they create and appreciate art. At the same time, assignments need to be roomy enough to leave plenty of space for the individual student's interests. A well-balanced assignment both channels and awakens perception, and in these ways supports the development of alertness.

Inclination. Inclination refers to the motivation to put one's skills to use. Inclination can be extrinsically motivated (i.e., work completed for a grade, to please someone, to fulfill a requirement), intrinsically motivated (i.e., work completed to discover an answer or a new question, or to satisfy curiosity), or can combine external and internal motivations (Amabile, 1996). An effective assignment challenges students to put skills to use in new contexts that engage them in the process of making–perceiving–reflecting (Winner & Simmons, 1992). In great assignments, extrinsic motivation begins to take its rightful backseat to intrinsic motivation, which develops as students engage in genuine inquiry and creation.

For example, Jim asked students to use the drawing skills developed through a year of instruction (e.g., composition, value, figure drawing, quality of line) to make drawings informed by Cubism, where objects are depicted in all three dimensions by showing multiple and conflicting views of an object simultaneously (see Example 11.4). Students struggled with this new way of drawing, while Jim showed examples from Picasso, Braque, and others who had approached the challenge of depicting three-dimensional reality on a flat surface. "I want to do that," a student said, as Jim showed her a Cubist work. She did not want to do it just because it was an assignment, but because she enjoyed the challenge. For this student at least, Jim had succeeded in creating intrinsic motivation for the assignment.

It is important to realize that alertness and inclination cannot be taught in the same manner as skills, which are usually demonstrated and then practiced—or, in a more constructivist vein, explored, named, and developed through iterative reflection and making. Alertness and inclination are attitudes, and these are developed through processes more like apprenticeship—through immersion in the classroom culture developed among teachers and students. Although it is easier to test for skills than to test for alertness or inclination, full assessment of any habit of mind requires assessing all three components of the habit: skill, alertness, and inclination.

In the chapters that follow, we discuss examples from the teachers whose classes formed the basis of our original research, Beth Balliro, Kathleen Marsh, and Guy Michel Telemaque from Boston Arts Academy, and Jason Green and Jim Woodside from Walnut Hill. We also mention examples from other educators currently using our framework, but for a more detailed look at current uses, see Part IV, Chapters 17–19.

FOUR

Develop Craft
Technique, Studio Practice

You start and you don't know how to do anything. You make a huge mess. You're out of control. You have no technique. It's so obvious [laughing], 'cause it's so messy. And then like any craft, you have to build and build and practice and practice. And the minute you create something with control and with technique—it's just a totally beautiful moment because you know you couldn't do it before.

—Beth Balliro

They know when they need to be there. They just work. They've just developed studio habits. And they work like artists. They just come in and do their work, and they know where everything goes. And that's what you want the beginning students to develop into.

—Jason Green

Perhaps the most obvious Studio Habit of Mind is Craft. When asked what they learn in art class, students are likely to respond that they learn to draw, paint, throw a pot—they equate learning art with simply learning craft. For example, they assume that learning to draw means learning to use conventions such as perspective, shading, and "rules" of composition. They rarely think about the other habits of mind that they are using as they work—for example, looking closely, imagining forms, conveying expression. But as Jim Woodside put it succinctly, "Art is beyond technique."

In what follows, we describe the two components of Develop Craft. Students develop the disposition to use skill attentively in various media and tools, and with conventions. We refer to this as Develop Craft: Technique. Students also develop the disposition to care for materials, tools, works, and studio spaces, and we refer to this as Develop Craft: Studio Practice. When we analyzed our videos and interviews, we labeled as Technique all instances in which students were being taught procedures and attitudes about using tools, materials, and conventions; we labeled as Studio Practice all instances in which students were being taught skills and attitudes for taking care of tools, materials, works, and studio spaces.

TECHNIQUE

Teachers demonstrate the use of tools and materials and guide students as they work. Students are meant to learn the varied properties of tools and materials and the range of ways that they can be employed in a skilled and mindful way. Students develop a sense of what they can and cannot do with different tools and materials, and they become more adept at choosing the right tools and materials for the piece they wish to make.

As students develop technique, they also learn about the elements of artworks, such as form, line, surface, value, and how to employ artistic conventions such as perspective or color mixing. While developing technique involves becoming familiar with artistic conventions, it does not require rigid adherence to them. Developing technique allows students to make informed decisions about whether and when to depart from conventions or use tools and materials in new ways.

TEACHING THE THEORY AND PRACTICE OF COLOR: INVENTING COLORS PROJECT   (EXAMPLE 4.1)

The classroom example that follows illustrates Developing Craft: Technique. In a color-mixing class at the Boston Arts Academy, Beth Balliro teaches her students about color theory and how to use the color wheel. They put this into practice by experimenting with color mixing using acrylic paints.

Beth's Inventing Colors Project (see also Examples 6.1 and 12.1), taught near the midpoint of her second-semester course with 9th-graders, is part of her multiweek Imaginary Creatures Painting Project in which students depict themselves as mythical creatures. Two paintings are assigned in this class. In the first, as mentioned earlier, students depict where their creature was born, focusing on using a set of complementary colors. In the second, they depict where their creature died, focusing on using a set of neutral colors. The class is intended to help students gain experience with acrylic paints before they begin using them on their final paintings, where they will put into practice some of what they have learned about color theory.

Demonstration–Lecture

Beth begins her Inventing Colors session with a Demonstration–Lecture on color theory that focuses on the color wheel. Beth tells students that color theory is a topic that can be taught at many levels and requires gradual building up of knowledge.

> You're getting the basics of color theory. This is a very, very first baby step. And when you're sophomores and make it back here, you'll need to know this. When you're juniors you'll further refine it. And, when you're seniors, you'll laugh because this will be so easy. OK, but right now it's the first, first step. It's the foundation. And, unless you know the foundation, you can't build upon it.

Beth directs students' attention to a color wheel she has drawn on the board. Using the wheel, she engages students in a question-and-answer session about aspects of color theory: primary and secondary colors, complementary colors, neutral colors, and color mixing. She builds on students' knowledge, elicits and corrects misconceptions, and models how to use the wheel to envision new colors. She also explains that the color wheel is a theoretical construct that provides guidelines for color mixing, but that learning about color also involves trial-and-error mixing with the specific paint being used.

Studio Transition

While students distribute the brushes, papers, and palettes (clean white Frisbees), Beth reminds them about how they need to care for materials (Develop Craft: Studio Practice) and shows them how to set up their palettes with only red, blue, yellow, white, and a gloss medium. She directs students' attention to writing on the board that describes the guidelines for the two assigned paintings. As students are setting up their palettes and materials, Beth checks in with individuals to make sure they understand the assignment.

Students-at-Work

As students work with the paint, Beth encourages them to experiment and mix a wide range of colors in order to build an understanding of the concepts of complementary and neutral colors.

- *Invent your own colors and use principles of color theory to move beyond basic colors.* Beth tells one student, "Yellow/violet. Those are opposites, so have it be mostly yellow and then mostly violet. So yellow doesn't mean only this [*holding up a yellow paint tube*]. You can mix it with a little red to have an orangish yellow, or a little white to have a whitish yellow."

Stopping to talk with another student, she reminds him to use the painting to develop facility with color mixing and not to spend too much time locked into detail. Moving to two other students, Beth advises one to explore "endless kinds of yellow." With the second, she clarifies, "You don't want it to be just red or green, you want it to be in the family of red or green."

- *Use principles of color theory to guide your color mixing.* To a student who asks how to achieve skin tone by mixing colors, Beth demonstrates as she tells him how to make use of the principles of color theory along with trial and error to create a desired color: "Whenever you go for skin, that's a neutral color no matter whose skin you're talking about. And that's made by mixing the color and its opposite." She also points out that she's using lots of water because she wants the colors to blend. Finally, she shows how to add white for a highlight, but cautions: "If you want to get darker, you can't use black because it will make it too gray—I want you to do what a group of artists called the Impressionists did, which is to use only color for dark. So I'm going to add [*adding blue*] and this will be your dark."
- *Think of these paintings as a vehicle to develop technique in color mixing.* Beth tells one student: "Try not to spend too much time on the drawing. Because even though we just spent lots of time talking about how drawing is the foundation of painting, today you need to learn how to mix color. That's the goal of today. It's not to create a great perspective drawing of a bridge. It's to mix color."
- *Recognize that trial and error help in learning to mix color.* Beth asks a student what he used to mix the color he wants to be a deep orange. As she demonstrates how to mix the color, Beth explains, "So if I said that orange is a little too green, add red,

the opposite of green. It's a back and forth. There is no recipe because each kind of paint acts differently."

- *Try other ways to mix color once you have grasped basic techniques.* Beth confirms a student's use of red plus yellow to make orange, with the addition of gel medium to make a translucent orange. Then she challenges him: "And now think about if you can pull in other colors to get it to be even more of a range of color. In other words, now that I've seen a lot of paintings I think, 'Oh, he made that with red and yellow.' You want me to look at it and not even care about how you made it. You want me to think, 'Ah, look at that red. How did he do that? It's a mystery red.'"

Beth Reflects

Beth explained to us in a post-class interview that she lectures on the color wheel and its history rather than just letting students learn through trial and error so that students will see that painting is scientific. Whether or not students become painters, "they understand that painting is not exclusively an intuitive, free, emotional process, but there is a real science supporting it, and a long history of color theory."

But theory is not enough. To explain why students also need to experiment with paint, Beth gave the following example of what colors do in practice to model differences from what the color wheel predicts:

> If you mix Yellow Ochre with Mars Black you get a green. So, without any kind of blue, you can achieve a green. And that's very different from what the color wheel tells you. And it's because how they make Mars Black is with probably some dark, dark blue pigment. It's a composite color so it's not a pure thing.

In her Demonstration–Lecture, she alerts students to this gap between theory and practice. This class illustrates Beth's belief that playful assignments that prompt students to Stretch and Explore help students develop technique. She explained that when students play around, they end up having to confront technical issues. Beth finds she can help them with technical issues in a low-stakes way without threatening their self-confidence.

With more advanced students, Beth uses a more complex and inventive approach to technique instead of explicitly focusing on the development of technical skills, as she does with beginners. "I believe in the standard 'you have to know the rules to break them,' and this connects to building technique first and then pushing beyond it

and its foundation," she explains. For beginners, Beth said she might ask them to use five complementary colors, while with advanced painters she might talk about achieving space through the sharpness of edges, or by *inventing* some kind of technique. Beth also added another example: "With 9th-graders I might talk about how you glaze. This is how you create a dry brush effect. With an upper-grade student, I might say, 'What technique have you made up here?'"

A Dispositional View of Technique

It is easy to equate technique with skill, but skill is not sufficient. Technique must be tied to its purpose, which is making an idea visible. Both alertness to opportunities to use techniques and inclination to pursue techniques lead to the expression of meaning. Teaching artistic conventions in isolation from what these skills are *for* fragments art education into mere training.

Skill. The skill of Technique includes the ability to use tools, materials, and the conventions of design. While learning technique involves becoming familiar with artistic conventions, it does not require rigid adherence to them. Students need to learn what they can and cannot do with different tools and materials and to select the right tools and materials for what they want to achieve.

Alertness. When artists notice weaknesses in craft, they show an alertness to Technique. Without alertness, all the skill in the world is insufficient: Artists need to recognize when and where to deploy their skills, and they need to be resourceful, recognizing the potentials of available materials. Alertness to the technical potential of materials lays the groundwork for making informed decisions and leaps of insight, such as when Picasso recognized a bicycle seat could be used to represent the head of a bull. Students learning to use a new material need to be alert to its range of possibilities: the textural qualities paint can make, the range of effects afforded by a filter in a graphics program, the different methods by which pieces can be attached in an assemblage. Developing technique allows students to make informed decisions about whether and when to depart from conventions or use tools and materials in new ways.

Inclination. Even when students are alert to what needs to be worked on, they must have the inclination actually to do so. Thus, when a teacher observes a weak element of technique in a student's work and the student responds simply, "But I like it like that," that student may be showing a lack of inclination to appreciate the importance of technique. Students can have the ability that is needed (skill) and be aware of what needs to be done (alertness), but still not be motivated to *use* their skills to address an issue (inclination).

STUDIO PRACTICE

Studio art involves making things, and students need facility with the tools and materials with which these things are made. But some instruction must invariably involve teaching the conventions for caring for these materials and tools. We call this kind of instruction *Develop Craft: Studio Practice.* Studio Practice refers to ways for finding, caring for, and storing materials (e.g., clay, paper, paint) and tools (e.g., brushes, wire cutters, erasers). Studio Practice also involves learning how to store one's works—labeling and dating them, spraying them, putting them in portfolios so they do not get ripped, and so forth. Studio Practice also involves learning ways to make best use of the physical space of the classroom (e.g., giving yourself ample room for materials, placing materials such that they are easy to use where and when you need them), as well as learning about procedures that are specific to working in an art studio (e.g., wearing smocks, wearing safety glasses when using power tools).

The two classroom examples that follow illustrate Developing Craft: Studio Practice.

TEACHING THE PRACTICE OF MAINTAINING THE STUDIO: SELF-PORTRAITS IN COLORED PENCIL PROJECT   (EXAMPLE 4.2)

At the Boston Arts Academy in Kathleen Marsh's class, Self-Portraits in Colored Pencil, taught near the beginning of her fall course with 9th-graders (see also Example 10.3), students engage in a cleanup session that shows many of the features of what we came to call Studio Practice. From the first days of school, Kathleen assigns specific cleanup tasks to students in her 9th-grade class as a way of encouraging them to be responsible for maintaining their work environment. Kathleen considers it foundational that students learn the studio practices of setting up, cleaning up, coming in and out of the studio space, and finding specific tools and materials. She notes, "It's going to be a huge change from what they've been doing." Workspaces inevitably get messy, and students must learn that cleaning up is just as important as setting up their work environment.

In interviews with us, Kathleen stressed the importance of students learning to maintain their work environment, which is especially important in a shared space. If students have their own studios, the level of mess is a personal choice. But in a communal space, courtesy and efficiency dictate cleaning up. "There are so many people that use that room. That room is in use all day long. And it's got to be ready and presentable for the next class." She used the example of Alexander Calder to acknowledge how working solo differs. "I don't think the man ever cleaned up. And it didn't affect his work any. Some people have to have a clean environment to work. But I don't think everybody does." In a shared space, Kathleen added, "It's about citizenship."

Kathleen teaches cleanup as part of a work cycle. "They have to understand that their work period has a beginning and an end, and at the end, you know, the work has to go in a place where you're going to be able to find it. And the tables have to be orderly. And the floor has to be swept. That's just basic." To structure the cleanup, Kathleen assigns specific tasks so students know exactly for which part they are responsible. Assignments provide training and solve the practical problem of making sure all work gets done. Kathleen also told us that at the Boston Arts Academy there is a schoolwide cleanup philosophy. "This is their workspace, so they need to work on maintaining it."

TEACHING THE STUDIO PRACTICE OF KEEPING A PORTFOLIO: LIGHT AND BOXES PROJECT   (EXAMPLE 4.3)

Midway through the first term, students in Jim Woodside's class are working on a Light and Boxes Project (see also Examples 3.3 and 8.2). They are making reverse charcoal drawings of a still life of boxes by using an eraser to pull light forms out of paper coated with graphite. Today students are also going to learn how to care for their work by constructing a portfolio, spraying their drawings so that they don't get smudged, and organizing and storing their artworks in the portfolio. During class, Jim takes students one at a time over to the side of the room, where he helps them make a portfolio from cardboard and duct tape.

Before students start to draw, Jim explains what they will be doing and why. "I think the easiest way, the most useful way to maximize our time is for me to ask you to come over one by one. And then the rest of you can keep drawing." He also reminds students to spray their drawings outside where there's fresh air, to preserve them. Jim makes clear to students that portfolios help them take care of their work. Additionally, he tells them that having work organized in portfolios helps him when he grades their work.

Jim Reflects

In an interview, Jim talked about the importance of students keeping portfolios of their work. Maintaining a portfolio helps instill a sense of professionalism in students about their artwork. Portfolios also allow students to see changes from their early to later drafts. Seeing this history of one's working process is part of seeing oneself as an artist, and this is the reason Jim encourages students not to throw away any of their work.

> It's really important, because it has to do with how they see themselves as artists. They see the work they've produced. They see the process they've been in. And they see the history of the process. This is why I don't want them to throw things away as well. You know, sometimes I say, "If you do something that you think is a mistake and you throw it away, it doesn't mean you never made the mistake, you know. So why throw it away?"

When Jim sits down to write comments and give grades, he looks through a portfolio to view a student's work from the beginning to the end of the semester. Students looking at their portfolios have the same window onto their work and working process. They see the peaks and valleys and how hard they've worked, and this allows them to reflect on their process and progress. Additionally, Jim told us that he worked one-on-one because students in this class were young, and he wanted to sit with each of them personally as they organized their work.

A Dispositional View of Studio Practice

Skill is rarely a challenge for students' understanding of Studio Practice—pick up the scraps, return tools to their designated places, wash the paint (carefully!) out of the brushes. More challenging is the need to develop proactive attitudes toward those skills so that the studio environment continuously supports one's learning. Artists arrange studio spaces to nurture the production of their work, and studio classrooms need to be maintained for the same reason. When teachers introduce cleanup as something artists do to help them in their work, rather than as something rigid and done because teachers say so, students develop alertness to *when* to do maintenance and the inclination to *actually* do it. What is usually seen as drudgery management becomes part of the learning agenda. It may still be unpleasant, but it is recognized as necessary and purposeful.

Skill. Gaining the skills of Studio Practice is not difficult. Skill requires learning how to keep one's materials and tools clean and how to store one's work and materials so that they are both safe and accessible. This skill involves learning how to organize one's space so that one can work optimally (e.g., giving oneself ample room for materials, placing materials so that they are easy to use where and when you need them), as well as learning about procedures that are specific to work in an art studio (e.g., soaking clay tools in buckets to avoid clogging sinks, working with masks and in well-ventilated spaces with materials that emit toxic fumes).

Alertness. Alertness to Studio Practice requires that students identify instances when cleaning or reorganizing materials, tools, and studio space will support them in making artwork. Disarray is useful for some and impedes others, but noticing the environment's effects on the artist's process is what provokes decisions to take the time away from creating and make physical adjustments to the studio. Recognizing when to change the music, repaint the walls, or adjust light sources are all instances of the alertness to Studio Practice.

Inclination. Studio Practices are routines artists develop to support their working process. When teachers straighten up the classroom, they model taking responsibility in the studio. When they define and assign specific roles and tasks for cleanup, they build the habitual expectation that maintenance is part of an artist's daily practice. A studio routine may also aid an artist's working process (e.g., cleaning or organizing the studio can offer a moment to think about a piece from a new perspective). Any task that motivates making changes to the physical environment's organization and maintenance of spaces, tools, or materials develops the inclination to develop Studio Practice.

STRUCTURING A CLASS TO FOCUS ON BOTH TECHNIQUE AND STUDIO PRACTICE

TEACHING CARE OF THE WHEEL AND THROWING TECHNIQUE: INTRODUCING CENTERING ON THE WHEEL   (EXAMPLE 4.4)

At Walnut Hill, Jason Green develops students' understanding of Studio Practice and Technique in his Centering Project, introduced in the first class of the fall semester (see also Example 13.1). Here students begin to learn how to use the pottery wheel to center balls of clay. To do this, they must gain familiarity with both rules of the studio and techniques for using the pottery wheel (see Figure 4.1).

Demonstration-Lecture

At the beginning of this first class, Jason shows students where the tools and materials they will need are kept. In

Figure 4.1. Develop Craft—Jason Green's Students Learn to Throw Clay Forms on a Pottery Wheel

A. Jason Green introduces tools to students in their first ceramics class

B. He labels drawers of ceramics tools to make them accessible

C. Jason demonstrates setting up to center clay on a pottery wheel

D. While students work, Jason advises them individually on centering

this 15-minute Demonstration–Lecture, he walks them through setting up materials and tools so they can begin to work. As he talks, he demonstrates each tool, shows how it works, and then gives step-by-step instructions as he models how to work the wheel, showing both correct and incorrect ways.

The following examples illustrate how Jason introduces getting set up to use the pottery wheel:

- *Jason tells students all about the tools they will need* (Develop Craft: Studio Practice). Jason informs students that they will each need a bucket for water. He shows them where the buckets are kept and fills one with water to show exactly where and how to fill them, as well as how much water to put in. He also shows students ceramics tools that they will need. He takes one of each and displays the collection on a nearby table as an example that they can refer to as they set up their own throwing materials—wooden ribs, wire tools, needle tools, and sponges—and other tools that they won't need today but will use later, like wooden knives.
- *Jason tells students how to get their clay ready for the wheel* (Develop Craft: Technique). Students will first need to get water in a bucket and set up a bat, the round flat surface on which their clay will sit as they turn the wheel and work the clay. Jason shows students how to cut clay and how to compress it. As he demonstrates, Jason describes what he's doing. "When I'm doing this, I'm trying not to fold the clay, like these folds, really trying to keep those compressed."
- *Jason gives a detailed description of the wheels* (Develop Craft: Studio Practice). Jason holds up a splash pan, shows how this large bowl fits onto the wheels, and notes that some of the wheels are a little bit different; these practical details are critical to the students' success with the tools. He next shows how each wheel has a pedal and where the buttons are that turn the wheels on. Students will also need a bat. Jason tells students where to get their bats and how to care for them: "Sometimes the bats aren't cleaned. You want to make sure everything's clean. So if you have clay here [*pointing to the bat*], or clay around these [*pointing to the wheel surface where there are pins that fit the holes in the bat*], you might need to take your needle tool and clean it a little bit [*holds up the needle tool*]." Once a bat is clean, it can be placed on bat pins, and students are told to be sure that the bat doesn't rock on its pins.

Next, Jason shows students how to form balls of clay. He makes eight balls to give students a chance to really see his ball-making technique as they work along. After they have made several balls themselves, Jason demonstrates how to center a ball of clay on the wheel. As he demonstrates, Jason carefully describes all the actions involved in each step of the process. He draws their attention to how his body is positioned, where his support is, and what he does with his hands. As he demonstrates the correct procedures, he also describes typical problems students may have and how to avoid them.

Students-at-Work

Following Jason's introduction, students choose a wheel and set up their own areas for work. Jason talks with students as they work, offering comments rich in information about the studio practice of getting set up. Sometimes Jason's comments remind students of what they saw in the earlier Demonstration–Lecture, as when he has to remind students where to get their clay. Other comments offer new information, as when he tells students which kind of bat to use.

When students begin to work on the wheel, Jason circles the room, closely observing students before giving advice on their technique. When he talks with students, he notes points of success and corrects errors, frequently demonstrating again as he talks. The repetition is necessary to support understanding, as each student sees new aspects of the process, depending on their constantly changing levels of understanding.

- *Jason reminds students of the assignment and gives advice as he watches them* (Develop Craft: Technique). When students first start working, Jason often reminds them of the assignment and what he has shown them in the Demonstration–Lecture. For example, stopping to look at the balls of clay one student has made, he reminds her: "Make these really, really round. Make eight and remember you'll need a bat, which is up front, to put them on. Try to make them the same size if you can. That's good, that's good. Try not to make them too big; you'll have to use lots of muscle."
- *Jason gives step-by-step instructions to help students attend to aspects of process as they work* (Develop Craft: Technique). To a student starting the wheel and centering a clay ball, Jason first advises, "Now, the first thing, you're going to put some water on it and press down on it." He then corrects how fast she is spinning the wheel. After the student has correctly adjusted the speed, Jason demonstrates and describes how to hold her hands and press the clay. Before moving to the next student Jason prompts, "Add a little bit more water now," and demonstrates again how the student should hold her hands.

- *Jason shows how the whole body contributes to centering* (Develop Craft: Technique). As Jason advises students, he moves students' hands, elbows, or feet to correct their position or demonstrates proper form himself. Jason tells one student, "Remember, your left elbow has to be braced, so you want to brace it against your hip. And then you want to put your right hand, lock it onto your left hand." As he speaks, he shows her this technique and how the clay is starting to get centered as he starts to apply pressure. After watching the student, he reminds her, "Keep that elbow down on your leg. Put pressure on the top and side at the same time, and add water very frequently."

Jason Reflects

In an interview after the class, Jason told us that he focuses on the technique of centering because that skill is a prerequisite to making any kind of pottery. He added that in the demonstration he shows how to center rather than how to make a pot because "students know they're going to be making pottery, and they know pottery is hollow. But if they don't have that basic skill of centering, then it's very, very difficult to make a pot."

Jason explained that centering is a complex and difficult skill that involves a variety of types of understanding—conceptual and physical—and that his goal in the first several weeks is for students to learn to center.

> Most of them have never touched clay before. And even if you know a little bit about throwing pottery, you know what centering is, but if it's brand new, you might not even know what that term means. In some ways there are mechanical and sensory aspects and the understanding that goes along with it— understanding the language of the medium.

Jason's focus on centering is one way he works to change students' general attitudes toward materials. Jason gave us the following reason for his emphasis on the properties of clay:

> Sometimes students will try to use clay to make something, and they're just making their idea and not *thinking* about the material. And they may fail, because they're not using the entire process. They're just using the clay as a construction material.

Without becoming responsive to properties of the material, entering into an ongoing dialogue with it, students are just implementing fixed ideas and might as well be using any material. He wants them to avoid naively underestimating the material's importance, which is typical of a beginning student. "They just happened to be in ceramics, so they're making this thing out of clay. But there's no reason for it to be made out of clay." This is the kind of thinking he wants students to avoid and to begin to understand how the clay is a partner in their creations.

More advanced students also have the same difficulty working with the properties of the clay. After Jason described one student's growing frustration and difficulties, he added,

> Sometimes you just can't do certain things because the materials you have won't work the way you want them to. One point I was trying to make to her is that she might not have to actually follow her design exactly, and she might have to allow the process to be more fluid.

Students vary in the ease with which they develop techniques such as centering. As Jason noted, "It takes some students weeks and weeks and weeks until they can do that." He added that sometimes he spends class time mainly going around the room individually helping those students, demonstrating to them, and correcting their technique individually.

Generative Connections With Develop Craft

In the third of his six Norton lectures at Harvard University, South African artist William Kentridge illustrated how artists combine Craft with other habits. As he walked back and forth between his drawing and the camera used to shoot his animation, *Mine*, Kentridge pondered how to create a transition between two scenes. This slow process required the maker (Develop Craft), the viewer (Observe), and the walker (Reflect) to converse with one another. It was during his walks back and forth between the camera and the drawing that Kentridge figured out how to solve a problem he had been pondering for days. The video, produced by the Mahindra Humanities Center at Harvard, is available at https://www.youtube.com/watch?v=cdKkmSqYTE8.

Kentridge's description of how he works mirrors the process described by Arts PROPEL, a collaboration among Project Zero, Educational Testing Service, and the Pittsburgh Public Schools (funded by the Rockefeller Foundation from 1986 to 1991). Arts PROPEL developed long-term projects (called "Domain Projects") involving three components: production, perception, and reflection. Production, or making, was always primary and central. Perception always grew from making: Students were encouraged to look closely at their works (and works of others) as they created. And all along students were encouraged to reflect about their process and to continually evaluate their work. Hence, reflection also grew out of making. This structure in which production, perception, and reflection interact was important to the development of our Studio Thinking Framework. The introductory handbook to Arts Propel can be downloaded here: http://www.pz.harvard.edu/resources/arts-propel -a-handbook-for-imaginative-writing

The teaching of craft is often—though not always—central to visual arts classes. Acquiring technique gives students control over their works. And as students acquire technique, they begin to "think" with it, and that means making connections to other habits. But although Develop Craft was emphasized as an intended learning goal for every class we observed, we never saw it being taught alone. Instead, teachers cluster technique with one or more of the other habits, introducing ways to use skills with tools, materials, and conventions in the context of larger projects that require students to "think with" these skills, and not simply as tricks to be mastered for their own sake. Similarly, teachers model practices that maintain the studio as a way to support the artmaking process, not as tasks to be carried out because someone said to. Teaching Develop Craft within the context of a project sets students up to learn alertness (recognizing when a new or better skill would improve the work they are engaged in making) and inclination (they are more likely to actually use skills to improve work they care about).

Using habits together develops all of the habits involved: Each one stimulates the others, since they are interdependent. In the example below, a senior from the Boston Arts Academy talks about capturing light and creating variations of value in his drawing. His comments show us how Develop Craft clusters with Engage and Persist and Observe.

> It's about capturing light on something. Once more it's about value. Because that's something I've been working on the past four years. I push myself to see more variations and to get more detailed and to compare the grays. Like when I was doing my self-portrait, comparing the grays between one area of my face and the other to try to show the difference. [See Figure 4.2]

Develop Craft pairs with Express whenever teachers assign authentic and engaging projects so that technique must be used to convey meaning. Develop Craft also clusters with Stretch and Explore and Engage and Persist (teachers might tell students to play around and keep trying); and also with Observe and Understand Art Worlds

Figure 4.2. Self-Portrait from a Senior at the Boston Arts Academy

(a teacher can encourage a student to look closely at how other artists use or approach materials and tools).

What Teachers Can Do

Focus on the Quality of Craft in Relation to What the Work Conveys. The most important understanding students can achieve about Craft is that it is a vehicle for *meaning and expression.* Therefore, it is important to teach in a way that makes this clear. A comment from Jim Woodside, a drawing teacher at the Walnut Hill School and part of our original study, makes this point sharply. Looking at one of his student's drawings that was strong in technique but devoid of atmosphere, Jim said that a drawing that is just technique is dead.

Teachers help students link craft and meaning as they discuss work. For instance, Jim asks students questions that highlight how their choices about edges in their drawings are connected to effects "Let's look at the edges of your shapes. See how this is a hard edge and this one bleeds into the next? This one has a gap, and this one is soft and transparent. What are you saying with all those different edges? If you mean them all to be bold, you'll need to keep working to make them all consistent. But if you want a sense of disarray, think about making them more different, and where each difference should be."

Likewise, when looking with students at the work of practicing artists, teachers might discuss how the artists' decisions about materials, techniques and conventions relate to what the work conveys. Contemporary artists often violate our expectations about craft and create surprise, either by using techniques in unusual ways or by using approaches that contradict expected fundamentals. For instance, Chinese performance artist Liu Bolin painstakingly paints a bodysuit on himself so that he can blend into various backgrounds as a barely visible figure. The purpose of this is to make commentary on the invisibility of the individual in the face of institutions, but the expressive effect only works with meticulous technique. Or to turn to a more traditional work of art, one might discuss how Michelangelo's use of Carrara marble and decision to depict a naturalistic pose both contribute to the emotionality of *The Pietà*.

Use One-on-One Conversations During Students-at-Work sessions as opportunities to introduce mini-lessons on skill. "Here's a tool that might help you," or "Let me show you something about mixing browns," or "Have you thought about how things are attached? Let's look at what you've done and what that tells a viewer." Teachers can also build Studio Practice into these conversations. These "just-in-time" teaching moments help students develop the alertness for which of their skills to use when. "If you put your water bucket on the other side, you won't have to reach across your work and risk dripping on it," or "Your workspace is awfully cluttered. Take a few minutes to get it organized—you'll be able to find what you need more quickly."

Develop Craft in Other Disciplines

Every discipline involves craft, and just like the visual artist, practitioners of other disciplines need alertness and inclination in addition to skill to practice their craft well. Both surgeons and sailors learn techniques for tying knots, alertness to which knot is needed in a particular situation that comes up, and the motivation to tie it so it holds. An historian learns to find and handle primary source documents without damaging them, alert to the need to preserve the fragile and irreplaceable objects for the future and inclined to do so even when it is inconvenient. A writer learns grammar and syntax to communicate clearly, is alert to errors and to the needs of different audiences, and makes the effort to speak and write grammatically, driven by the need for listeners and readers to understand. Astronomers learn to use telescopes and to care for them, chemists to accurately weigh and measure substances because minute differences can change reactions. A singer learns the skills needed to support her breath from the diaphragm, but must also learn to recognize when to adjust her breathing technique (alertness, for example, to the shifts needed when singing long melodic vs. punctuated phrases), and be driven consistently to employ different skills as different needs arise (inclination). And every kind of work has Studio Practices. In all disciplines, professionals need to maintain their working spaces, tools, materials, and storage of products that are in process and completed: Sailors develop the motivation to care for ropes and singers to foster the health of the voice, and both develop alertness to when that is required (older ropes beginning to fray; how to sing when a cold is coming on). In each of these examples, Craft is used for disciplinary purposes.

In the next chapter we look at how classes are set up to teach students to work through frustration, to not give up, to persist and remain engaged.

FIVE

Engage and Persist
Committing and Following Through

I think they learned how to work through frustration.

—Kathleen Marsh

Teachers in rigorous visual arts classes present their students with engaging projects, and they teach their students to connect to the assignment personally, to persist in their work, and to stick to a task for a sustained period.

In both schools we observed, this culminated in high school seniors being able to pursue a self-directed line of inquiry for a full semester. Students are taught to identify their own passions and interests and connect these to art projects, whether assigned or developed autonomously. They are also taught to focus, to develop mental states conducive to working, and to develop self-regulation (Baumeister & Vohs, 2007). They are taught to break out of ruts and blocks, and to feel motivated to go on. For instance, a senior at Walnut Hill pursued a semester project that resulted in several dozen expressive and painterly oil portraits and other studies. He told us that his teachers gave him some feedback as he pursued his independent study but that they mostly had a "hands-off approach," allowing him to focus on what he termed his "personal learning." In his words: "I think that's where I am currently as a result of doing a lot of work and just learning from what I was doing. And a lot of it, I've found, is my personal learning. I mean, the biggest element is, I think, I care about it. It's like I really want to advance where I'm going."

Teachers also push their students to stick to projects and not to give up. One 9th-grader at the Boston Arts Academy told us why he practices his drawing every day outside of class. "You can't expect to be great at it without practicing." In the words of artist Sister Corita Kent (Kent & Steward, 2008, p. 176), Rule 7 in art is "The only rule is work. If you work it will lead to something. It's the people who do all of the work all the time who eventually catch on to things."

When one is engaged, one is intrinsically motivated to persist. Persisting for intrinsic reasons is what matters, not simply following directives to persist or persisting out of fear or a desire for approval. It is this habit that

becomes the "still small voice" that drives intrinsic motivation, turning students from "school-success" orientation to working to pursue a full and passionate life.

Engagement is what makes someone *want* to persist. Personal engagement means that one gets pleasure out of the work itself, rather than simply working at something for some future goal. Mihaly Csikszentmihalyi (1990) calls this "autotelic" experience—experience that is self-rewarding and leads to states of flow—when one is truly engaged, lost in concentration, unaware of time, and fully focused on the moment.

In what follows, we present two classroom examples in which we see students working on projects that require sustained attention and motivation. In both classes, students wrestle with frustration and must work hard over time to meet a deadline.

DESIGNING IN CLAY: COMPLETING THE TILE PROJECT (EXAMPLE 5.1)

Toward the end of the school year at Walnut Hill, students are hard at work on a tile project in Jason Green's ceramic sculpture course. This project requires considerable technical skill and the willingness to stick to a task for several weeks without being able to see the end product. In an earlier class (see Example 6.2), students have designed a grid composed of nine tiles, and today their task is to finish their tiles. Students are asked to think about the shape, color, and texture of their tiles and to use the grid as a sketchbook in which they experiment with design options. As students come into class, they know what they are working on and go right to work. Jason calls this a "working class" (see Figure 5.1).

Students-at-Work

Today students must keep working hard if they are to finish the assignment by the deadline. "We will actually

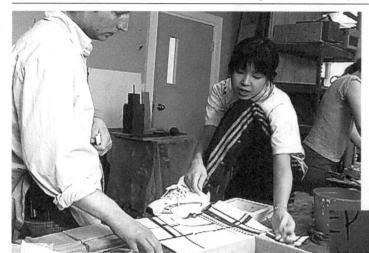

A. Jason Green urges a student to continue the work she has begun

B. His students go right to work as they enter class

C. He advises a student not to judge her work so early in the process of making ceramic art

D. Jason urges another student to try to finish by the end of class as he consults about her design decisions

try to finish these tiles today, and that's a lot of work for some of you," Jason says, acknowledging that the students have a difficult task ahead of them.

Jason consults with students as they work, helping them focus on their work and stick to the task:

- *Stick to what you've begun.* Jason opposes a student's plan to start over, urging her to stick to the work she has begun. He also reminds her there is a deadline: "It won't be done by the show. That's all I can say if you want to start a new one. I would finish this."
- *Slowing down is sometimes a form of persisting.* To another student, Jason says, "So you just need to relax and take your time and build it."
- *Even if you're not happy with your work right now, it's important to keep going.* When a student says she feels her work looks "stupid," Jason gives her courage to keep on going. "You shouldn't be critical at this point, because it's so early in the process."
- *Learn to manage time as you work.* Jason suggests to a student that she find time to come to the studio outside of class so she can finish. He reminds her that she should glaze soon. "It's going to take you a while to glaze those pieces, I think. So you want to make some time in your schedule. This weekend. Friday."
- *Keep going even when you may not feel like it.* Jason tells a student to keep on going, even if she is not in the mood. "You should try to finish this today even if you don't feel like doing it. It's your last chance to get it done."

Jason Reflects

In our initial interview with Jason, he talked about how the medium of ceramics requires self-discipline because the material is continually changing and always drying out.

I think it helps students develop habits—speedier habits that hopefully will allow or force them to think about things—and think about their artwork a little bit when they're outside of the classroom, so they don't just leave and forget about it. They have to remind themselves—you know, think about it sometimes.

In our interview following this class, Jason talked about how students learn by following through, even if they don't like what they have made. By going through the process and coming up with something, students realize that not everything works.

Sometimes a class is just about working until the job is done. Jason characterized this class as a "working class"

and the last "wet day," so students needed to get right to work.

Just get work done so that we can finish things up. The goal was to really get people to make decisions about things and do it, and that's how art works when you have a deadline. And you know sometimes that's a good thing because you know your process is accelerated a little bit and you know you might have to make a quick decision or it changes the pace a little bit. So that's sort of the overall goal [of this class]—do the work that needs to be done.

Jason also noted that students come to understand that art projects require work over extended periods of time. Jason acknowledged that this was a frustrating project, and students would never have completed it if they had not been pushed to persist. He added:

The students didn't like the project very much, but they liked the results a lot. Almost across the board I think they were really frustrated with the whole thing, because they had to use so many tools and measure things, and I think they just really had to struggle a little bit, and, also, we had a short time line.

FINISHING THE PROCESS: MAKING PUPPETS PROJECT (EXAMPLE 5.2)

As the final project in Kathleen Marsh's fall term, 9th-grade foundations class at the Boston Arts Academy, students are working on 3D projects. They have learned to encase an egg in a package strong enough to keep it from breaking when dropped 100 feet (see Example 11.6). This was followed by a joinery workshop with Barrington Edwards, a colleague in the visual art department. In the class featured here, students are working on a culminating project designed jointly by Kathleen and Barrington: making a 3D puppet with two kinds of joints and five moveable parts. Kathleen and Barrington have stressed the importance of linking craft and design in building the puppets, a technically demanding project.

Just as Jason recognized the difficulty of the multistep Tile Project, Kathleen is well aware of how challenging this project is. Students are frustrated because their puppets look unfinished. They have not yet gotten them to the envisioned endpoint. Like Jason, she feels the need to encourage the students so that they will stay engaged. For example, at one point she asks, "How many of you feel frustrated with your pieces right now?" Many students raise hands. Her next comments offer encouragement:

> I want to say for all of you that you've done an amazing job. . . . To take something [paper] that's inherently two-dimensional and make it three-dimensional is really difficult. This is a really hard thing we're asking you to do. And you're doing a really good job. So, don't lose heart, okay?

Students are given clear information about just what they need to do to finish this project, to help them stick to the task by making it clear what the task demands. "I hear a lot of extra conversation. I know you guys are really ready to begin, OK? And I know you are really antsy, but I want to make sure that everybody is clear about what's required."

Kathleen also reminds students of expectations, "Part of the culture of this school, and not just this department, is that there is an expectation that you are going to spend time outside of class on your work." At the same time, she tells students why there is this expectation:

> Our expectation is that you spend a little time outside of school working on things, because we do want you to challenge yourself. We do want you to go above and beyond the very basics of what we ask, and sometimes that requires more time. OK? So, sometimes you need to get into the habit and culture of staying after school.

She reminds them that all of the visual arts teachers are available in the classrooms Monday through Thursday after school. This is a clear example of a verbalized expectation that students stay engaged and keep persisting.

Students-at-Work

As students work, Kathleen offers encouragement to both individuals and to the whole class.

- *Don't give up. You've done a good job.* As she helps students, Kathleen pushes and encourages at the same time. She looks at one student's sketch and prods the student to continue. "Where are your moveable parts?" "You have a lot of work to do, but you have a good start. You've got to really focus." At the same time, she offers praise for what the student has done so far.
- *Remember the task at hand.* As Kathleen walks to help a student, she expresses her concern for the way the whole class is starting to lose focus, "I'm very worried by you. You're all over the place, and you're not focused."

- *Re-engage with a "good-enough" vision and a feasible plan of action you can carry through.* As Kathleen pauses to help a student joining paper strips, she offers advice: " Don't fall in the trap of having a vision that's so far away that you can't satisfy the basics of the assignment, and don't get so caught up in disappointment that it's not matching your original vision. You and many others like you fall into that trap, and one of the things an artist needs to learn is that sometimes you just have to meet deadlines and meet the criteria being asked for rather than being too perfectionist."

Kathleen and Students Reflect

In an interview after the class, Kathleen reflected on the project and on helping students to Engage and Persist. Some students need to be monitored so that they stay on track. Others Engage and Persist on their own, yet even these independent students need to be checked in a large class so they don't get lost. "You have to keep checking everybody. Making sure they're still all going in the right direction. Making sure they're not losing focus, and it's hard 'cause that class is really big." Kathleen thinks that her students need support to stay focused; she notes "A lot of kids who come to this school do not have the kind of external support that kids who are middle-class or upper-class have, so we have to create structure and support." She finds that students learn to stay on task for increasingly long periods of time. "I noticed that their attention span is lengthening. They're learning to work in longer studio sessions. They aren't asking me for breaks anymore."

One senior said learning to persist in work was the most important thing she learned in her 4 years at the Boston Arts Academy.

> Here they force you to stick with a piece. I remember in middle school you just started drawing something, you just leave it on the table and walk away. You don't have to finish it like that. And I had a real difficult problem with sticking to my work, because I'd have an idea and I'd be all happy about it and I'd start it. And then by midway, I'd have another idea. And I'd get the idea from the piece that I started, and so I'd just digress again and start over. And they had no problem with that in middle school. It's only like keeping you busy. It doesn't matter what you're doing. Then I got here. It was only Boston Arts Academy when I really started finishing pieces, and that was a big thing for me, because it's like wow, I actually completed something! And I like it! [*laughing*] So it was huge,

Figure 5.2. Charcoal Self-Portrait by a Senior at the Boston Arts Academy

Figure 5.3. Wood Sculpture by a Senior at Walnut Hill

it was like a big deal for me just to finish the work. [See Figure 5.2]

A senior at Walnut Hill talks about her persistence and shows us how sticking to a project also involves the habit of *Envision*. The end product that she holds in her mind motivates her to keep working:

"I think I've learned how to work really hard" is the first response of the Walnut Hill senior who created the sculpture shown in Figure 5.3 when we asked her what she saw as her important learning over 4 years of art classes. The sculpture is inspired by her idea of creating a 3D mosaic with wood blocks and is a good example of her work ethic. Working from a pixelated image of gears, she describes her initial process: "I put [the image] in a gray scale so that for each different scale I made a block a different length—the lightest blocks were the longest ones and the darkest blocks were the shortest ones. So I had to plan everything out before I actually started to do it." However, after cutting all the blocks to scale, planning their assembly, and constructing it nearly to the top, she realized that the sides of the circle were not going to connect properly and the structure was not stable.

She had to disassemble the parts of the circle, figure out how to make it work to her envisioned goal, and then recut the wooden pieces. Her engagement in creating this piece, envisioning how it would look when done, and her commitment to good craft combined together to help her to persist: "I'll get halfway finished and I'll just be like, 'ugh, I don't want to do that anymore.' But when I get to that point I'll just look at what I've done. That's what gets me through it, just thinking about what the end product is gonna look like." She told us that as a senior she explicitly set challenges to make herself work hard: "I pick ways of building things that are very tedious, very meticulous work. I make it really difficult for myself to get done. I like it when I get stuck, because I have to work so much harder. I don't know, I just like to work."

In our final interview with Kathleen, she talks about the importance of passion, which we see as the high end of engaging and persisting:

The thing that we talk a lot about as a school is that other thing that you look for, which is the unmeasurable thing, which we call "it," or "the twinkle in the eye," "the hunger," "the desire," and we don't measure it. We certainly talk about it, we certainly note it, we do write about it, but we don't measure it. There is no way to measure it.

Both Jason's Tile Project and Kathleen's Puppet-Making Project challenged students and grabbed their interest. The projects were within the students' abilities yet were novel and exciting. The projects also gave plenty of space for students to take a personal approach to the task. Teachers often played the role of gently keeping students on task and making sure they persisted in their engagement.

A Dispositional View of Engage and Persist

Engage and Persist extends beyond just working hard. Developing this habit involves figuring out how to start and keep working in meaningful ways.

Skill. The skill that makes engagement possible is self-awareness. Students need to be able to identify their interests. Skills of persistence include strategies to work through obstacles to continuing, such as taking a break, asking for someone to comment on one's work, standing back and looking at one's work from a new angle, or working on something else for a while.

Alertness. Alertness to engagement requires that students recognize what engages them and notice when they feel engaged. Alertness to persistence means recognizing the obstacles to persistence, such as feeling stuck, overwhelmed, sleepy, distracted, or frustrated, and knowing that this is the time to pull out all stops and use the skills of persistence.

Inclination. The inclination to engagement means seeking out opportunities that are engaging and discovering interest in work that is assigned. The inclination to persist arises when one is engaged—if you genuinely care about what you're doing, you push through obstacles until you are satisfied. The inclination to persist also depends upon self-efficacy—the belief that you can get better. As Carol Dweck (2000) has shown, when students believe that intelligence is something that can be improved through effort, they work harder.

Generative Connections With Engage and Persist

In Jason's Tile Project and Kathleen's Puppet-Making Project, Engage and Persist was not taught in isolation. Engage and Persist often pairs with Reflect when students become aware of obstacles that need to be worked through. Engage and Persist pairs with Express because working on a project to convey personal meaning is engaging; in addition, the most engaging projects are usually ones that allow expression of personal meaning.

Engage and Persist also frequently pairs with Observe and Understand Art Worlds—when students look at artists' work and practices and use these as inspiration. For example, a 9th-grader at Boston Arts Academy identified as a graffiti artist and resisted broadening his skills. By his senior year he had become interested in his African heritage and chose to look closely at African masks. This study resulted in a painted self-portrait in the style of an African mask (see Figure 13.1). Observing the art of another culture broadened him, and he found that graffiti was only one of the ways of working that engaged him.

The example below shows a cluster of Engage and Persist, Envision, and Stretch and Explore, as Jason helps a student sustain an experimental attitude rather than rush to a premature solution in the initial stages of envisioning her unit sculpture.

Jason: Before you start that, I want you to think about the little coil. Think about that and think about other forms or shapes of clay that you might use rather than just that little coil—maybe three or four different pieces of clay that you could repeat to build. . . . (Envision)

Student: So you don't want me to do the pine cones?

Jason: I didn't say that.

Student: You want me to experiment first. (Stretch and Explore)

Jason: First, yes, rather than just starting, I want you to experiment with some different types of units. Some might be very geometric, some you might just grab and shape in your hand quickly. (Stretch and Explore in the service of Engage and Persist).

What Teachers Can Do

Teachers can help students engage by setting up projects that include choice, a practice often underemphasized (Douglas & Jaquith, 2009; Jaquith & Hathaway, 2012). They can ask students to think about the activities they choose to engage in during their free time—such activities are likely to be what they care about. They can also ask students to keep personal sketchbooks to gather ideas and images that intrigue them and that can be used later. This helps not only to get students to work in the moment, but also to develop their disposition to engage continuously in their work.

Video clips of artists often show how they engage in their work or provide biographical accounts. These stories can inspire students to engage in their work in more serious ways. Students might be surprised to learn that artist and architect Maya Lin submitted her winning design for the Vietnam War Memorial when she was just an undergraduate student.

Teachers can highlight artworks that demonstrate the extremes of artistic persistence, such as realist painter Vija Celmins's careful graphite representations of water or Latoya Ruby Frazier's performance piece in which she destroys the Levi's jeans she is wearing through repetitive body motions on the sidewalk, to critique Levi's advertising campaign that misused her hometown of Braddock, PA (documented by Art21 at art21.org/watch/new-york-close-up/latoya-ruby-frazier-takes-on-levis/).

Sometimes teachers need to encourage and praise efforts at persistence. Teachers might also create tension (e.g., remind students about deadlines) or reduce tension (e.g., playing relaxing music) to help students focus. Perhaps most importantly, teachers can help students Engage and Persist by nurturing their self-efficacy—reminding them to be alert to excessive self-criticism and encouraging them not to give in to negative self-talk.

Engage and Persist in Other Disciplines

Getting good at anything requires persistence. Much has been written about the 10,000 hours required for expertise, whether the activity be gymnastics, violin playing, chess, or feats of verbal memory (Ericsson, 1996; Ericsson et al., 2009). Even the most gifted child prodigy needs to work hard to develop and actualize her inborn abilities. And engaging work is the key to persistence in any discipline.

SIX

Envision

Thinking in Images

I try to get them to think about how they would choose an object as a source, and then abstract from that object to make a sculpture.

—Jason Green

In studio classes, students learn to think in images when they are developing their works. They think in images as they come up with an idea, as they progressively re-conceptualize their work, and as they imagine the steps to get there. Envisioning and Observing are the ends of a continuum. When observing, one looks closely at the outside world. When envisioning, one imagines and generates images of possibilities in the mind.

Consider the relationship between Observe and Envision in observational drawing. The artist observes and then uses a medium to give form to what she sees. The translation from model to representation requires envisioning. Artists aim to capture not only the surface aspects of their models, but also the underlying structure and geometry—for example, the axis of the head versus the axis of the body, the torso as a trapezoid. Artists may also emphasize aspects of a pose (e.g., location in space, tension in a part of the body) or choose a composition that suggests associations or narratives.

In work that is not done from observation, the continuum is less clear, but it also exists. Artists work from mental images that are themselves derived from having observed the world, and they observe in the process of making what they envision.

Here are some of the many ways students were encouraged to *Envision:*

- Generate a work of art solely from their imaginations, rather than from observation.
- Imagine how their work would look if they made specific changes. Here, the skill of *Envision* is used in planning a work.
- Make a "unit," repeat it, and then combine the units into sculptural forms. This is an example of another kind of envisioning focused on "improvisational" planning.

- Imagine all the ways to vary a line, a shape, a color, or a composition.
- Imagine implied forms in their drawings—forms that cannot be seen in full because they are partially occluded.
- Observe the underlying geometry of a form and then envision how that geometry can be shown in their work.

Two classes are featured in this chapter, and both demonstrate two kinds of *Envisioning*—imagining and planning. Imagining is an activity that is required for planning a work, and it can be done in a host of ways.

PLACES FOR AN IMAGINARY CREATURE: INVENTING COLORS PROJECT (EXAMPLE 6.1)

At the Boston Arts Academy near the conclusion of Beth Balliro's spring term course with 9th-graders, we see students continuing to work on the Imaginary Creatures Project. They are using acrylics to paint a mythical creature situated in the landscape in which it was born or died (see also Examples 4.1 and 12.1). The creature cannot be seen; thus, it is envisioned.

Students-at-Work

As students work (see Figure 6.1), Beth repeatedly finds ways to focus students on one form of Envisioning—generating images from the imagination:

- *Imagine where your creature came from and create a landscape for the creature.* Beth asks a student to think explicitly of what he is trying to represent. "Wherever you think that beautiful creature can burst out of a seed. Where would it be? . . . a green-

A. Beth Balliro works on color with a student

B. Beth and a student consider how a landscape expresses character

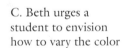

C. Beth urges a student to envision how to vary the color

D. She wonders with another student how to expand the range of colors in a work

house, or a pot, or a windowsill, a crack in the sidewalk."

- *Create an imaginary landscape that tells a narrative.* Beth tells a student: "I want you to have a landscape that has a story, and, in this case, I want you to think more deeply about your character."
- *Envision where the light is coming from in the landscape.* Beth asks a student to think about light. "Where is the light in this forest coming from . . . day or night? What time of day? What kind of light? Is it foggy? Bright and shining?" Beth also asks students to look closely at their work (Observe) as they plan, to see how it might grow (Envision).
- *Determine where on the page a new color could be used.* Beth asks a student, "Think about if there is a place where you want to include a color that's different than these."
- *Envision variations of a color.* Beth prods a student working with two colors to envision more variations of the colors. "OK, so you have red plus yellow . . . you have orange, think about how many oranges you can get."
- *Think of how to make color translucent and layered.* Beth asks students to think about how to layer colors "so you can still see the value shining through."

Beth Reflects

When asked to give this class a title, Beth called the class "Inventing Colors." As explained in Chapter 4, students were learning to envision new colors out of primaries, motivated by their struggles to envision a mythical creature that could in some way represent themselves, in landscapes of its birth and death. When asked why students should learn to invent rather than copy, Beth replied that when students just follow tradition, their work is "so much less interesting than when they invent. So, that's why I didn't want to lead them by requiring that they look at references." Beth also thinks it's important to have students learn the relationship between drawing from imagination and drawing from observation because "fantasy drawings will be much better if you work on observation." (Figure 6.2 shows a painting resulting from this project.)

DESIGNING IN CLAY:
BEGINNING THE TILE PROJECT   (EXAMPLE 6.2)

In Jason Green's classroom at Walnut Hill, students are beginning a tile project near the end of their second-semester course in ceramics. In this class, they are assigned to create nine tiles pressed from molds. They place objects into the molds to press out individual textured tiles. They must think of each tile in relation to the

Figure 6.2. Birth Painting by a 9th-grader at the Boston Arts Academy

whole, as in painting, because the nine tiles, each 5 inches square, must form a piece that can be hung on the wall (see also Example 5.1).

Students-at-Work

As students work, Jason frequently asks them to envision the next steps in their work. Below are Jason's interactions with two students as he prods both to think of what they might do next with their work:

- *How might individual tiles function as a single piece?* Jason tells a student, "I want you to think of how the tiles relate. Have something that connects them together between the tiles." To another, he says, "You need to know what each tile will look like before you start making it." He further warns her to avoid carving all nine pieces separately; she will need to think in terms of a grid.
- *What would your work look like if you tried something else?* Jason asks the student to think of the basic things that make up the design. He then asks her, "What would happen if you did it on each tile, so you didn't have to carve nine pieces of plaster?" (This also nurtures the Studio Habit of Mind Stretch and Explore, because Jason is encouraging the student to play with options.)
- *What do you plan to do?* Jason asks a student what she plans: "You have to decide if you want the middle out, coming closer to you. That means you will have to cut these little squares."
- *What technique might you employ?* As the student struggles with her grid drawing, Jason suggests that she

think of how she might execute what she plans: "You could cut something like this [he picks up a straight piece of wood] and have it go into the mold, and you would get a nice straight line."

Jason Reflects

In an interview after this class, Jason noted that the project requires advanced planning, which we refer to as Envisioning. "They're making all the decisions about their artwork when they're not actually working on the clay." He also stressed that in this project, students have to "figure out" ahead of time the end product before beginning to build the object. They must envision how the forms will be reversed after clay is pressed into the mold.

Jason said his goal was to have students envision their own product and not follow a set of automatic steps: "What I don't want to do is give them the recipe for making art, because there is no real recipe." Instead, Jason's goal is to help students find their own solutions: "I want to give them the tools so that they can be innovators and come up with their own problems and their own solutions and their own questions."

One might at first think that Envisioning occurs only when artists work from imagination. But Envisioning also occurs when working from the model or when combining imagination and observation in works. Every time artists plan next steps they are Envisioning. Every time they step back and ask themselves how the work would look if they made some kind of alteration, they are Envisioning. The teachers asked students to plan and to imagine revisions in their works. Thus students gained considerable practice in working from mental images. Envisioning—the ability to imagine and to generate mental images—is a disposition important in many domains. And visual arts classes are perhaps the arenas in which this disposition is most consistently fostered and demanded.

A Dispositional View of Envision

Skill. The skill that makes Envision possible relates to using mental imagery. Students need to be able to generate and manipulate visual images in their minds as they imagine how they want their finished products to look.

Alertness. Alertness to envisioning requires that students recognize when it is important to reimagine their work. Students creating observational work need to recognize that the translation from model to work is not direct; it is mediated by their imaginations. There are many ways to represent what is seen, and it is up to them to imagine how they want to show what they see as they translate observation to the work of art they are creating. Students creating work from imagination need to recognize moments to reimagine their product and realize that there are many ways to proceed.

Inclination. When artists put their imaginations to use as they are planning and/or creating works, they show the inclination to Envision. Without support, students often skip or give short shrift to the envisioning process and move directly into making, without doing the mental work of exploring their ideas. Without specific attention to Envisioning, clichés come to the surface, students stay stuck in their existing schemas, and works tend to be uninspired and say little that is new. The envisioning process is what sustains artistic investigation and leads to innovation.

What Teachers Can Do

Some typical approaches to support the skill of envisioning include regular use of sketchbooks, making thumbnails and storyboards, and suspending the commitment to final decisions by, for example, gluing collage elements only after trying out many different compositions.

Teachers can help students envision by setting constraints, like saying "Make ten sketches before you start the work," or holding back the glue until students have arranged a collage three different ways. Another technique is playing the "What if?" game by asking students to imagine how their work would look if. . . . What if you moved this part over here? What if you darkened this corner? What if you repeated this red over here? What if you showed the figure more from the back? All of these prompts push the student to generate and manipulate a mental image, to put off the final decision, and to imagine greater possibilities in the work.

An antidote to the problem of "first idea" is shown by a practice in Olivia Gude's Spiral Curriculum (a Saturday program that was held at the University of Chicago), where she taught her pre-practicum art-teacher students to employ Surrealist games as envisioning tools that surface unconscious ideas, forms, and intentions useful to the creation of provocative works. By smoking paper, preparing papers with inkblots and splatters, or using random selection processes of dice, spinners, or blind choice, students' imaginations open in ways that avoid the constraints of their usual ideas.

Students can also learn to envision how to work by studying artists' envisioning processes. For instance, Julie Mehretu envisions large abstracted spaces that contain and connect references across time and geography. Trenton Doyle Hancock envisions entire worlds and lives for his fictional mythical creatures, the Mounds.

Generative Connections with Envision

Envision, the habit of thinking in images, commonly clusters with Observe and Develop Craft, resulting in a kind of embodied thinking—making envisioned ideas real by crafting with materials, observing what is done, and then tinkering both with the idea and the material.

Envision also often pairs with Reflect, the habit of metacognition. Asking students to talk about their works can help them become clearer about their goals and their judgments, prompting them to re-envision and go on to revise. Judging when a work is finished also requires that Envision interact with Reflect and Express—to recognize when one's vision has been achieved.

Envision also clusters with Stretch and Explore and Engage and Persist. When students are dissatisfied with what they have made, they have to envision something new. And this often requires being willing to stretch beyond what they know how to do well and to play around. One must be sufficiently engaged in the project to persist in exploration.

Envision also frequently interacts with Observe and Understand Art Worlds. Students can look closely at works by other artists—in museums and galleries, in books and reproductions, among their peers, and online—to help them envision what they might do in their own work.

Envisioning often surfaces in complex clusters of habits whenever artists describe their process. A freshman at Walnut Hill explained his thought process as he responded to a drawing assignment:

> Well, when I did the drawing, it was supposed to be about the way the whole room looks and the way everything just comes in to the subjects. But there are a lot of things around that would distract from what I was trying to draw. So I did change things around a little bit. I tried to make things as much as I could point to the middle here. I think it's mostly the stuff that I left out that helps support the piece. (Envision, Express, Observe, Reflect) (See Figure 6.3)

Envision in Other Disciplines

Envisioning—the ability to imagine and to generate mental images—is a disposition important across domains. This disposition is consistently demanded and fostered in visual arts classes.

Athletes often rehearse what they are going to do using mental imagery. For example, Mary Whipple, coxswain for the rowing team at the 2012 Olympics, explained how she visualizes what she will say in a race and how she gathers her rowers together in a quiet dark room

Figure 6.3. Drawing of a Studio Class by a First-Year Student at Walnut Hill

before every competition; they all close their eyes as she talks them through the coming race (Macur, 2012).

A scientist envisions patterns to form conclusions; a historian avoids the problem of presentism by envisioning the mindset of a different era. Choreographers envision dances; composers and conductors envision the sounds and silences of music; and playwrights and directors envision dramatic stories. Writers imagine and reimagine plot structure for writing scenes. Filmmakers imagine a narrative in time and motion while creating storyboards for a film. Architects use sketches and Computer Assisted Design to imagine a building that is translated into models to convey their vision to others for execution. Engineers envision how parts of machines can work together efficiently—in their minds, in sketches, and using digital 3D modeling and fabrication. All these responses employ envisioning and moving back and forth between envisioning and observing.

In the next chapter we consider how students learn to go beyond technique to express a personal vision in their work.

SEVEN

Express

Finding Meaning

The strength of the drawing is going to depend very much on the evocative nature of the space.

—Jim Woodside

Express is commonly associated with arts classes. Often people equate expression with free and undisciplined venting of emotion. But expression is really about meaning of all sorts—feelings, concepts, and ideas.

Works of art convey meaning through the symbol system of the art form. In *Languages of Art* (1968), philosopher Nelson Goodman distinguishes two ways of symbolizing: *representation* and *metaphorical exemplification*. A painting of a crying child is a representation of sadness. It is literally a picture of a sad person. When works of art symbolize through metaphorical exemplification, they convey qualities that the works do not literally possess: A painting can be metaphorically sad, loud, or agitated just through the way it uses line, color, composition, and allusion. A piece of music can express brightness or ease through its timbre, tempo, and consonance. Dance uses such elements as gesture, force, level, and speed to convey meaning.

When we look at a work of visual art, we do not see only what is represented (a landscape, a portrait); we also grasp its metaphorical properties. When a violinist plays with great skill but no feeling, the audience is left cold, and the critics take their revenge. When listening to Beethoven's 3rd Symphony, the *Eroica*, the audience is meant to feel a host of emotions, from triumph and nobility to mourning and solace. Works of art cannot be reduced to verbal messages to convey their meaning, and great works of art are always more than great craft.

A senior at Walnut Hill told us how she learned about the centrality of expression:

I came to this school and I basically just was thinking about skill and showing skill and, you know, trying to create depths and dimension and just show what's real and show that I can present it in a real way. And that's the perfect example [Fig 7.1A]. But with my self-portrait [Figure 7.1B], it clearly shows how I'm more working with myself

and who I am. It's very personal, it's more deep, and it's not about presenting something in a realistic way. It still has a lot of skill in it. But the whole general idea of what I'm trying to present has changed. And I grew a lot through that because basically when I came here I started to have a lot of skill but I didn't really know what to do with it or how to connect it with my thinking.

While representation as a form of symbolization is not limited to the arts, metaphorical exemplification is specific to the arts. We named this habit Express to refer to the making of meaning in both ways.

In the following two classes, we see students learning aspects of expression. In both, we see examples of class structures and interactions with students that encourage them to go beyond technique to create something with evocative meaning.

DRAWING FOR FEELING: FIGURES IN EVOCATIVE SPACE PROJECT (EXAMPLE 7.1)

At Walnut Hill in Jim Woodside's Figures in Evocative Space Project (see also Examples 11.1 and 14.2), students learn to convey a mood or atmosphere in their drawing that evokes something about the psychology of the figures in the drawing. Jim moves students away from thinking about representing a single figure, as they had in previous classes, toward thinking about figures in relationship, telling a story in an evocative space (see Figure 7.2).

Demonstration-Lecture

Five months into his drawing class, Jim introduces his students to the concept of drama and narrative. He poses two students together at opposite sides of a space. He asks the rest of the students to think of the models as kids just hanging out. He contrasts this kind of drawing

**Figure 7.1. (A) Drawing of Apples Focused on Skill
(B) Self-Portrait Focused on Expression**

(A)

(B)

with more standard fare in which he had asked students to draw an isolated figure he set up for them. He makes comments, encouraging them to be expressive in their drawings.

- Jim asks students to use drawing to express a dramatic relationship.
- I'm trying to set up a kind of dramatic lighting, a lighting that seems almost mysterious or evocative. I want this to be set up like a kind of stage. You know, when you think of actors on a stage, you don't just

think of the personalities, but you think of the whole story being told. You think of the lighting. You think of the kind of environment being implied, right?
- Jim asks students to think about what is implied, suggesting that they think as if they were movie directors and show their decisions in their drawings:
- These two people are elements in a drama. What I'm asking you to do is move beyond the idea of just drawing a figure in an art class, which is what we've done for the last couple of weeks. Now I'm asking you to think more about the emotional content, the relationship between the two, the drama, the mystery.
- Jim asks students to express the relationship between the two figures in the empty space between them:
- You're going to have to include all this space, this empty space. Now that's going to be a big challenge in your drawing, because something is going to be in that space, you know? There's gonna be the wall, the blackness of the window, but more importantly, what's the sort of emotional content and character, and what do you get out of that drawing? Let me rephrase that—the strength of the drawing is going to depend very much on the evocative nature of this space.

Jim also introduces paintings by Edward Hopper and Richard Diebenkorn and leads a discussion about these paintings' evocative, emotional content (see Example 11.1). In addition to his focus on Express, he fosters Understand Art Worlds as the students learn how their work relates to that of professional artists. He helps them Observe, as students learn to see light and value by looking closely at works of art, and he asks them to Reflect, as they are asked to describe qualities in the work.

Students-at-Work

Jim consults with students as they work on a series of quick, compositional sketches (3–5 minutes each), and then on a longer drawing on better paper:

- *Notice the expressive light on the face of the female model.* Jim directs a student's attention to the strong, very clear light on one side of the model's face and the dark values on the other, and says, "That can be all the information you need. A sort of very mysterious, wonderful light across one side of her body." This consult also fosters learning to Observe as the student is shown how to look closely at the model.
- *Create a dramatic sense of receding space by exaggerating perspective.* Jim puts tracing paper on the drawing to demonstrate as he suggests to a

A. Jim Woodside focuses students' attention on light as a source of drama in drawings

B. His students begin drawing figures in dramatic lighting

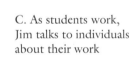

C. As students work, Jim talks to individuals about their work

D. Jim encourages an uncertain student to heighten contrast in his drawing to show the dramatic relationship between the figures

student that he include in his drawing pictures on the wall "because if you put them on in perspective, it's the perfect way of telling the viewer that the space is going back. But you can make that even more dramatic if you like, exaggerating the diminishing side of the picture." This consult also fosters the learning of Develop Craft, as the student is encouraged to use the rules of perspective mastered earlier in the semester, and the learning of Observe, as the student is encouraged to notice space around the models and use it to express an intended effect.

- *Use the technique of erasing to convey a dramatic feeling of light.* Jim suggests that a student use the technique of erasing. "This drawing is the type of drawing that sort of works from darkness backward instead of putting darkness on." He also asks the student to recall a project from several months ago, when he covered the paper in charcoal and erased into it (see Examples 3.3, 4.3, and 8.2). "In a way, there's a similar thing going on here, where bits of light are worked out of darkness." Jim asks for permission to erase the student's drawing a bit and describes what he's doing. "In certain areas where it's important to show the weight of the figure, go back in with your eraser. You know, heighten that contrast in certain areas." This consult also fosters the learning of Develop Craft: Technique, and is a good example of how students are taught to be alert to craft (and develop technical skill) in the service of expression.

Critique

During the class, Jim uses several short Critique sessions to discuss how students' compositional decisions suggest the relationship conveyed between the two figures. Students' works, taped onto drawing boards, are leaned against the wall for all to contemplate. Jim praises students' success at making decisions in their sketches about what they want to express. He directs students' attention to expression as "powerful decisions starting to be made, starting to emerge out of your sketches."

During the Critique, Jim notes how one student has created a strong statement of isolation by the choices made. He points to small, discrete figures and suggests the power of really exaggerating the distance between them. "Maybe it's a statement about the lack of communication between the two figures."

Jim further compares the expression of the deep space in the drawing to another student's drawing that is flatter. He points out how the dramatic angle gives the picture a less stable effect and how the student's choice to include architectural elements (wall and floor) is really

the substance of the drawing. "It's not a portraiture, it's just arrangement of shapes."

Jim also shows the class a finished drawing of the same kind of scene by a student in another class and points out the power of the open space and the way the drawing is done with just a hint of light around the otherwise anonymous figure. He comes back to the idea of a stage set. "When I talk about telling a story, I'm not saying that you're illustrating an event, a story, but I'm saying that you're implying a drama, a sort of living drama between figures."

Jim Reflects

In our interviews with Jim, he talked about how he strives to teach students to find personal relationships in their art and how he never teaches technique alone. "It is about connecting the art to your life and to the world and your place in the world." Jim talked about why he never wants to teach just skills and then go on to content and expression. "It is not [only] the skill of drawing that they are learning. It is very much the making of a mark in the world as expression; and, to me, that might be something that is more interesting and more exciting for them."

For Jim, the teaching of technique is only part of the picture. "I have had kids in drawing that could draw better than I could, but they really couldn't push it to another level. There is just not depth in their work." He tries to help students see how an idea, like drawing the figure, connects to a world that they relate to and understand. "Whether it's them with their parents in the kitchen or whether it's kids hanging out in Harvard Square, there's a kind of drama to everyday life." And what hits you first when you look at a work of art is not its technique but its evocative properties.

In our final interview with Jim as he reflected on the year, he said that the assignments get more interpretative as he moves through the year. They are more evocative in terms of expression, but he stressed that expression cannot be conceived of in isolation from other aspects of drawing. Expression emerges from the drawing process.

DRAWING FOR MEANING: IMAGINARY CREATURES PROJECT   (EXAMPLE 7.2)

At the Boston Arts Academy, in Beth Balliro's Imaginary Creatures Project in the middle of her second-semester course with 9th-graders, she stressed that students should express personal meaning in their work. The students are each making a mythical creature that expresses something about their own personality. They are going beyond representation to create something with connotative, evocative meaning. In an earlier class, students wrote about what inspires them ("What is your muse?") (see Example 9.1). Now, with this inspiration in mind, Beth helps them to do a pencil sketch in which they think of themselves as a mythical creature—part human, part animal. As students worked, Beth encouraged them to identify properties through which to convey personal meaning in two ways:

- *Decide which aspects of character to express in the mythical figure.* Beth asks a student several questions to get him to think about which aspects of his character he wants to express in his mythical figure. "If you could be any character, would this be the one? A warrior? What about you is the most dominant part of you?"
- *Decide how your drawing will express that character.* Beth urges a student to put her figure of a mermaid into action so that it expresses more power, and so that the mermaid expresses something about the student's self. She encourages the student to make "not just any old mermaid but your own mermaid. Instead of having a portrait of a mermaid, see if you can put it in action." When the student responds that mermaids have power over the waves, Beth replies, "Yes, so that tells part of her power."

Beth and a Student Reflect

In an interview, Beth talked about how she was indirectly trying to influence the student who chose to make a mermaid—trying to get her to think about the viewer and make a creature that conveys something to that viewer. Although she really didn't want the student to do a mermaid, she didn't want to tell her not to do a mermaid because the student was invested in a lot of draft drawings of mermaids, and "she was pretty psyched up about the mermaid thing. But in my mind I'm thinking, uhh, a mermaid!" Beth wanted the student to avoid being "clichéd":

> Art that is clichéd doesn't engage the viewer, and art that presents something intriguing does engage the viewer. So, I don't know that she's ever thought about the viewer before. I'm trying to get her to see the work outside of herself as something that conveys something to a viewer.

In our initial interview, Beth told us why learning to be expressive is so important for her students. "They have equally not really found their voice, in a way that it can be heard. I think being an artist is figuring out how to get yourself heard." In a later interview, Beth talked about how it is that students can discover their voice in

an art class but still struggle in an academic class. Here she has brought up the vexing issue of transfer (Perkins & Salomon, 2012). Whether students can discover their voice (and thus something about their identity) in an arts class and have this discovery generalize outside of art class is a question ripe for investigation.

A Dispositional View of Express

People often think of expression in art as the unruly expression of feelings. As we define it in the Studio Habits, however, Express requires a great deal of skill to work its magic.

Skill. Gaining the skill of Express means learning how to create a work that goes beyond craft to convey meaning and feeling. And this can be achieved both through literal representation (e.g., expressing agitation by depicting an agitated crowd) as well as through metaphorical means (e.g., expressing agitation by using vibrating colors).

Alertness. Alertness to Express requires that students become familiar with and exploit the expressive potentials of the media in which they work. For example, when working with the concept of memory in collage, a student might use familiarity with translucence, transparency, and opacity to create layers suggesting the history of an event dimmed by time. Or when working in clay, familiarity with a wide range of surface treatments might allow the creation of objects like those by artist Marilyn Levine in which clay takes on the look and feel of leather jackets, purses, or shoes (www.marilynlevine.com/artworkframeset.html). Artists are alert throughout the making process to the potential implications and interpretations of the aesthetic choices they make with craft.

Inclination. The inclination to Express means actively pursuing meaning when making and viewing artworks. We do not mean by this, however, that works are coded representations of ideas. Making expressive work is not a linear process, since meaning often evolves along with the piece, and sometimes artists do not consciously or explicitly understand where a work is taking them. But the inclination to Express means following the work as it evolves into its final form, remaining aware of its meaning and feeling.

Generative Connections with Express

Express often pairs with Develop Craft, since artists manipulate materials into forms that convey meaning. By using Develop Craft in the service of expression, students learn to use techniques as intended—to convey visual meaning. But any number of habits might surface in a cluster with Express and Develop Craft, including Stretch and Explore (playing around with ways to use materials that might suggest various meanings); Engage and Persist (pursuing expression of some meaning over a sustained period of time); Observe (noticing qualities of materials that evoke some idea or feeling); and Reflect (explaining how meaning is conveyed).

Express also pairs naturally with Understand Art Worlds. An artist who paints the figure in 2022, for example, paints in the context of painting's history. Female nudes were the object of the male gaze for centuries, which has implications for figural subject matter now—who is looking or meant to look (e.g., issues of power and powerlessness). Some artists decide how to think about audience in relation to the expressive intention of their works, as when designers negotiate with their clients or artists explicitly address particular audiences. Others claim fealty not to the audience at all, but only to an idea—that is, to how the artist perceives an idea's representation.

What Teachers Can Do

The most central support teachers can offer is to keep meaning at the center of the artmaking process, immersing students in ongoing discourse about meaning. Assignments need to address meaning, either by specifying a theme or helping students to find their own from their explorations, brainstorming, and reflections.

Teachers can help students learn to express by viewing and discussing examples of artists' work and videos in which artists think aloud about their works and working processes. How do the artists think about meaning in their works? How does meaning evolve?

Art21 supports this effort by tagging and sorting artists by theme, such as Consumer Culture, Race in America, or World Building (art21.org/artists/). Teachers can share artworks where the material of the work conveys meaning: Doris Salcedo's *Atrabiliarios* displays encased worn shoes to represent victims of violence in Colombia (discussed on the website of the Museum of Contemporary Art Chicago at www3.mcachicago.org /2015/salcedo/works/atrabiliarios/). Or they can discuss the impact of political, socially engaged works such as Shepard Fairey's Barack Obama "Hope" street poster or Yinka Shonibare's 2018 work *The American Library*, made of books with names of immigrants and their descendants who have impacted American culture.

Instead of creating assignments by media (e.g., our "clay" unit or our "watercolor" unit), teachers can help students identify what they want to express and then show them how to use materials, tools, and the elements and principles of the visual arts to explore that meaning. Even a beautifully crafted work of art can be empty and without interest, just as an ugly one can be evocative and moving. This realization can motivate young artists to strive for more than just high-quality craft. Critiques, too, need to focus as much on meaning as on craft, identifying possible relationships between them. It makes no sense to perfect the craft first and then think about what to convey.

Express in Other Disciplines

All of the arts involve expression. Poetry uses words and punctuation for rhythm, sound, and connotation as much as denotation. Interior designers arrange furniture and use light, color, and texture to create environments that evoke particular feelings or functions. In theater or dance, the performance conveys meaning and feeling through the style of the set, costumes, and props; the manner of speaking or body language in dialogues or duets; and the movement and energy of a character's entrance or exit. And music, too, expresses meaning, whether nonliteral or narrative—for example, through dynamics, rhythms, and harmonies.

Expression in the form of metaphorical exemplification is seen outside of the arts as well, in any kind of good writing, regardless of the discipline. Writers strive to write with a personal voice that evokes atmosphere and feeling and that strengthens the meaning they want to convey. This is true not only for poets and novelists but also for nonfiction writers such as historians, science writers, or political columnists.

EIGHT

Observe

Really Seeing, Not Just Looking

Keep investigating things around you. Looking is the real stuff about drawing.

—Guy Michel Telemaque

Artists use the habit of Observe everywhere. They observe the world around them, the works of other artists, and their own works as they develop them. Students in the art studio are taught to look more closely than people ordinarily do and "learn to see with new eyes." When teachers tell their students to look, as Guy Michel Telemaque does in the quotation above, students may think they really see already. But observing goes beyond looking and means moving beyond habitual ways of seeing. Students need to learn to notice things that might otherwise be invisible and therefore unavailable as content for thinking. Really seeing is the Studio Habit of careful, mindful Observation.

Students are taught to look closely at the following:

- The model or source from which they are working
- Their own artworks as they evolve
- Art processes modeled and artworks created by the teacher in demonstrations
- Artworks created by other students
- Artworks by artists past and contemporary

Teachers help students notice more by pointing out nuances of color, line, texture, and form. They point out the underlying geometry of a form and describe the expressive properties of a work, including its stylistic and compositional elements.

In the two classes that follow, we show how students are taught to observe. Both teachers have their students use a viewfinder (a small piece of cardboard with a rectangle cut out of its center), a tool artists have traditionally used to aid observation.

SEEING WITH NEW EYES:
USING THE VIEWFINDER   (EXAMPLE 8.1)

In Guy Michel's first design class of the term at the Boston Arts Academy, students learn to look through a viewfinder with one eye, so that they can learn a new way of seeing—seeing the world as elements in a composition. He tells them, "Instead of painting what we see, we're going to see what you would paint." This is meant to help them select what they want to put on a page.

Demonstration-Lecture

Looking through the viewfinder helps students learn to see objects as only lines, shapes, and colors in a frame. Guy Michel tells students:

> Forget that you are looking at a bucket or a person's hair, or a table and a chair, and all these things. Forget that these are objects that have any real definition. I want you to simply concentrate on the lines that are created in what you see.

Guy Michel talks about what he sees when looking through the viewfinder. He turns and holds the viewfinder up to a desk.

> Right here I am paying attention particularly to the way this line goes diagonally across this frame, and then there is another little line underneath it that I can see has a little bit of a distance. It's a different color, different texture, and the line is thicker because from my perspective this line is a little thinner than this line down here.

Guy Michel explains how, when you look through a viewfinder with one eye, you lose depth perception and start to see the world as if it were a two-dimensional picture. Instead of seeing one thing in front of another "all you're seeing is [that] one thing stops where another thing starts. And that is all design, because one color in a shape stops and the other starts."

Students-at-Work

Guy Michel hands out viewfinders, and students practice seeing the world as design (see Figure 8.1). As they look around the classroom and hallway, Guy Michel keeps students focused on this new way of seeing by engaging in observations with them. He asks individual students, groups of students, and sometimes the whole class to do the following:

- *Vary how the tool is used.* Guy Michel explains what to notice when looking through the viewfinder with one eye. "Think about how things look different when you hold it close to your eye or closer to the object."
- *Focus on design elements.* Guy Michel asks students to forget what they are looking at and just think about the surfaces. "Is anybody having trouble forgetting that they're looking at something that they already know? . . . Forget that you're looking at somebody's arm or a table. Just think about the shapes, the colors, the lines, and the textures and the value of things as they change as you move the viewfinder around."
- *Notice, think, and respond.* Guy Michel asks students to talk about what they see differently by using the viewfinder: "Do you notice something that you're not used to paying attention to?"

Demonstration-Lecture

After students have investigated the classroom and hallway, Guy Michel gathers them in the classroom and uses a magazine cover with an image of a building and a poster on the wall to help synthesize what they've learned: Paintings don't have to be seen as what they represent; rather, they can be seen as simply a surface of colors, shapes, patterns, textures, and forms. "That little change in thinking is what I want you to concentrate on." He concluded by introducing a homework assignment that connected the "new way of looking" to the course focus on design: Students created sheets of numerous thumbnail sketches that each combined one circle, triangle, and square, in an effort to find those designs that best conveyed the idea of motion.

Guy Michel Reflects

When we asked Guy Michel to give this class a title, he called it "A New Way of Seeing," or "Seeing the New." He explained that his goal is to "change how they look." "We're seeing what we are going to paint," he says as an explanation for using the viewfinders.

The goal of looking more closely, he explained to us, is to demystify the act of drawing and realize that the challenge of drawing a complex object is no different from the challenge of drawing a simple one.

> What happens is they think, "I can't draw a person." But if you say, Draw this pencil, they probably won't say that. But really, the lines are just different. So make the line that corresponds to what you see. Turn it here. Shadow it here. It's stripping away what it is and just painting the lines.

Guy Michel is, in short, teaching students to look closely so that they can begin to draw what they never thought they could draw. The first step, he tells them, is to learn to see.

SEEING THE WORLD AND PUTTING IT ON PAPER: LIGHT AND BOXES PROJECT (EXAMPLE 8.2)

For Jim Woodside's Light and Boxes Project at Walnut Hill, students learn to think about the relationship between the world and their drawing. Students use the viewfinder to see the world anew and then go one step further and think about how they can put what they see onto paper.

Early in the fall semester, students file into Jim's classroom to find a pile of wooden and cardboard boxes in neutral tones stacked at a variety of angles in the center of the floor (see also Examples 3.3 and 4.3). The students gather around this unusual still life, and Jim gives them each a viewfinder. As did Guy Michel, Jim teaches his students how the viewfinder helps them see, and as a result, helps them draw more accurately.

Demonstration-Lecture

Jim shows the students how to look through the viewfinder at the still life from many angles, and he explains how the viewfinder can help them decide about the composition of their drawings:

> This is a really great way to isolate what you want to work on to get a sort of preview of it, to figure out, most importantly, how it relates to all four sides of the paper. If you look through that you'll start to get a sense of, "Is there enough in that composition to occupy my drawing? Is there too much? Do I need to move in closer? Do I need to step back?"

Jim explains that students are also going to be working on perspective:

> We're still talking about line, but the main emphasis of what we're going to work on today is going to be perspective, geometry, one- and two-point perspective, how to arrange these shapes in a logical

A. Guy Michel Telemaque asks students to use a viewfinder to "see what you would paint"

B. He guides students to see design in the environment outside the windows

C. He tells students to forget that they're seeing objects and focus on just lines

D. Guy Michel explains that viewfinders help people see objects as just lines, shapes, and colors in a frame

way, in a way that makes sense, in a way that is representative of the space that exists here in real life, on your two-dimensional surface.

Before students start drawing, Jim holds up the viewfinder and explains to the class how to use it to plan a composition:

> As you look through the viewfinder, look at all four sides. Don't just think of the top and then the bottom, you know, like we tend to look at the earth and think of the sky and the ground. Look at all four sides of the hole in the cardboard, because that's how you're going to start to think about all four sides of your piece of paper, in terms of the composition. Think about how the lines work, intersect, interact, with all four sides.

Students are given newsprint, tempera paint, and brushes as their drawing tools and materials. They are told to draw the outlines of the boxes only, and to concentrate on how one form relates to another in space. "Learn to see shapes," Jim tells them.

Students-at-Work

Jim circulates, watches, asks questions, and encourages students to use the viewfinder. Occasionally he speaks to the whole group, but usually he talks to one student at a time. For example, Jim helps one student see the major vertical organizing lines that structure the still life. "Most of the things in the still life are set straight up and down, OK?" He also suggests what the student might do next:

> So if I were you, I would stop on this part right now and get some of these straight verticals in, like maybe that big pedestal there, or maybe that box down there if that's in your view, so you can work these big diagonals against that.

Critique

After students have made a preliminary drawing, Jim puts all the drawings up on the wall and holds the first Critique of the 3-hour class. He begins the Critique by asking students to look at their own drawing and think about what's *wrong* with it. The Critique moves fluidly into a Demonstration–Lecture.

Demonstration–Lecture

Using student drawings as a reference, Jim puts up a blank sheet of paper on which he draws boxes as he talks about principles of perspective drawing. He introduces some terms, writing them and illustrating them simply—horizon line (eye level), one-point perspective, vanishing point—and draws boxes in various positions above and below the horizon line. Jim shows students an old movie projector case and demonstrates how perspective helps to understand the simple overall shape of the case and to look beyond the minor details—handle, latch, etc. He explains why they should first draw the general shape of the rectangular projector case, as he lifts the cover to reveal the projector itself, and only later alter that same shape when depicting the specific details of the projector:

> Whether you're drawing a person or the most complicated thing in the world, you want to see it in simple terms first. It really helps to understand things in simple geometric terms first.

Jim makes a connection to the way he asks students to think of the figure:

> This is the same thing as when you draw a person. I'll tell you as we draw the figure to learn to break it up into geometry. If you just think of like the chest and muscles and arms and everybody's different shape, it can be overwhelming. But if you think of someone as just a cube and another cube attached, it can really help to simplify it.

Much of what we hear in this Demonstration–Lecture is similar to how Jim talked to individual students in teacher–student consults during the Students-at-Work session. But here, he talks to the entire group, making reference to individual students' works, thereby moving seamlessly back into Critique.

Critique

Before beginning another round of Students-at-Work, Jim helps students talk about what they see in their own and others' works that they think is more or less successful. Students discuss point of view in different drawings and the importance of intentionally choosing the point of view in a drawing. Jim concludes by telling students, "So these are the kind of thought processes and choices you should make with every single drawing."

Students-at-Work

Following the Critique, students return to working on the still life, this time drawing it armed with the rules of perspective. With one student, Jim demonstrates perspective drawing by placing a piece of tracing paper over the student's drawing and then drawing from the student's viewpoint. As he draws, Jim explains and points out to the student aspects of the display and how he is capturing these in the drawing. "Where is your horizon line?" he asks the student. To the student's reply he answers, "Right, so that means this is significantly below your horizon line, right? OK, so let's just say that the vanishing points are off here, they're somewhere but it's imaginary, off your piece of paper." Jim continues to draw and direct the student's attention to the drawing.

Jim also focuses the group's observation on other students' work. He holds up a drawing and directs students to observe the expressive quality of charcoal in this work.

> She's got this beautiful, very hard angular drawing of the objects, OK? But for the interior it looks like she's just sort of pretty much rubbing her fingers in toward the inner shape, taking that charcoal and pushing it in. Pretty simple solution, but I think it comes up with a really powerful expressive result, don't you?

For a student who is really struggling, Jim demonstrates how to get the horizon line right by working directly on the student's drawing. While marking on students' work is controversial among art educators, Jim and his students share an understanding that this classwork is an exercise, not a work of art, and therefore, his marks do not violate the integrity of the students' expression. Nevertheless, Jim respectfully asks the students' permission before adding his own lines to the paper. Then, as he draws, he explains his marks:

> OK, where is your horizon line? Do you know? It's about right there, right? So why do you have these going up? I'm going to do it right over, OK? [*Drawing on student's drawing.*] Your horizon line is right there, OK? You'd see a little bit of the bottom, don't you? So if I'm looking at it, it's going be like this.

Jim and Students Reflect

In an interview, Jim spoke about some of the reasons he taught this class as he did. He explained that if you look through a viewfinder at the still-life, "you're basically looking at an abstract piece of art" by becoming aware of all four sides of the piece of paper. "If you look through the viewfinder at a still life, which is just boxes and shapes, you become immediately aware of lines intersecting on all four sides." This is a complex way of looking at a work, and most students don't think

that way, "but the viewfinder helps them to and it's a great thing. It just gets the visual clutter out of their assignment."

The value of critiquing your own work is to help students learn to see and "to be able to look at your own work after you've done it and do more than just be pleased with yourself." In looking at the work of others, you learn. In reflecting with us after class about the Critique, Jim explained, "I wanted them to look at their own drawings and analyze them in a right–wrong/yes–no fashion." This was not intended to be a deeper critique of their thinking and expression in their work. Students were simply to find a box that just didn't look right. The form that the Critique takes follows its purpose.

Jim explains how the goal of teaching perspective is to get students to see the simple geometry underlying the forms: "It's hard for kids to see things simple. I think that simplification is a goal in art." He explains,

> Brancusi, the sculptor, had this great quote that I might even have said to the kids, "Simplicity is complexity solved." It comes up in big sophisticated ideas in art and also in things like this. So when you draw the human figure I try to get them to see the form. It's the forest through the trees sometimes—you see the big picture.

When asked to give this class a title, Jim called it "Living Use of Perspective and Composition." He means to show students how the skill of perspective drawing can be used in all drawing—it is a way of grasping the architecture underlying form. In his post-class interview, Jim explained why he does not teach perspective just by having students draw a box in isolation, but rather asks them to Observe the principles of perspective in what they see. "By having them draw a whole still life, they're making a work of art. They're not just drawing a box and learning how to do it." By embedding the skill to be learned in the context of artistic challenges, students don't merely learn the skill itself, they learn to use the skills for their own purposes.

As students learn to see, their observational drawing skill improves. One 9th-grader at Walnut Hill realized how far he had come in his ability to Observe when he talked about his first still life. He told us why he thought the drawing was not accurately drawn: "I didn't really *look* at it. I just saw what I thought I saw and just drew. And I didn't really, like, break it down" (see Figures 8.2 and 8.3).

Students carry the habit of Observation outside of the classroom. A Boston Arts Academy senior told us how she began to notice perspective in the environment after learning about it in an observational drawing class:

Figure 8.2. A 9th-Grader at Walnut Hill Explains That in His First Drawings He Drew "What I Thought I Saw"

Figure 8.3. Late in the 9th Grade, a Student Explains That He Looks More Carefully Now by "Breaking It Down"

I remember walking down Lansdowne Street. I looked at the way that the street goes in, and it's exactly what he was talking about how things fade into space and it's a vanishing point at the end. And I was like "OK, and so this art stuff does make sense." [I noticed it before] but I didn't understand why I saw it like that.

Even a beginning student noticed how he was starting to look at things differently. A 9th-grader at Walnut Hill commented on this: "When you're painting, it's an extremely different way of looking at things than when you're not. Because you see things, or at least I see things, in huge blocks of light and color. You look at things differently."

A Dispositional View of Observe

David Perkins (1994) refers to the habit of observation as having an "intelligent eye." Students who spend time in classrooms such as Guy Michel's and Jim's are getting continuous eye training. There is looking, and then there is seeing. Students learn that looking is not always seeing. Their eyes are now opened.

Skill. The skill that makes Observe possible is really looking. When artists look carefully they can override the schemas that lead people to draw hands too small, eyes too high, far away objects too large. The art historian E. H. Gombrich (2000) refers to the process of *making*, which always involves schemas, and *matching*, when schemas are complexified by observation.

Alertness. Alertness to when to employ observational skills requires that students recognize the need for careful observation during the artistic process. Such opportunities arise regularly. They arise when noticing something unusual and before committing to a composition (an interesting face on a bus, an oddly shaped object on the sidewalk, the way the shadow of an easel interacts with a pattern on the studio floor). They arise from the realization that something is "bugging you" (Jim Woodside's words), or not working, or that a work seems stuck. Even when a work seems finished, artists alert to the possibility that there may be more work to be done will stand back and look more deeply or invite others to look at the work with them. These kinds of alertness prompt artists to consider what they are seeing, how they are looking, and what might extend their looking and renew the process of taking in information.

Inclination. Experienced artists spend significantly more time looking at a model from which they are drawing than do novices, who look primarily at their drawings (Solso, 2001). When artists notice something that would benefit from further observation, they are challenged to put their looking skills to work. By making the effort to look longer or more broadly, they demonstrate the drive or *inclination* to Observe. An artist might remind himself to stand up and look at his work from various angles, levels, and distances. Or she might pause her making to look at other artists' works—by her peers, on the Web, in the library, on videos, or in galleries and museums. She might take out her sketchbook and browse through it or make new sketches. While responsive actions may vary widely, the point is that the artist does something to see more and better, and that informs the process of making.

Generative Connections to Observe

Observe pairs naturally with Envision—it is sometimes difficult to see where one of these habits ends and the other begins. When teachers guide students to imagine ways to change their work, they are prompting students to observe, then reflect and envision. Observe looks out to the world; Envision looks back into the mind. They are interdependent habits, often with a nearly instantaneous connection from the observed to the envisioned, and back again from an envisioned image to further outward observation.

Teachers can ask students to observe the works of other artists and to think about how to use what they see in their own work (Observe, Understand Art Worlds, Reflect). Observe clusters often with Understand Art Worlds and Reflect since the works made by others define the aesthetic context in which every artist's work is seen and judged.

Teachers can help students learn to observe how and how well their choices of materials and tools affect the meanings expressed in their work (Observe, Develop Craft, Express, Reflect). Reflect comes into this process when students use information from observation to consider how well they are conveying their intended meanings. They must think about what they are trying to express, look closely at their work, and decide what to change and how to make alterations.

What Teachers Can Do

Teachers can help students develop the skill of Observe by encouraging them to remember to look and to slow the looking process down. They can point out interesting observations they make in the normal flow of the day— nuances of color or light, line or texture, interesting shadows, unusual illusions or effects, or the underlying geometry of a form (Perkins, 1994). They can describe the expressive properties of a work, as well as its stylistic and compositional elements. They can also suggest common strategies used by artists to help themselves see more: using viewfinders to see possible relationships and compositions from a variety of angles, looking from different distances and levels, using lenses to magnify objects, squinting so that images blur, focusing on negative space, and closing one eye to flatten shapes. Teachers can help students develop the inclination to Observe by

Figure 8.4. This student's painting shows generative connections between Observe and other habits of mind, such as Develop Craft, Envision, and Express

having them keep sketchbooks to capture impressions and gather information as it comes to their attention, archiving a resource of images to be used at will. They can highlight works where careful looking deepens our understanding. For instance, Hans Op de Beeck's *The Boatman and Other Stories* (2021), life-size installations where interpretation requires combining many observed details. Or James Turrell's *Skyspace* series, domed rooms with an aperture open to the sky and passing clouds, inviting viewers to see the sky as a framed and moving painting. Teachers can expand the concept of Observe to include Listen (or more broadly "Attend") by sharing the work of multimedia artists who incorporate sound, such as Laurie Anderson or Guadalupe Maravilla.

Observe in Other Disciplines

The centrality of Observe in the visual arts is easily apparent, but this habit is important in all art forms, even though sometimes it takes a nonvisual form. To develop their craft, dancers watch themselves work in front of mirrors, and choreographers pay close attention to the movements of people, animals, and objects to get ideas. Actors observe people, settings, and situations to develop an interpretation of a character, and they review rehearsals and performances of others and of themselves (attending to their own behaviors on stage and in mirrors, photographs, and videos) to assess effect and quality. Musicians observe, too, with eyes, ears, and bodies—their postures, embouchures, and fingerings; the conductor's facial expressions, gestures, and body language; musical scores; and, most obviously, the sounds and silences of the music itself.

Observe is also central to the sciences. The photographer Eadweard Muybridge used photography to study how animals and humans move. Similarly, a biomedical engineer might use contemporary imaging technologies to study human movement while designing prosthetic devices for amputees. Chemists observe chemical reactions, physicists observe the behavior of matter, and biologists form conclusions from observations of the natural world. Historians observe photographs, films, and events as well as texts. Mathematicians observe phenomena and logical relationships in order to model them algorithmically. Linguists and language learners observe patterns of speech and behavior. Observation is so fundamental to understanding that it seems almost superfluous to name its occurrences. But recognizing the ubiquity of observation across domains may help identify connections among the many different ways that have been developed for investigating the world.

NINE

Reflect

Question and Explain, Evaluate

My goal is to have them question the way they do things. And lose bad habits and develop new good habits.

—Beth Balliro

I'm trying to give them the questions that they should be asking themselves while they're making something. Or after they've made something.

—Jason Green

When we're talking about looking at artwork, whether it's one in the museum or your own or your classmate's, it's still that slowing process; it's still that trying to separate the difference between interpretation and description.

—Kathleen Marsh

Reflecting about artistry, making judgments about art, and thinking about what constitutes beauty are processes at the heart of the field of aesthetics. The classes we observed were filled with aesthetics discourse—which we refer to as the habit of Reflect.

We make a distinction between two forms of Reflect. Artists reflect *metacognitively* when they consciously consider the form of their artwork—thinking about why they made the decision to use a color, a technique, or a compositional structure, or about the intended meaning. We refer to this type of thinking as Reflect: Question and Explain. Question and Explain is used by professional artists during critiques and reviews, in artist's talks and statements written by artists to accompany their work, in curatorial statements for an exhibition, and in art history and art criticism.

Artists *evaluate* when they interpret and judge the aesthetic success of their own and others' works. Evaluation involves some kind of direct or implicit comparison of a work with other works or with envisioned criteria or goals, and it always involves considering quality. We refer to this type of thinking as Reflect: Evaluate. Evaluating shows up in professional artists' working process (e.g., deciding on next steps or when a work is finished), during critiques and reviews, and centrally when viewing works by other artists and in the related fields of art history and criticism. Sometimes artists just know

when something works even though they cannot say why. Because our research focused on teacher–student interaction and teachers used language to help students learn to Reflect, our examples emphasize verbal forms of Reflect: Evaluate.

Making evaluations of works of art is a sophisticated process. In the words of Elliot Eisner:

Making judgments about how qualities are to be organized does not depend upon fealty to some formula; there is nothing in the artistic treatment of a composition like the making and matching activity in learning to spell or learning to use algorithms to prove basic arithmetic operations. In spelling and in arithmetic there are correct answers, answers whose correctness can be proven. In the arts judgments are made in the absence of rule. (2004, p. 5)

Both kinds of reflection involve students thinking about their artistic goals and those of others. Both also involve self-knowledge: Students learn about themselves and their reactions and judgments as they evaluate work, whether their own or that of others. And both involve consideration of quality: Describing work is prerequisite to evaluating the effectiveness of its elements. Evaluation involves comparison of the work with other works, with accepted rules, or with the envisioned final work not yet achieved.

QUESTION AND EXPLAIN

In the two classes that follow, we show how students are taught to Question and Explain. In both of these classes, teachers use questioning to help students focus on a particular aspect of their work and to reflect on what they are making and how they are working.

DRAWING YOURSELF AS MYTHICAL: IMAGINARY
CREATURES PROJECT   (EXAMPLE 9.1)

Near the middle of the second-semester class for 9th-graders at the Boston Arts Academy, students in Beth Balliro's class have recently visited the Boston Museum of Fine Arts. Beth talks about how a museum is a house of muses, and the muses are the keepers of the arts. Today students are asked to paint their muses—themselves as mythical creatures. The creature must be semihuman and must express something about the student's self. Students look at themselves in mirrors as they imagine their muse (see also Example 7.2).

Demonstration-Lecture

Beth first asks students to write about what inspires them. On the board she writes the following three questions for students to answer:

- What/who is your "muse?"
- If you had mythical powers, what would they be?
- What would your weaknesses be?

    As she gets pens and brushes out, Beth pursues these questions with individual students. Next, she hands out ink and packets with photocopies of mythical creatures from African and Native American cultures that students can use to help them envision their creatures.

Students-at-Work

While students draw their mythical creatures, Beth circles from student to student, pressing them to explain how the character they are drawing reflects something about themselves (see Figure 9.1). Here are some of the questions she asks students to encourage them to develop the habit of Question and Explain:

- How would this be you?
- What part of this character would be you looking in the mirror?
- How's it going to be you?
- Tell me about it. How is he part you?
- What kind of character is this? Do you really want to be this character?

- And how is this you, the glasses and the eyes?
- So this is you plus what? Some type of cat. . . . So how do the eyelashes make it seem half-human, half-animal?

    Beth sometimes points to specific parts of a drawing and asks students to explain what they did or are trying to do there:

- So did you just use a brush?
- How did you get this detail? It's beautiful.
- Tell me about those ears.

Beth Reflects

In an interview after class, we asked Beth to say more about her questioning techniques. She talked about two ways to help students learn to Question and Explain: Asking students to answer their own questions for the next 10 minutes, and having students keep journals in which they write about process on a daily basis. In this class, though, she has a minimal goal in mind: getting students to talk about their artmaking process. That seems clearly attainable for all her students and is a first, simple, and concrete step in their development.

    The habit of reflection helps students become independent workers and become "able to self-monitor so that they can eventually be autonomous," Beth explains. She believes that becoming reflective can help art students gain confidence when they are in academic classes in which they may not be strong students. "I want them to be able to articulate their process and articulate how they're different from other students." They can "figure out how to be more of a presence and how to advocate for their own growth in a way that allows people to hear them."

    Learning to be reflective about one's work and to advocate gives the emerging artist power in today's art world. "Part of their responsibility, I think, as artists is figuring out how to get yourself heard."

BUILDING OBJECTS IN RELATION:
COIL SCULPTURE PROJECT   (EXAMPLE 9.2)

In Jason Green's Coil Sculpture Project near the start of the second term of ceramics at Walnut Hill (see also Examples 3.2 and 11.5), when the focus has shifted from wheel-throwing to sculpture, again we see students being asked to Question and Explain their work. Jason asks students to look around the room to find two objects that could serve as the referents for a hand-built ceramic sculpture created with coil technique. The assignment is challenging because students are not to make a copy of the objects, but rather to create a new object that combines parts or all of the two

A. Beth Balliro prompts a student to pause and think about his work

B. She leads students in reflecting on their visit to the museum—a "house of muses"

C. Beth guides students to reflect on their personal muses

D. She urges students to consider what personal characteristics they could emphasize in their mythical creatures

objects they are using as models, varying scale as their intention dictates. Additionally, the sculptures must not have a flat bottom. The students are not making pottery, which is flat on one side so that it can stack on a shelf, but sculptures, which are built to be viewed from all sides. Students also have to make two experimental tiles with textures on them. From these tiles, they will choose the patterns that they want to use as the "skins" of their sculptures.

Students-at-Work

All of the techniques students have learned thus far will be used in this project. As students begin, Jason circles the room consulting with individual students.

- *Describe your plans.* "Do you know what you're going to do?" Jason asks a student as he prompts her to explain how she plans to use a light bulb. Later he returns to the same student to ask, "What about this form? What's the whole thing going to look like?" Jason questions another student to help her think how she might build with coils. "What's your object?" "Do you want to make the whole thing?" "Which part of it?" (Notice the connection to Envision)
- *Justify your choice as an aesthetic decision.* "What do you think is interesting about this? What do you like about it?" As Jason probes further, he asks the student to look closely at her chosen object and think of how it is used. Then he asks how her sculpture might be like the toy she has chosen. To a student combining a funnel and shell, Jason asks, "What do you like about the shell?" (Notice the connections to Express)
- *Assess as you work.* "How is that coming?" After the student nods that it's OK, Jason talks with her about what she might do next. "What are you doing now?" The student and Jason talk about what she might do next because her sculpture is too wet to work on any more today.

Jason Reflects

In an interview after this class, Jason said he hopes the students will begin to internalize the questions he poses and improve in the habit of Question and Explain. He explained that posing questions helps students become aware of the choices they make as they work, "They have to identify the choices they've made during the process and experiment as well, and just be able to reflect on the process or reflect on what they've made afterward." He added that "when students say, 'Well, this is the way I like it. This is the way I want it.' I say, 'Why do you want it that way?'"

A Dispositional View of Question and Explain

People sometimes distinguish between making and thinking. This is how art classes come to be seen as "nonintellectual" or "nonacademic." But artmaking requires serious thinking. One form of thinking called for in art classes is metacognition about one's working processes, which we refer to as Reflect: Question and Explain.

Skill. The skill of Question and Explain requires developing the technical and expressive vocabularies needed to explicitly consider one's goals, works, and working processes. It also requires the ability to think metacognitively, conveying that thinking by speaking and writing.

Alertness. Alertness to Question and Explain comes when students recognize occasions when self-questioning and explaining could be helpful to advance the process of making. Such occasions arise when artists are stuck, blocked, or confused, when a work seems to be finished, or at the beginning and end of work sessions or classes. There are also times to silence talk. In the words of Sister Corita Kent (Rule 8): "Don't try to create and analyze at the same time. They're different processes" (Kent & Steward, 2008, p. 176). As the quotation implies, artists also need to develop an alertness to times when self-talk or comments by others constrain the forward movement of work; at these times, they need to learn to shush their too-critical interior voices for a time or find quiet spaces away from others whose opinions are not yet welcome.

Inclination. The inclination to Question and Explain develops when students recognize the *need* to pause in the making process and think about what they are doing and where they are going. Pausing often feels unnatural during the flow of making, but it is important to take the breaks that disrupt the flow periodically. In Jim Woodside's 3-hour afternoon classes, he insisted that students put down their materials about halfway through and take a walk outside—just to clear their heads and see anew once more. While walking to the cafeteria for a snack, the students talked with each other and made notes in their sketchbooks. Similarly, Jim frequently paused the action of classes for mid-process critiques in which students generated new ideas from others' responses and their own new perspectives. As students see the value of such pauses, they can internalize the inclination to pause and reflect.

EVALUATE

Near the beginning of the school year at the Boston Arts Academy, the new 9th-grade students in Kathleen

Marsh's class have been working on a series of four self-portraits in colored pencil (see also Example 4.2). Kathleen begins today's class with a Critique followed by a Students-at-Work session (see Figure 9.2). We briefly describe the Critique and several Students-at-Work interactions to show examples of comments likely to help students learn to Evaluate.

DRAWING VALUES IN COLOR: SELF-PORTRAIT IN COLORED PENCIL PROJECT (EXAMPLE 9.3)

Kathleen asks students to put up their partially completed drawings. Then she asks students, one at a time, to select a peer's drawing and describe it using some of the vocabulary terms listed on the board. Students were then encouraged to Evaluate the work in process by thinking about choices they had made and envisioning changes that they could make to their own drawings. Kathleen said that she placed the Critique at the start of class so that she could redefine the goals of the self-portrait assignment through this low-stakes evaluation. She wanted students to focus their attention on value and composition. To support this shift in focus, she highlighted student work that showed good use of value, and she asked students to think more about background (to develop Express) and the placement of the face on the page (to Develop Craft in the techniques of composition).

Critique

Kathleen initiates the Critique with a reminder to use this chance to practice vocabulary to articulate positive evaluations of each other's draft work:

> I'd like a few people to pick out the vocabulary words—and here they are listed on the board—that you see evident in your classmates' drawings. You guys have really done an excellent job. And I'd like you to describe what it is that is excellent about these pictures. Pick one image and describe what you think is skilled or excellent about it, and use some of the vocabulary words in describing it.

A student begins, "OK, I like the outline there and . . ." When the student hesitates, Kathleen asks, "Can you walk up and point to it?" With this prompting the student points to a drawing and explains more: "Because it has a lot of *value*. Because on the right side it goes from dark to light and you can see different colors on the dark side. And on the light you can see just light. Like a little yellow and that's probably it."

Kathleen reinforces the student and turns to the student whose drawing is being discussed for self-evaluation.

"I'd like to hear what you have to say about this. Apparently, what you're doing is you're building up layers of color." The student responds. "Yeah, but I only did it on one side. I was going to get started on the second one." In what follows, Kathleen prompts the student to evaluate possible next steps in using color and value.

> *Kathleen:* OK. So what else are you going to do today? What are your other plans for this piece?
> *Student:* I'm going to make it look like real flesh, like flesh color.
> *Kathleen:* OK, and . . . [She waits for him to finish her sentence.]
> *Student:* And I'm going to leave it that light on one side.
> *Kathleen:* OK, and what are some of the other colors that you're planning to use to create your skin tone?
> *Student:* I was using like the yellow and light brown and peach and pink. I'm trying to get it to look like real flesh.
> *Kathleen:* OK, can I make three suggestions?
> *Student:* Uh huh.
> *Kathleen:* Yellow, red, and a tiny bit of blue.
> *Student:* Blue?
> *Kathleen:* Yeah.
> *Student:* OK.
> *Kathleen:* Why would I say blue?
> *Student:* Because it's a cool color. You want to mix two warm colors and a cool color.
> *Kathleen:* It's a cool color. Blue is the color of your veins [*pointing to the veins in her face*]. And there is some of that in the transparency of your skin. A tiny bit. And also what makes brown? And I actually said this to a bunch of you on Monday. What are the colors that make brown?
> *Student:* Red, yellow . . .
>
> *[Kathleen calls on another student.]*
>
> *Student:* Red, yellow, and blue.
> *Kathleen:* Red, yellow, and blue. All the primaries make brown.

Having evaluated the need for mixing primaries to achieve flesh tones, Kathleen demonstrates the need to create different colors of brown because of the variety of flesh tones. Kathleen has all the students extend an arm into the middle of the table and observe their skin.

Students then move to discussing color in another student's work. When a student points to a self-portrait that he really likes, Kathleen probes for more explanation of that judgment. "OK, what is it about this that you really like?"

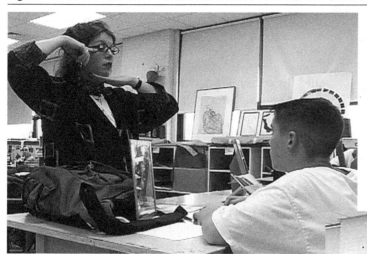

A. Kathleen Marsh shows proportions of a human face by using her own face as an example

B. She guides a student to evaluate his own work

C. She talks with a student about how his drawing can control where a viewer looks

D. Kathleen explains how she is evaluating a student's drawing

Student 1: Opposite. It's like the whole different contrast of the white and the brown is just there, you know.

Student 2: [the student whose work is being discussed]: It works out smoothly.

Kathleen: OK, but are you finished? How much white do you plan on leaving in your drawing?

Student 2: Umm, not much. Only the eye and some of the light . . . are coming from the other side. Like where the white is now is where the light source is coming from, but it's not done.

Often evaluation requires metaphorical thinking, as shown by the next student to speak, who says, "I don't think he finished it, but I still think it looks really cool. It's all . . . it looks like you're standing there and all of a sudden a big flash of light comes and just brightens everything." Kathleen responds that this is a good perception, and another student adds, "I thought of nuclear war."

Kathleen offers further information to enhance students' abilities to articulate their evaluative observations about the challenges of using the color wheel:

All of you guys are taking very different approaches to the use of color. [Student 2] has decided to make his colors really intense and keep that intensity throughout his drawing. And we've discussed how that might become problematic, because you're really working with that saturated color and you're going to continue to do that. Right? So I think you're figuring stuff out about color. Right? Because normally I would say start with thin layers and build up. But he's sort of layering as he goes. And that can be dangerous because you may run into problems that you aren't able to fix later. But you're figuring it out.

Students-at-Work

After the Critique, students work on their own portraits as Kathleen consults with individuals. To foster the habit of self-evaluation, her evaluative comments mix praise with advice for how a student might proceed:

- *Look at the subtle changes in skin color.* Kathleen draws the student's attention to a place where he has shown the subtle change of skin color when seen through glasses. "Nice contrast in your skin between what's behind your glasses and what's on your actual skin. Remember we talked about that? How the glasses change the color of the skin behind them? You did a really nice job with that."

- *Decide if your composition is accurate.* Kathleen helps a student see that the viewer does not know where to focus because of his composition.

  This still isn't touching any side of this page. You've got a floating head there. You need to at least connect this to the bottom and somehow figure out how to connect [the] drawing to [the] sides of the page. Why would I ask you to do that? . . . It makes that a bigger scale, but why is that important in terms of composition?

- Kathleen points to parts of the drawing as she continues. "I am your viewer right now, so I am looking at your drawing and you want to be able to control where I look. So your glasses really help and draw me into your face. But you need to figure out ways to lead me around your page."

- *Compare your drawing with your face.* Kathleen asks a student to see how her drawing does not capture the way her face is actually built. "My sense is the light is not hitting you exactly in half like that." As she talks, Kathleen gestures to her own face to demonstrate relationships. "Look at yourself. Generally speaking, your earlobes meet the bottom of your nose. So I think your ears need to be maybe a little bigger, and that will inform where the bottom of your nose is. And that will tell you where your lips will be. Also look at the line of your lips. It's much curvier than what you have here, OK? Close your lips and look in the mirror."

This comment from Kathleen also prompted the student to Observe.

Kathleen Reflects

Kathleen believes that her 9th-grade students are not yet ready for a full-blown critique.

I think it takes time to work up to that point. So we're not there yet in the 9th grade. Just to get everyone [to] talk in an orderly fashion and listen to each other talk. That's where we are. We're not there yet, the full-blown critique yet.

Kathleen used to consider effort as part of the grade, but she now believes that grading for effort does not show students where they need to improve. "It's not fair to them, because it's not giving them a really clear picture of what specifically they need to be working on." Critique helps students learn about the qualities of work that matter. They are a kind of formative assessment.

Critiques also provide students with the vocabulary they need to talk about their work. She described many of her students as "intuitive artmakers." "They do what they feel without much vocabulary attached to it. So we give them this vocabulary that begins to really describe what they're doing." This helps students set clearer goals and also provides a basis for conversations between teacher and student.

Kathleen said that reflecting on one's portfolio and exhibiting work are two other ways students learn the habit of Evaluating. By keeping a portfolio and reflecting on it, students can see and articulate how they've grown, both of which help structure a student's thinking. She believes that exhibiting one's work is like a formal extension of an informal class critique.

> Assessment happens on many, many levels, and of course in the older grades, I really believe that exhibition is a really key assessment tool, because I think in the act of sharing a work, and showing your work, you begin to—it's like releasing your baby. Once you release it, then it really becomes a separate entity. And that's when I think we really begin to look at the work and begin to grow.

As discussed in Chapters 3 and 15, when students graduate from the Boston Arts Academy, they must exhibit their work formally and talk about their work to a panel of outside experts. They must talk about their goals, their working process, their strengths, and their weaknesses, and they must answer questions. Students reported the value of this, saying, for example, "My perspective changed after my review, because I was treated not as a child artist, but more as a young adult with artistic abilities." In short, when students are asked to reflect about themselves, they see themselves being taken seriously; they see their own interpretations valued and thus they gain confidence in their abilities to think about themselves as artists.

A Dispositional View of Evaluate

Evaluation is a central reflective habit in the arts because of the omnipresence of both formal and informal critiques and because of the continual push to step back and judge whether something is or is not moving in the right direction.

Skill. Underlying the skill of Evaluate is the ability to make interpretive claims and judgments about works of art and to justify these claims using evidence. Of course, there are no absolute "right" or "wrong" judgments of the quality of works. Judgments are shaped by sociohistorical context and individual taste; revolutionary works that were once reviled, such as Duchamp's *Fountain* (a urinal mounted for display in a gallery) may be revered later as an historical benchmark (i.e., as an original icon of the type of work called "ready-made").

Alertness. One of the dangers of evaluation is that students may become paralyzed by self-consciousness. Alertness about when, how, and what to evaluate calls for students not only to realize when to make judgments but also when to suspend them. Sometimes students simply need to keep working and hold off on any evaluation—silencing their internal critic so that they can work from intuition without second-guessing themselves in the process. At other times they need to pause their making for moments of "light" judgment—taking a step back from their work to think about where they are going, what is working and what is not, and why. And at still other times, they need to be able to listen to judgments of their works that others offer, even when these are critical. Deciding what to do with such judgments is yet another piece of alertness; some are good to keep and others should be let go. Discerning which is which requires alertness to the delicate balance between internal and external demands.

Inclination. The inclination to evaluate requires that students do not get stalled by taking a stance of relativity. Just because there are no right or wrong answers does not mean that every response is equally good or bad—in fact, quite the reverse. There are many rich solutions to any given challenge, but there are even more poor ones. Students need to experience for themselves the difference that tiny choices make in how a work is perceived, in their own works and in the works of others. As students get into the habit of learning from non-hurtful criticism, they come to value the potential of the evaluative process more and to recognize how it helps their artistic process move forward.

Generative Connections to Reflect

Whenever Reflect is added to the operation of a habit or cluster of habits, those habits are strengthened and deepened. Every habit can link with Reflect. Teachers can pose questions to help students talk about their techniques (Develop Craft), their levels of investment (Engage and Persist), how they are coping with mistakes (Stretch and Explore), how thematic meanings are conveyed in works (Express), and so forth.

Question and Explain is tightly linked to Observe. When teachers circulate during Students-at-Work sessions, they ask students to describe what they are doing, explain why, and make judgments. None of this can be done without looking closely. Evaluate and Observe connect, because as people evaluate, they focus attention to specific aspects of the work, honing observational skills.

Careful observation also keeps students from making facile evaluations (e.g, "I like that work, because it's graffiti, and I like graffiti"). When teachers evaluate, they are typically evaluating something specific, whether the technique, the expression, or the observational skill is revealed. Thus, when a comment aims to teach the student to Evaluate, it usually is also teaching another habit as well.

What Teachers Can Do

To help students build the disposition to Reflect, teachers regularly ask students to step back and focus on some aspect of their work or working process. This kind of metacognitive talk about process occurs far more often in art classes than in traditional non-arts classrooms. Teachers might ask students to keep notes in their sketchbooks and write blogs about their changing processes to foster development of a reflective inner voice, to supplement the emphasis on visual symbols that students think with when they work with art tools and materials. Teachers can share videos of artists talking about their practice that highlight how reflection is embedded in their creative process. Or they can share works where a reflective process is embedded in the art itself, such as Stephanie Dinkins's ongoing work, *Conversations with Bina48*, which is documentation of her ongoing conversations with an advanced social robot, in which they discuss emotions, their families, racism, and friendship.

Teachers can nurture Evaluate by setting regular (even daily) reflective assignments, asking students to Reflect privately in front of a video camera (sometimes called "video confessionals"), and holding frequent, mid-process critiques that allow peers and teachers to offer information in response to work in progress. Art teachers frequently evaluate student work informally as they move around the room while students are working, and they also evaluate during Critique and in culminating reviews of students' portfolios of work. Students can learn from these consultations and critiques how to evaluate themselves and others. Thus, students in visual arts classes are learning to make aesthetic judgments and to defend them. They have the opportunity to learn to be self-critical and to think about how they could improve. Creating such a classroom culture and immersing students in it is probably the most effective way a teacher can positively influence a student's disposition to Evaluate.

As a senior at the Boston Arts Academy told us, "When I was younger, I wanted to hear people tell me, 'Oh you're doing so good. That's so beautiful.' And now I just want to grow. So by just hearing the good things, you don't grow"

Figure 9.3. A Senior at the Boston Arts Academy Describes How This Reclining Pastel Figure Shows That He Has Learned to Learn from Critique

Figure 9.4. Late in the 9th Grade, a Student at Walnut Hill Reflects on How He Used to Draw Figures "Piece by Piece Instead of Drawing the Whole Figure"

(see Figure 9.3). Another student shows us that already in his first year at Walnut Hill, he has become able to evaluate his own work critically. Looking at some work done early in the year, he tells us, "I don't think these are particularly well drawn. Because when I did it, I'd draw the head and finish it and then move on down the neck and into the arm. Draw everything piece by piece instead of drawing the whole figure, which is what I gradually learned to do" (see Figure 9.4, which the student felt was *not* drawn piecemeal).

Reflect in Other Disciplines

It is impossible to do great work in any discipline without reflection, but too often schools do not expect students to reflect. Public reflection happens more often in arts than in non-arts classes because of the ubiquity of the critique structure. But classrooms can all benefit from public reflection. For example, in Japan, which

ranks high in international comparisons of mathematics education, an observer might see elementary students working in groups on a single, open-ended problem for an entire class period. The groups then present and are critiqued on how they approached the problem rather than on their final answers. By reflecting publicly, as is traditionally done in studio classes, these mathematics students internalize a focus on process that supports their success in mathematics.

As another example of public reflection in non-arts classes, Hetland asked her 7th-grade history class to present their research in process and respond to questions from their peers. As a result of challenges from their peers, the students refined their research focus and buttressed their conclusions with stronger evidence. Whenever student work in progress is made public and students engage in peer review, students have the opportunity to Reflect on their processes and those of others and to Evaluate products as they evolve into their final forms.

TEN

Stretch and Explore
Taking a Leap

I hope to teach the kids how to think differently.

—Guy Michel Telemaque

You ask kids to play, and then in one-on-one conversation you name what they've stumbled on.

—Beth Balliro

At its core, Stretch and Explore is creative thinking. By that we mean that it is transgressive—it breaks boundaries. It combines thinking that opens up ideas (divergent) with thinking that sets ideas (convergent), so that we reach an adaptive solution that is novel. New ideas come from pushing at constraints. In the words of John Cage, "We're breaking all of the rules. Even our own rules" (Kent & Steward, 2008, p. 176). Artists try new things and reach beyond what they have already done. They play, take risks, explore novel associations, and make mistakes, not deliberately, but routinely and inevitably. For artists, mistakes are opportunities—they lead to problem-solving as well as to something more at the core of creativity—problem-*finding* (Getzels & Csikszentmihalyi, 1976). New problems to solve are discovered through exploration. In the words of artist Sister Corita Kent, Rule 4 in art is "Consider everything an experiment" (Kent & Steward, 2008, p. 176).

Artists Stretch and Explore by using the practice of conditional thinking: What if I try it this way, or this way, or that? They seek out the unusual, push beyond the limits of what is understood, and stride into the unknown as if they knew where they were going and what they were doing. Artist Bunny Harvey once said that she looks for odd found objects on daily walks, then plays with these forms in juxtaposition to inspire new ideas for her paintings. Artist Brice Marden used three-foot dowels as an unusual tool to paint a series of large works with a continuous line in the 1990s. And artist Rachel Perry expands what people normally consider to be art media by making art out of the detritus of daily domestic life, such as twist ties, fruit stickers, gum wrappers, and voicemails.

In what follows, we describe two ceramic sculpture classes that show how students are taught to Stretch and Explore. Both teachers encourage students to reach beyond what they can already do and to play with alternative possibilities.

INTRODUCING THE MEDIUM: SKETCHING IN CLAY (EXAMPLE 10.1)

At the Boston Arts Academy, Beth Balliro begins her ceramic sculpture unit for 9th-graders in the first class of the semester by having students "sketch in clay." Many of the students have never touched clay before. Now they must play a game in which they mold creatures out of clay and then destroy them. The end product is not important; only the process matters. The goal of the first part of the class is to get students used to digging their hands into clay. By working quickly and then smashing what they have made, students lose their inhibitions and learn to experiment—to sketch in clay—rather than create a perfect finished clay product. After the game, students work on a final creature that they will glaze and fire, so they experience in short order the entire process of wet clay to fired piece.

Students work in groups, sitting around small tables. A chunk of clay sits on each table, and Beth starts the game by telling one student to pick up some clay at his table and make "a creature that flies." After a minute, Beth stops him, holds up his creature, and notes how it conveys a sense of flight. Then she asks him to smash it. To the class she says, "The first thing I want you to get at is how to work quickly. The second thing, which is maybe even more fun, is destroying it."

Next, Beth asks one person at each table to pick up the clay and quickly make "a creature that slithers." After a few minutes, Beth tells each maker to smash what has been

77

made and pass the clay to the next person, who will then make a "ferocious" creature. The process is repeated again when the next student at each table is asked to create a "gentle" creature. As they work, Beth moves from group to group, commenting on how each is doing. She tells them it is hard to just "dive in" to the clay and "smush things around." She adds, "Some of you guys might have trouble doing that. Especially some of you that like really clean lines and perhaps like to draw with pencils. Sometimes it's a really different thing to work with clay. So I want to commend you for all diving in. That's why we did that."

Students are learning to be messy and experimental—learning that this kind of mucking around is an important part of the artistic process.

While Beth moves among students as they work, she finds ways to encourage them to keep working experimentally. "You might say, 'Here's a pencil, and I'm going to use the back of the pencil and roll it across the clay, and I'm going to experiment.'" The following are other examples of comments meant to help students learn to Stretch and Explore:

- *Don't worry about how the piece will end up.* Beth encourages a group of students to play freely without concern about how their pieces end up looking. She says that she wants them to have something in mind, "and then I want you to play and play and play."
- *Experiment with expression through texture.* Beth encourages a student to "think about what kind of texture it might be. Is it a furry part or is it sharp and shiny like a beetle?" She suggests that he can explore ways to create texture and should remember the finger marks another student used in her piece.
- *Experiment with tools.* Beth offers ideas of tools a student might use to experiment: "There's a couple of screws and things on the window sill over there and they make really good tools, sometimes, things that aren't really tools. You might play around with that, too."
- *Discover new techniques through play.* Later, Beth will teach specific techniques, but right now she wants students to discover techniques on their own, through play. Such experiences reinforce an understanding that techniques are solutions others have come up with for problems they have encountered. Students learn that when they have a problem, they can use techniques others have created or can invent a technique to solve it themselves. To a student struggling to stick clay together, Beth says, "There are specific ways to do it, but I want you guys to play around in this first project. Just go with that and see what happens, and maybe you'll learn a new technique with doing that."

Beth Reflects

Beth talked to us about this class and about teaching students the habit of Stretch and Explore. Taking risks is an important part of growing as an artist, which Beth says she is constantly trying to reinforce in her students. Her students "need to be able to risk what they're already good at" and not be trapped by the "safety net of style." Beth also talked about her own growth as an artist and the importance of stretching beyond her comfort zone.

> When I'm really working hard and doing good work, it's not fun at all. I hate it, and that's how I grow as an artist. I struggle through it, and I feel out of my comfort zone, and I'm exhausted, my arms hurt, and that means that I'm working hard, and that I'm growing as an artist.

One of Beth's goals for the Sketching in Clay class was for students to lose their inhibitions about working with the medium of clay and about being "precious" regarding their work. She wanted students to free themselves of the goal of trying to make everything perfect and smooth. She had them smash their first pieces so they learned to let go, a strategy she has also tried with painting. When asked why she did not teach students about hollowing out their forms so they were not too thick to be fired, Beth told us that this was just one more constraint she wanted them to be free of at first.

As much as she can, Beth wants students to learn from the materials rather than through explicit instructions.

> If I had more time, I would have them learn entirely from the materials. And let them learn, and then fail, and then have things, you know, break and explode and all that, and then they'd learn that way.

Capitalizing on mistakes, she says, is a major consideration in ceramics.

> It's not all about perfection and dominating a natural material, but it's letting the natural material do what it will. So if something cracks, if somebody has a piece that cracks, I don't want them to freak out and think it's broken. If you have a crack, well, let's fill it with gold. And let's make that what the piece is about.

When students are playing, Beth believes they are more able to take suggestions and criticisms than when they are working on a piece that must be finished in final form. She told the story of a student who had a "white page issue" and how "it's easier for him to address it, deal with it in kind of a low-risk painting, which was a play painting, than in a highly refined major project." She added, "I think my hope is when they play around, stuff will come to the surface and then we can address issues in a less tense way." Beth also reflected more generally on how students at the Boston Arts Academy are not allowed to learn passively: "This is not just going to school. You can't just follow these rote things that other schools may have asked you to do. You have to really step outside your comfort zone and push yourself in all kinds of areas."

BUILDING FORM:
REPEATING UNITS PROJECT　　　　　　　(EXAMPLE 10.2)

For Jason Green's third ceramics project in the second semester of his mixed-age (grades 9–12) introductory ceramics course at Walnut Hill, students learn to plan in a responsive or "improvisational" way, by creating a unit and then repeating that unit to build a larger form. Students are learning to adopt the attitude of "What would happen if . . . ?" They cannot know what the end product will be like from the initial unit. They discover as they go.

In their first two projects, Jason's students learned traditional methods of hand-building—coil and slab. Today they learn a method of building based on repeating units, a method that is common in nature and often used in clay, as when walls of clay bricks or roofs of clay tiles are built. They are to create a unit and then repeat that unit over and over to build a larger form. He talks to them about different kinds of units and explains how the way that the units are put together determines the form of the resulting sculpture (see Figure 10.1).

Demonstration-Lecture

Jason encourages students to begin by playing around with different kinds of units. "I want you to experiment," he says. He discusses examples of forms from nature that are built up out of repeating units—a wasp's nest, a pine cone. He shows a small wall of bricks and a sculpture comprised of stacks of the same cast bottle, layered over and over. The task for today's class is to create small experimental models trying out various units and exploring ways of joining these units into a whole.

Students are asked to decide how units will be joined. Jason tells them to consider whether they are "going to be piled or stacked or are they going to be compressed together or glued together." Students are told to play with showing how the units are stuck together to reveal rather than conceal the building process.

"You want to think about showing, if you stack things together, if you stack coils together, and assemble them; when you score, leave the connection and don't smooth things over." Jason refers to this kind of experimentation as "thinking with the clay." Here are some examples of how Jason helps students learn to Stretch and Explore as they think with the clay:

- *Experiment with a range of different forms.* Jason stops to talk with a group of students. When one tells him her plan, Jason tells her, "Rather than just starting, I want you to experiment with some different types of units. Some might be very geometric, some you might just grab and shape in your hand quickly." Jason suggests to another student in the group that she go even further and build using "dramatically different units."

- *Experiment with techniques for making and joining units.* Later, Jason returns to both students to talk further about different ways they could work with building from their units. To one, he suggests she might build something large by connecting together the pieces she has built already. Jason tells the other that he can tell her unit was made with the slab roller and suggests, "Think of touching the clay in a way you haven't touched it before. Is there a way you can make a unit just from your hand or from another tool that's not a ceramic tool?"

- *Think conditionally and experiment with what the clay can do.* Jason uses conditional "what if" language to urge a student to think of possibilities for building a unit based on a wing. He asks, "What if you just tried flattening pieces of clay and building a wing out of this?" "What happens if you start alternating and building the sculpture up this way?" He also asks a student to make clay do unusual things: "Think about Jackson Pollock, because his painting was a result of his process. He would drip the paint in a certain way. How could you drip clay?"

- *Invent some different tools.* Jason tells a student to experiment with tools, including invented tools: "I want you to also do some more experimentation before the end of the day and make some things with your hands and with other tools that aren't ceramic tools."

- *Take advantage of accidents and let things just happen.* "You are actually building a sculpture over there but didn't know it," Jason says as he points to a small pile of similar pieces of clay. He tells the student this is because they have a certain similarity and suggests maybe she try to see what she could build from them. He adds, "Those are interesting units because

Figure 10.1. Stretch and Explore—Jason Green Asks Students to Consider "What Would Happen If . . . ?" in His Unit Sculpture Assignment

A. A student consults with Jason Green about the units she has created from which to make a sculpture

B. Jason encourages a student to play with her idea of "wings" for her unit sculpture

C. He tells a student that he wants her to experiment

D. Jason demonstrates combining natural forms such as wasp's nests and pine cones

you weren't thinking about them too much when you made them."

- *Experiment with different versions.* Jason talks further with the student who originally based her unit on a wing and explains why he is urging her to think about several versions of the same idea. I want to put you through different ways to think of getting at the same idea. So if it seems like I don't like what you're doing, I like everything you do, I just want you to sometimes do different things so you can learn some more and see different ways of using the clay.

Jason explained to us that one of his goals for this class was to get students to explore ways to act on the material of clay: "I want them to research the material more than their idea of what their sculpture is going to be in the end, which is tough for them because I'm setting them down this road, and they really have no idea what they're going to be making."

Jason and Students Reflect

Jason further explained why he wanted a particular student to think about the unit and not the final product: "The final product will emerge. Thinking about what the end result was going to be limits her." He added, "I'm really trying to get them to stretch and push the material and themselves, and take some risks and do some things that they might not normally do."

Jason also talked about his own habit of stretching and exploring as an artist: "That's what I do. I try to continue to ask questions, and because of that, my own processes are continually changing. I don't make the same things over and over and over again." A freshman at Walnut Hill said the same thing to us:

If you know what you're good at and you just repeat that over and over again, you're never going to get anywhere. You're just stuck doing the same thing over and over again because you know you can. And that's taking the easy way out. And you're not really going to go really far with that, I don't think.

A senior at Walnut Hill identified the habit of going beyond the given assignment as central to what she learned in high school: "Coming up with interesting solutions to interesting problems." She told us about how, in response to a multimedia assignment in her junior year that asked her to make a book, she explored different ways of conceiving of books. "I didn't want to make just any old regular book, so I started thinking of different structures that kind of had pages or had covers." She ended up creating an Asian-inspired fan with the different segments representing pages of a book. She further explored by wrapping recycled container lids and bottle caps with ribbon and string to create a layered "elegant effect" (see Figure 10.2).

And another senior at Walnut Hill told us what he had learned about not focusing always on creating a finished piece of work: "I think you get to a point when you're doing art where you have more to learn from going and doing a new piece than refining the one you've already got. You can see the progression through different works."

Figure 10.2. A Junior at Walnut Hill Pushed the Form of Her "Book" and Transformed Recycled Materials into an Elegant Fan. (A, B)

A.

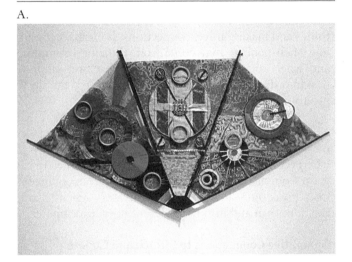

B. (detail)

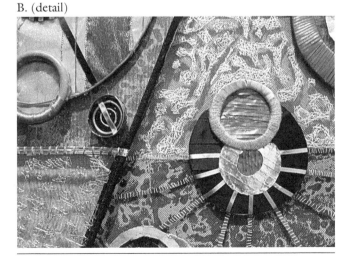

A Dispositional View of Stretch and Explore

The disposition to Stretch and Explore may be less dependent on skill and more a matter of an attitude—alertness to creative connections and the inclination to put them into action.

Skill. The skills involved in Stretch and Explore include the ability to make novel associations, to diagnose by analysis how outcomes failed, to conceive of tasks that take off from illogical premises and follow them to their logical conclusions—even when this pushes beyond the artist's ability level and makes failure likely. Stretch and Explore is the skill of dismissing the censors, deciding to push beyond the urge to merely repeat previous successes, and keeping critical voices at bay while adopting the unconscious abilities of a child adept at play. This is what leads to problem-finding.

Alertness. Alertness to Stretch and Explore means recognizing the possibilities everywhere for trying new things and making novel connections. It means recognizing when benefits may come from thinking divergently and when to infuse artmaking with play and randomness in order to move the process forward strategically. It means seeing errors as creative opportunities.

Inclination. The inclination to Stretch and Explore means the willingness, even the desire or need, to go wherever your first steps takes you, to innovate. It can grow from dissatisfaction, from curiosity, from confusion, from boredom—anything that motivates a reach beyond the quotidian and into the realm of novel possibilities.

Generative Connections to Stretch and Explore

Stretch and Explore often pairs with other habits that support and extend its creative core. For example, teachers pair it with Develop Craft when they ask students to experiment with new materials and techniques; students can invent new techniques with tools and materials, such as when Sara Stillman asked her kindergarten through 5th-grade students in Oakland to do everything possible to alter cardboard. This pairing easily becomes a cluster when Express is added, since messing around produces unusual outcomes, which convey new meanings if they are recognized and used in artmaking. Extending the cluster by adding Envision (imagining what's to be made) and Reflect (thinking about what's been made) further extends and consolidates what is learned.

Stretch and Explore becomes more generative when combined with Envision. When teachers ask students to think about "what if," students begin to envision new possibilities and then try them out. Adding Observe into this pair results in explorations being noticed, which then can catalyze further investigation.

Stretch and Explore is also tightly linked to Engage and Persist. When students are highly engaged, they are more likely to keep on trying new things; and when students persist for long periods of time, they are more likely to find the edge of their competence and step off that edge. As discussed in Chapter 6 on Envision, another common cluster is the triad of Stretch and Explore, Engage and Persist, and Envision.

What Teachers Can Do

Teachers can help students develop the inclination to Stretch and Explore by infusing their conversations with encouragement to try new things: "See what would happen if . . ." "How else could you have done this?" "Don't worry about mistakes, just be brave." They can encourage students to be willing to embrace mistakes, stumbles, and failure as steps along the way to innovation. Artist Oliver Herring's "Task" events are effective ways to introduce students to the value of play. In Task, participants each write "something someone could do" on a slip of paper and put it in a box. Each participant then takes a slip and carries it out in some way. When they finish, they write a new task slip, put it in the box, and take another. The process unfolds with the development of more and more playful tasks, releasing a spirit of possibility that is hard to match. Similarly, MassArt professor John Crowe assigns students the task of "making fifty mistakes" and surprises them in the next class by asking them to choose one mistake to "elevate to a work of art." Students may not at first have the intrinsic motivation to generate ideas. Assignments such as Task and Fifty Mistakes provide extrinsic motivation; the goal is for this motivation to become intrinsic.

Teachers can share the works of artists who experiment with materials, such as Cai Guo-Qiang who creates work with gunpowder (though we suggest with a warning not to try at home!) or Deborah Butterfield's iconic horses which were first built from mud, clay, and sticks. Or they can share artists who employ exploratory processes such as Matthew Barney's *Drawing Restraint* series where he makes marks as he swings, trampolines, climbs walls and so forth. The aim is not necessarily for students to work in the same ways as these artists, but rather to model a spirit of exploration.

When teachers encourage students to Stretch and Explore, they strive for what David Perkins calls "optimal ambiguity"—tasks that are clear enough to communicate a direction and open enough to allow infinite solutions. Teachers who want to encourage this habit do not tell students exactly what to do. Instead, through the level of challenge in the assignments and the responses teachers make as students work on those assignments, teachers urge students to play around, to take risks, to discover what can happen, and to try out alternatives.

Teachers also allow students adequate time to stay with a line of inquiry long enough to pursue the kinds of conditional thinking involved in Stretch and Explore. At both Boston Arts Academy and Walnut Hill, students were gradually supported to move from responding to open-ended assignments given by the teacher to pursuing a self-directed and sustained line of inquiry that allowed them to explore the possibilities in an area of interest, and to build their artistic agency (as we discuss in Chapter 16). As one senior working on a series of expressive oil portraits describes the process,

> We [the student and Jim] have a little bit of a back-and-forth, and then it gives me a little bit of a direction, and it gives me something to think about, and then I go out and implement that in the next, say, ten pieces I do. I think they almost have a bit of a hands-off feeling or approach to it. And a lot of it, I've found, is my personal learning.

I mean, the biggest element is, I think, I care about it. It's like I really want to advance where I'm going.

This sustained self-directed stretching and exploring is also an expectation of advanced art classes, such as those in the International Baccalaureate, Advanced Placement in studio art, and Teaching for Artistic Behavior (TAB) (see Jaquith & Hathaway, 2012; Douglas & Jaquith, 2009).

Stretch and Explore in Other Disciplines

Teachers of all subject areas typically hope their students will learn to think creatively. Although it is in the art studio where creativity is stressed most explicitly, no creative breakthroughs are made in any discipline without a stretch, and exploration is the way thinkers stretch. Stretch and Explore is therefore the core of creativity across all disciplines. Viewing creativity as the sole purview of the arts curriculum is a common problem in schools. Students need to learn to Stretch and Explore in every school subject. Mistakes in non-arts classes are often seen by students as shameful, humiliating, and to be avoided. Teachers in academic disciplines could learn from art teachers' emphasis on playful mucking around and embracing mistakes as opportunities.

ELEVEN

Understand Art Worlds
Domain, Communities

Part of my role is to demystify art throughout the year.

—Jim Woodside

The most powerful experiences in art history that I have witnessed have been in my studio classes, not necessarily in my art history classes.

—Beth Balliro

There's strength in ideas and working together toward a common goal.

—Kathleen Marsh

By "Understand Art Worlds," we refer to the process by which students come to understand the many art worlds in which artists (including designers and architects) engage: contemporary, modern, ancient, prehistoric, non-Western, outsider, folk, popular culture, sub-cultures, non-arts disciplines and domains, and so forth. Even outsider artists do not work in total isolation; artists and artworks always respond to works that have come before, consciously or not. We divide this Studio Habit of Mind into two components, *Domain* and *Communities.*

Understanding the *domain* means familiarity with the full range of art: from contemporary art practices (e.g., Damien Hirst's dead animals in formaldehyde; Félix González-Torres's candy spills; Marina Abramovic's interactive endurance performances) to the origins of human art (e.g., knowing that, as reported in *Science Magazine,* the earliest known forms of human art were nonrepresentational designs rather than the famous bison on the cave walls of Altamira and Lascaux [Pike et al., 2012]). As students gain access to fuller ranges of artistic responses throughout time and across cultures, they can develop their own voices in response to those conversations.

Understanding *communities* means learning about and participating in the discourse community of artistic practice—people who are concerned and knowledgeable about art (and even audiences who are naïve), including artist-teachers, student-artist peers, families and friends, teaching artists, local artists of all kinds,

contemporary artists everywhere, and past artists. Artists are in dialogue, real and imagined, with communities that speak the languages of art around the globe and throughout time; those working now and those from the past. Understanding *communities* also means learning about what Csikszentmihalyi (1990) has called the "field" of art—the galleries and museums, and the people who guard and open their gates, including museum curators, gallery owners, and other artists. Together, these gatekeepers decide whose work will be exhibited and immortalized. While social media and other cultural forces are breaking down traditional systems of control, access, and authority, gatekeepers still exert powerful influence on what the public and specialized audiences consider to be great or worthy. Artists need to respond to the gatekeepers in one way or another along a continuum running from acquiescence to transgression, and student-artists need to come to understand those interactions.

The community component of Understand Art Worlds also includes working with peers. When students collaborate on a group project, such as the creation of a library of ceramic molds (Examples 3.2, 9.2, and 11.5), or the Egg Drop Project (Example 11.6), they work in a team. When they work on individual projects, they share tools and materials, help each other by providing suggestions, and learn by looking at each other's work. In all of these ways, students come to see artmaking as an activity that is carried out in the company of peers.

One Walnut Hill senior told us, "I think working like this made me be able to respect other people a lot more and have a better understanding of other people and who they are."

DOMAIN

Students are taught about the *domain* of art (works of art, both contemporary and historical). While art history is not usually taught in a systematic fashion in studio arts classes, teachers often ask students to look at works or reproductions of works of art that relate in some way to the project in which the students are engaged. Students are taught about their own relationship to the domain of art, considering the similarities between the problems explored in their own works and those explored by established artists.

Students often talked about how their own artmaking grew from looking at how other artists had solved problems. One of Jason Green's students tried to imagine the process behind artists' work so she could connect it to her own work: "When I see the other sculptures, I imagine about them, their process—how did the artist make this? How did they work? I imagine about the process. When I think about that, I can get ideas."

We first present examples that teach about the domain of art (artworks) and help students see the relationship between their own works and those made by professional artists. In these examples, students come to see that they are working on visual problems similar to those that artists are dealing with now or have dealt with throughout the centuries. They also come to see how they can learn from and be inspired by these artists.

CONSIDERING REPRESENTATIONS: FIGURES IN
EVOCATIVE SPACE PROJECT   (EXAMPLE 11.1)

Recall Jim Woodside's drawing project, Figures in Evocative Space, described in Examples 7.1 and 14.2, in which he sets up a "scene" with two student models, far apart from each other, just "hanging out." He emphasizes that "these two people are elements in a play here, elements in a drama." He wants students to use drawing to express a dramatic relationship.

To illustrate his point, Jim provides examples of artists expressing relationships evocatively in paintings by Edward Hopper and Richard Diebenkorn:

> This is a very famous painting done by Edward Hopper called *Nighthawks*, done in 1942. OK, now, if you can see it, what's the sort of feeling you get from this, what's the emotional content? [Students suggest quiet, late, drowsy.] Quiet, late, drowsy,

how is that implied? It's a very quiet painting, that's a really, a really perceptive remark. And I really like that you said that, 'cause what you're starting to do is describing it not just in paint terms. It's a very quiet painting, it's late at night, the figures are small in relation to the space, the way that they're relating to each other; if you look closely they're all sort of in their own worlds. He thought very carefully about the relationship between the figures and how that was going to be implied.

> This [Jim shows a book with a reproduction of Richard Diebenkorn's 1957 painting, *Man and Woman in a Large Room*] is by a painter called Richard Diebenkorn, and while this painting is not as emotional as the Hopper *Nighthawks* painting, it is very much about how figures relate in a larger space. You can see the artist working in his studio, and this is maybe the model. It's a very standard scene, a very ordinary scene. The figures themselves are not really individual, are they? They're just elements there, just sort of props in an overall drama.

Jim has shown the students the paintings to inform their thinking about the current drawing challenge he has posed to them. He explains, "So this is the kind of thinking I think will be helpful if you need to have an image in mind as you begin something like this." During the Critique following the assignment, students discuss how they expressed emotions similar to those in the Diebenkorn and Hopper works.

Jim Reflects

After the class, Jim spoke with us about how the image helped the students appreciate the challenge of the assignment, how he hopes students will move beyond "academic" art to expressive art, and how such paintings can help students understand what he is getting at:

> When they look at [the Hopper] they don't think, "Look at the figures," they think, "It's a late mysterious night." And there's figures in there and they don't seem to be talking to each other and they can all understand immediately, even though it's a very dated image, they can understand that idea of hanging out late at night.

DRAWING INSPIRATION FROM IMAGES:
AFRICAN POTTERY PROJECT   (EXAMPLE 11.2)

Students working on Beth Balliro's African Pottery project near the beginning of their second-term 9th-grade class at the Boston Arts Academy are making a textured clay surface inspired by the patterning in African pottery (see also Example 3.1). They begin by looking at ceramics from three areas of Africa. Beth explains that this will give them some context within which to consider what they are about to start making. She focuses students' attention on images that illustrate varieties of African pottery. She asks them to notice the patterning and select three designs that they like. To get the students to think more deeply about patterns, she also asks them to make sketches of the patterns they see around their house. The students also learn about John Biggers (1924–2001), an African American artist who studied the art of several African cultures. Students look at his drawings, as well as at images of pottery from Africa. Beth explains that she has chosen Biggers because he's an artist whose work was inspired by African art, as theirs will be. The goal of the project in class today is to begin to make three coil vessels, each of which has elements from the pottery of the three regions of Africa that they have studied, both here and in their humanities class. The challenge is to connect form and pattern.

Beth Reflects

After the class, Beth explained to us that she wanted her students to learn to respect another culture's art as John Biggers did. She hopes that her students will be inspired by this and will go on to research the art of another culture on their own. She also hopes to get her students to understand that art can be functional and does not just need to hang on museum walls; again, Biggers exemplifies this understanding. "I want them to think about art in everyday life and how they can actually make things to use and have them be artful and share them with people."

DESIGN INSPIRED BY OBJECTS: CERAMIC SETS PROJECT   (EXAMPLE 11.3)

The final project of the term in Jason Green's beginning ceramics course at Walnut Hill is to make a ceramic set, a group of objects that work together, and that includes one pouring vessel, such as a tea set (see also Example 12.2). Before they begin, Jason shows them a wide variety of "sets" made by ceramicists, objects that he has brought to class for the students to study and touch. He holds up specific objects and talks about how they were made. He explains how a glaze was applied. He holds up an ewer and explains what it is. He holds up some jars, pointing out how they were crafted:

> Look at how these handles are made. These are pulled to give this sort of elegant curve. This spout and this spout are made from slabs, flat pieces of

clay, see, and they're joined right here [*pointing to the joint*]. You can look at these different types of lids and how they work. This is a special locking lid [*removing the lid from the pot and reinserting it*]. That's a nice handle [*pointing to the handle*], huh?

Jason also points out that some of the objects have designs stamped onto them. "These are put in with stamps [*motioning to impressed designs in the teapot*], so if you wanted to try stamping, we have pieces of, lots of pieces of scrap wood or pieces of plaster. You can use anything as a stamp." Jason points out how some of the pieces are made using techniques the students have already learned. "This is made using that wax resist like I showed you and just taking a very small brush and putting the glaze where I want it."

Jason compares one free-form pitcher with Jackson Pollock and abstract expressionism: "This is abstract expressionist, using the clay very quickly, then using lots of slips, very quickly dripping slips." Jason holds up another object, explaining that it was a sculpture made on the wheel. "Just a sculpture with this hole as the aperture where light is supposed to shine through and then hit the table." And about another object by the same artist, "The bottom is added on and this is just an oval thing, but you can see how this easily could be some sort of pot." Jason is trying to stretch his students' conceptions of the possibilities of ceramics (also nurturing the disposition to Envision).

After studying the actual objects, students are directed to look at books and postcards and images on the computer (including images of ceramics from the Sung Dynasty in China) for further ideas. "I want you to think about just the different varieties of form and different approaches to touching the clay." Like the students in Beth's African Pottery class, Jason has his students draw their inspiration here from the art of varying times and cultures. Such exploration extends students' imaginations through connections to the ongoing conversation conducted in the world of practicing artists. At the same time, teachers are careful to discuss tensions around cultural appropriation, especially of indigenous art traditions where individual artists are often not identified and there is a colonizing history.

Jason Reflects

After class, Jason spoke to us about how he believes that looking at works by ceramicists can open up students' minds to new possibilities. He wanted them to see many options. He particularly wanted them to see subtle variations in form and to relate form to function. He believes that this kind of looking will encourage students to try new ways of working with clay:

I brought in some historical stuff for them to look at; some of them have seen some historical ceramics. It's just to show them these slight variations in forms and how they might relate to how the object is used. And just again in many ways trying to open up their minds to all the different possibilities and variations that are available to them. I want them to be able to investigate new ways of working and touching the clay. So I think it's good for me to bring in examples that they can look at visually and also things that they can touch, and you know, learn as much as they can from that and observe as much as they can. One thing I think I'm trying to also show them is there's such a huge variety of vocabulary available to them.

**STRUCTURING A WHOLE CLASS
TO FOCUS ON DOMAIN:
CUBISM PROJECT   (EXAMPLE 11.4)**

After presenting the examples above, we want to describe one class in depth to show how learning to Understand Art Worlds: Domain can become a thread through the three structures of Demonstration–Lecture, Students-at-Work, and Critique. Jim Woodside at Walnut Hill invites students to examine Cubist paintings and encourages them to understand the "why" behind this way of working—what the artists were trying to accomplish—in order to inform students' own work with Cubist ideas.

Demonstration–Lecture to Present the Project

Late in the spring term of his year-long drawing course, Jim introduces students to Cubism and has them make drawings based on what they have learned and seen. Jim shows a Cubist painting by Picasso and explains that this is in the style of Analytical Cubism. "It's the first kind of Cubism," Jim says. "Literally invented by Braque and Picasso together. OK? They literally made it up around the first decade of the 20th century—1907, 1906, around that time period."

Jim holds up a reproduction of a painting by Delacroix to show the contrast case—a painting that is *not* Cubist. What differentiates it from a Cubist painting, Jim explains, is that it has depth. The surface is two-dimensional, but the artist created an illusion of the third dimension. For the Cubists, the illusion of depth was "a lie" and so they rejected it. Instead, they wanted to show what was real. "What's real is this piece of paper, the flatness of it. So in a way, they were sick of lying. Now

that's an exaggeration. Don't ever tell anybody that that's why Cubism started, because they were sick of lying. But there's a little bit of truth to it."

Jim goes on to explain how Cubism differed from perspective drawing:

All art at that point, around say the turn of the century, the 19th to the 20th century, all art was about depth, perspective. You're looking into it. You're looking into a picture. Cubists come along and here they're looking at their canvas. Here's their big white canvas [*holding up large piece of paper*], and it's flat. It's flat. Two dimensions. One, two. How can we draw a picture of the world and somehow honor this flatness? Make that part of the idea? Make that part of the directness, the honestness of it. They come up with this idea which ends up being called Analytical Cubism.

Jim follows this explanation with an example:

And what they thought was that if I'm going to draw [student] sitting there and I want to do it on a flat surface, I'm going to somehow acknowledge all sides of her. The front, the side, the back, and I'm going to put it all on the same piece of paper. So in a way, I'm taking the three-dimensional world and I'm putting it on a two-dimensional surface in a way that makes sense, that's logical and that's honest. It's important to understand why it ended up looking like this. It's not just a style. There was a reason behind it.

As he holds up several reproductions of Cubist paintings, Jim asks students to talk about how each one "denies depth." He points out how one of the paintings violates perspective:

You know how I taught you in two-point perspective that as things go away, they get closer together? Look at this. This artist makes them get wider right there. That's not by accident. Why is the artist doing that? To make it flat. Why would they want to make it flat? Because the paper's flat and that's more honest. That's more logical. That's more contemporary, any of those words. But that's more real. Do you understand the idea? It's pretty deep stuff. It's pretty heavy stuff.

Jim then shows students Picasso's revolutionary Cubist painting, *Les Demoiselles d'Avignon*, and offers an explanation. "Picasso is trying to imply all sides of the figure, the front and the back at the same time." He shows them a few more Cubist works:

> These are what early Analytical Cubism looked like. What does the word *analytical* imply when you hear it? Analyze. It sounds pretty dry, doesn't it? It sounds pretty boring. It sounds pretty, like, analytical. And they wanted it to be that way. Think about it. Think what I'm saying. They wanted to honor the flatness of the surface. It's about analysis, like a doctor almost. It's not about wild expression. It's about how we can make it more clear, analytical, logical, honest. They didn't even want to use a lot of color here. Maybe I'm making too much of the word *honest*, but it's not trying to trick anybody. It's not trying to show you a picture that doesn't exist.

Students-at-Work

Jim immediately moves students into their own drawing. "Think about trying to draw in that style today. Think about trying to draw the front and the back of somebody's head at the same time." He engineers this by placing a model in front of the class for 10 minutes, then rotating the model a quarter turn each 10 minutes that follow. Students must continue with the same drawing. As Jim explains, "You're going to be forced to draw several sides of him on the same drawing."

As students draw, Jim circles the room speaking with individuals about their work. He often reminds students about the core idea of Cubism. When he spoke with one student, he said, "What you end up with is something that generally looks pretty flat. You know, meaning that you don't really look into deep space." He tries to connect what a student is doing to Cubism: "They were inventing a new way to make art based on the materials. The flat paper. . . . . So you already know how to do this. It's just you're feeling, like, how can I draw like Picasso? If you need answers to this stuff, try to think about the Picassos." He is teaching his students that paintings by master artists can provide them with answers to problems that they are trying to solve in their own work (see Figure 11.1).

Demonstration-Lecture

Before the Critique session, Jim uses a short Demonstration–Lecture to reinforce the challenges and solutions of Cubism. He brings out another Cubist painting to show the similarities between this painting and the students' work. He directs students to look at the mouth. "It's a profile of a mouth, isn't it? And yet the lips are in front. So he shows you side and front in this almost ridiculous cartoon-like way. That's what we're doing." He also underscores how what the students did today is a continuation of the same things they had worked on in large drawings last week.

Jim stresses why Cubism is something worth understanding:

> It's a really important part of the way art is taught, the art of the last 100 years. Cubism is a part of what you should understand about art, about Western art, 20th-century art. And it's a very big part of the way that we work, the way that we study. And Cubism itself is just a style, but that idea of the flatness is what I want you to remember.

Again Jim relates Cubism to other things his students have studied:

> If you need a simple way to think of it, think of it as the opposite of perspective. I showed you before, months ago, weeks ago, about two-point perspective [*drawing*]. And how a railroad track goes way back in space. And this is your canvas [*drawing*]. And this is your railroad track going back in space. If you're doing a Cubist painting of it, there's your railroad track [*drawing*]. Right. It's flat. It's right here. Now this is really a simple illustration, but I'm only saying it to you as a way of thinking about a kind of oppositeness of perspective. And why? Because remember, the canvas is two-dimensional. Cubists thought that the image itself needed to be a reflection of the two-dimensional canvas.

Jim Reflects

When we spoke to Jim after class, he offered these reasons for wanting students to understand Cubism. First, students should understand the logic behind the emergence of Cubism:

> Cubism was the most important new movement in painting. Kids can get a handle on this. I think that they can start to understand or be curious about underlying concepts in other contemporary art. There are fairly concrete things to grasp on to, in terms of understanding it. It's important for them to understand that it's not just a new look, it's not a new style that came out, there's a reason behind it. There's logic to it that somebody was after.

He went on to explain that students should learn to use works by professional artists on a regular basis:

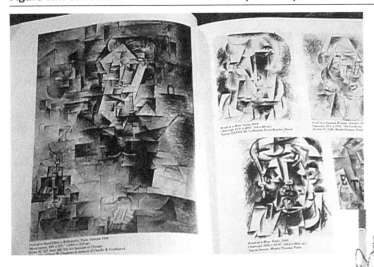

A. Jim Woodside shows students Picasso's paintings and drawings to support their learning to draw in Cubist style

B. Jim wants students to develop a "casual relationship" to art in the past

C. He explains that Cubism was motivated by wanting to depict the three-dimensional world honestly on a two-dimensional surface

D. Jim wants his students to understand that "art doesn't happen in a vacuum"

Students need to develop a kind of casual relationship to art in the past. To just go look at books, just flip through them, just get the stuff in their head. It doesn't have to be this almost religious event. You can flip through a book, and read a little bit here or there, browse around on the internet, and you develop a relationship with it, just as you would with a person. To develop a casual relationship is also to develop a living relationship. The work has purpose for you beyond just historical significance. It's living, and interesting, and alive, and maybe you can imitate some of it [and make it] part of your work.

He also explained that students need to recognize that one can learn from art without copying.

It's really important to understand the difference between the copying and learning from, and art doesn't happen in a vacuum, it's not all magically generated from inspiration. [Art] happens from work, and it happens from knowledge, and it happens from seeing other works. In some cases imitating them, borrowing things . . . this is what artists of the past have done.

We asked Jim if he thought students should study art history in a separate course. He explained that he prefers his method—making connections to historical works of art when these works are relevant to what the student is working on at the time. He added, "I try to get them excited about it and draw connections. In my mind, that's more important at this age than an official art history class." Thus, the disposition to Understand Art Worlds is inextricably fused with *making*. Students, Jim believes, gain a deeper understanding of works from the past when they see a direct relationship between these works, brought right into the art studio, and their own efforts.

A Dispositional View of Understand Art Worlds: Domain

When students work in isolation from work made by others, such separation leads to solipsism, triviality, and "school art" (Efland, 1976, 1983). When students learn about the domain of art, they can use artists as models of thoughtful process and see the potentials of artworks as sources of new ideas and standards of quality.

Skill. The core skill of Understand Art Worlds: Domain is the ability to seek information and stay informed about the cultures of art and artists. The skills of Understand Art Worlds develop when students actively seek to learn from artists' works and practices in order to inform their own artmaking. Both browsing and careful examination of the works and practices of other artists in relationship to their own projects are ways to build skill in this habit. Sometimes this means researching a particular question (e.g., How do artists create depth in two-dimensional works? or Which contemporary artists create impossible spaces in their paintings?). Skills include calling up the resources for specific topics by searches on the web, in libraries, and in museum archives. Once resources have been identified, artists need to know what to look at and for, and how to document and store the information acquired for later reference.

Alertness. Alertness to the domain of art is recognizing when, in the process of making, an artist needs to seek something within the works or practices of other artists. In response to a teacher's or peer's comment, a student might stop working to go look up a particular artist or artwork or a collection of works from a particular era, style, or medium. Similarly, alertness might move from looking to making: When students look at the works of others, they should be alert to what they might use in their own studio work. Alertness to the domain also occurs when looking at the work of others in Critiques: By noticing particular technical, conceptual, or aesthetic qualities in the works of others, artists can make connections to their own works and process.

Inclination. The inclination to understand the domain of art requires a willingness to pursue new ideas, techniques, materials, and formal solutions by using artworks made by others and by interacting with other artists. Some students hold the misconception that artists should not take ideas from others, and thus resist this process. It also is easy for novices to become immersed in making and not want to pause long enough to be informed by the work made by others. Artists build inclination by using that muscle. They set up regular practices to familiarize themselves with art and artists by going regularly to museums, galleries, and openings, following museums and artists on social media, reading arts journals and so forth.

COMMUNITIES

Students are meant to learn about their own relationship to broader art communities. They practice with their peers in classes and think about how they might fit into art communities, what they might do after graduation, and what they have to do to get there. They learn how to present themselves as artists by creating a portfolio, hanging a show, presenting their work online, and so forth. All of these activities are ways in which students are learning to become professional artists. Of course, most students in art classes will not go on to become artists. But learning to understand the challenge of balancing tensions between autonomy and collaboration in creating works of art is important for both serious and casual students of art.

In this section we describe two classes in which students are learning about community as they collaborate on group projects.

CREATING A LIBRARY OF MOLDS: COIL SCULPTURE PROJECT   (EXAMPLE 11.5)

For Jason Green's Coil Sculpture Project in the middle of the second semester of his year-long introductory ceramics course at Walnut Hill for a mixed-grade group of high school students, students create a library of molds to be shared later by all the students in the class as they make "skins" for their individual ceramic sculptures, an assignment that encourages students to share while at the same time pursuing their own work (see also Examples 3.2 and 9.2). Each student is going to make three different kinds of plaster molds. One will be a large slab with a texture all over the surface (the texture mold). Jason tells the students that "this is a very fast way to get a whole bunch of texture. So we're going to start building our sculpture using all different textured slabs. And we're going to share, OK?" Students will also make a sprig mold and a stamp mold. A sprig is a small mold that yields a piece of clay that can be attached to the surface of a sculpture.

After all the students have made these molds, they will then begin to make a textured surface for their ceramic sculpture. Making this "skin" will be "a very additive process. You're going to keep adding to the surface. And it's going to be lots of different types of textures."

To make their ceramic "skin," students will be able to make use of parts of the textured slabs created by other students. "So we're all going to be making a lot of molds. And we're going to have a library of molds, so that you can have a sculpture made from all different types of textures." While students spend this class period working individually on their molds, they know that they are working to create a library of textures to be shared. As they work with the plaster molds, students also share batches of plaster.

Jason Reflects

Jason stressed the importance of collaboration when we spoke to him. He thinks it is important for students to see how others have solved a problem and for them to learn from that solution. Students can also learn by eavesdropping: When he works with students, Jason responds to the individual, but he is aware, too, that other students are listening.

FOCUSING ON STRENGTH AND FORM: THE EGG DROP PROJECT   (EXAMPLE 11.6)

It is not difficult to create collaborative projects in studio classes, and, indeed, visual artists such as muralists, filmmakers, or architects do create work collaboratively. However, such collaboration has not been the norm in the discipline of visual arts. Perhaps this explains why we rarely saw team projects and more often saw teachers set up ways for students to support each other even though they were working autonomously.

Kathleen Marsh's class described here, the introduction to the final sculpture unit in the first term of the 9th-grade class at the Boston Arts Academy, is one of the few examples we saw of a group project. She divided the class into teams and gave each the same challenge—to create a container that will keep an egg from breaking when it is dropped from a banister down several flights of stairs. Each team is given one piece of foam core, three pieces of oaktag, ten straws, and a raw egg. They have an hour and a half to come up with a solution, to "create a safe haven for your egg," as she tells them. Students know there will be a prize for the winning team (or teams), and that winning means dropping the container and not breaking the egg. Another prize will go to the team that makes the best visual design. Thus, there is one prize for strength and one for aesthetics. Students must work together to solve this problem—there are no individual contenders (see Figure 11.2).

As students work, Kathleen moves around, directing comments to the groups as well as to individuals. In the interactions that follow, we see Kathleen focusing her students' attention on working together:

- *Look at a solution devised by another group.* "And can I just show you this?" Kathleen asks as she shows one group what another group of students has done to help them think of what they might do in their own work. "If you make strips out of your oaktag and fold them like this, you can make springs."
- *Remember you are not working alone on this project.* Kathleen continually reminds students that they are working together on the project. "Maybe two of you can do that while [she] is doing this?"
- *Keep in mind that resources are shared, and don't be selfish.* One group has used several eggs, leaving none for some teams. Kathleen expresses her displeasure: "You guys really put another team in a jam, and I'm not happy about that."

Figure 11.2. Understand Art Worlds: Communities—Kathleen Marsh's Students Work in Teams to Create Containers That Will Keep an Egg from Breaking When Dropped Four Stories

A. Kathleen Marsh offers suggestions to groups as she circles the room

B. Kathleen shows a group another possibility to consider in their design

C. She tells students to "create a safe haven for your egg"

D. Kathleen reminds students to work as a group

Kathleen Reflects

When we interviewed Kathleen, she explained why she believes collaboration and teamwork are important:

- Each student brings a different kind of skill to the group.
- Collaboration is a way to gather ideas and is also motivating because it is fun.
- When students work in a group, they keep each other in check so that the teacher does not have to play this role.
- Working in groups toward a common goal helps students transcend barriers of class and race.
- Collaboration is a skill that artists need, and many of her students hope to go on in the arts.

Although many visual artists still work individually, collaborative teams that use ensemble techniques, which historically were more central to methods in the performing arts, are increasingly common in the field of contemporary visual arts. Learning to work in and with artistic communities is valuable to art students for appreciating current practice. Working in communities also offers possible connections to the performing arts and to non-arts endeavors, such as science or interdisciplinary projects in which teams of disciplinarians from a range of domains work together toward shared ends. Again, though, whether the collaborative skills and attitudes learned in visual arts classes transfer to other learning contexts is a question worthy of empirical investigation.

A Dispositional View of Understand Art Worlds: Communities

Skill. The core skill of Understand Art Worlds: Communities is the ability to work with others, not only by collaborating but also by learning how to talk to others about their work (using specific language during critiques, rather than merely saying "I like that" or "That's awful") and by learning ways to respond when work is criticized—either by considering and/or using constructive advice or by dismissing respectfully advice that is off the mark (e.g., "Yes, that would be interesting work; it isn't the work I'm making, however"). Other times it's creating and using libraries of resources, as when MassArt student-teacher Robert Leyen hired five figure models for his students to photograph (they wore spandex because they were being photographed). Students created a a library of photos of poses and gestures to share as resources for works they were developing about social attitudes.

Alertness. Alertness to communities is required for times when interacting with others might catalyze progress on a work in process. Or alertness might involve being attentive to opportunities to participate in a collective artistic experience or to submit work for exhibitions or prizes, resulting in field recognition.

Inclination. The inclination toward Understand Art Worlds: Communities means the willingness to work on collaborative projects, and even when working solo, to listen to and seek out the advice and reactions of others.

As students learn about artists' worlds, they connect what they do in school art classes with what practicing artists do now and did in the past. They learn about art history by consulting the works of artists to help themselves solve visual problems. When working on portraits, they compare how artists have depicted people in the past and the ways they are doing so today; when working on light, they consider the range of ways that artists have grappled with portraying light. Understanding art history is thus always connected to the student's own making. Students also learn about the artistic community—the people and institutions of the art world. This is part of teaching students to become professional artists, which is something many of the students we studied aspire to be. But even for students planning to study and work in other fields, learning how galleries and museums operate, learning to present their work professionally, and learning to respond to and critique the works of others are skills that help them connect their school artwork to the art world outside the school walls. And of course as students begin to work collaboratively (when art projects, for example murals or videos, call for teamwork), they come to see the act of making works of art as an ensemble activity.

Generative Connections to Understand Art Worlds

Understand Art Worlds never operates alone. It can be used in pairs or larger clusters involving each of the other seven habits. It often pairs with Observe, since it is by looking closely at, listening to, and reading about artworks and working processes of artists that students learn about the domain and communities of various art worlds. Teachers encourage students to ponder what they see in words (Reflect) and in images (Envision) and to convey their ideas in writing, drawing, and speech. This four-pronged cluster of Understand Art Worlds with Observe, Reflect, and Envision allows students to consolidate understanding of the connections among their work and that of others, including works by professional artists.

Similarly, when this core cluster of Understand Art Worlds, Observe, Reflect, and Envision focuses on the aesthetic approaches of other artists, it attunes students to the meanings conveyed in their own works and works by professional artists (Express).

Understand Art Worlds also links with Engage and Persist. One route to deeper engagement in a work is to search for opportunities and ideas in the work of other artists. When students are deeply engaged in an investigation of particular styles, artists, and/or works (using the core cluster described above of Understand Art Worlds, Observe, Reflect, Envision), the artists' works and practices may open students' minds to new possibilities and make them more likely to play with the ideas and techniques they notice (Stretch and Explore). That motivates them to make their own works (Develop Craft). Develop Craft, of course, is also a common pairing with Understand Art Worlds: Students can study the works of other artists to learn new techniques.

What Teachers Can Do

Students in visual arts classes need to connect what they learn in art class to what practicing artists do and to what art worlds are like, now and in the past. As teachers teach toward Understand Art Worlds, we hope they will include artists from a range of periods, styles, locations and demographics—not just Western art but art from other cultures, and not just the greats of the past but also artists at work today. They can discuss how new discoveries can reshape our understanding of art history. For example, some historians now believe Vermeer and even earlier Northern Renaissance painters used lenses to project images which they copied (e.g., Steadman, 2002; Hockney, 2001). Should this change how we think of the works of these great masters? Teachers can highlight how some artists combine artistic traditions, like Japanese artist Tabaimo, whose animation work combines influences from ukiyo-e and anime (tabaimo.site.seattleartmuseum .org).

Teachers can also present artists whose work comments on the domain of the art world itself, such as Fred Wilson's influential 1992 *Mining the Museum* which examines which art or artifacts are shown and how they are displayed and how these reflect sociocultural dimensions of race and power. They can share work that challenges

traditional art forms, such as Lorna Simpson's *Stereo Styles* or *Five Day Forecast*, which confront issues of representation of Black women by challenging the conventional form of portraiture by not showing faces.

To support the Communities aspect of Understand Art Worlds, students can learn how artists have formed movements such as the Dadaists, Surrealists, or Impressionists, and knew each other's works intimately and learned from one another. Or how artists from the past as well as today often use teams of assistants or apprentices to construct works that the artists have designed. Or how artists have worked collectively, such as the Coral Reef Project, the Gee's Bend quilting collective, the Postcommodity art collective, the Raqs Media Collective, and The Propeller Group, just to name a few.

We draw a clear distinction between teaching students to Understand Art Worlds and teaching students art history. In an art history class, the goal is to teach a body of historical knowledge. When studio teachers help students to Understand Art Worlds, their goal is to help the students develop, as Jim Woodside says, a casual relationship to art of the past, and to see connections from the works of others that enrich their own process and works.

Understand Art Worlds: Parallels in Other Disciplines

Understand Art Worlds helps students connect their own work to that of professional artists. Students in all school disciplines benefit from making connections between what they are learning and what professionals in that discipline are doing and why. Thus, students in a history class would benefit from learning what contemporary historians are writing and thinking, the variety of methods that they use, and how publishers decide what gets into history textbooks. Students in a biology class would benefit from learning the kinds of unanswered questions being tackled and who makes decisions about which research questions are funded. Every area of study has a domain (works and knowledge created) and a community (gatekeepers and colleagues). Familiarizing students with these resources inspires and informs their efforts to develop understanding in that discipline.

We next consider how the Studio Habits of Mind are integrated with each of the four Studio Structures for learning.

Part III

INTEGRATING STUDIO STRUCTURES OF LEARNING WITH THE STUDIO HABITS OF MIND

Imagine walking into a studio classroom. Students are standing behind easels, using vine and compressed charcoal and black oil pastels on newsprint to draw a human model who sits hunched against a wall. Cool jazz plays softly, and bright lights cast shadows on and around the figure. The teacher is standing behind one student, silently observing him at work. After a while, she speaks to him briefly, points to the model, and lays a piece of tracing paper over the drawing. She quickly redraws several lines, says a few more words, and moves along to other students. She continues her rounds, stopping, looking, talking, and modeling processes and possibilities in short conversations with individuals.

A knowledgeable observer might surmise that the lesson's focus is value—students seem meant to learn to represent the variations of light and shadow on the figure. The spotlights are set up deliberately to emphasize the natural shadows that fall from the figure's contours; charcoal and oil pastels, black, without the confusion of color, are media that readily convey variations in light and shadow. But as we listen in more closely to the conversations between the teacher and her students, we only sometimes hear her emphasizing this element of developing craft. Yes, she talks to her students about value, but she frequently mentions other elements of drawing—line, edge, composition. She also talks about the "feel" or "directness" of various marks and areas of a drawing, as well as accuracy in representation. She engages in a discussion about "how to take that further," and another discussion about the similarity of one student's approach to a particular contemporary artist, Philip Pearlstein.

She's talking about everything! In these brief personal conversations, teachers may focus on a single idea or process or Studio Habit of Mind, but, often, they address as many as five or six, or even all eight of the Studio Habits of Mind in a single, short consultation.

What's going on here? Is the teacher not focusing her instruction on what she really intends students to learn? Or perhaps this example shows that the Studio Habits of Mind are too narrow or too broad to be useful? Actually, we think all is well, both with the teacher and with the habits. The habits easily make explicit the quick and nuanced moves of an expert artist's thinking. An artist's mind flows dynamically from one way of addressing artistic problems to another, and the teacher's conversational shifts make that visible. Once a teacher makes her tacit expertise explicit, she can work on the elements of it that are of most interest, refining her teaching as she might her artwork.

So, perhaps the artist-teacher comments first on how she sees the work and the referent, focusing momentarily on the disposition to Observe. Next, she considers how she might depict the idea differently (Envision). Then, she may play with the idea a bit (Stretch and Explore), as a way to refine or create new techniques (Develop Craft). Without a pause, she might model different ways to approach the visual problem (Stretch and Explore), thinking aloud as she draws and describing what she sees (Reflect: Question and Explain; Observe), how well it works (Reflect: Evaluate), and how it "reads" to her (Express). All this can occur in under 3 minutes!

While the example above depicts the dynamic and broad reach of habits as they are taught and learned in a Students-at-Work session, the Studio Habits of Mind are embedded throughout all of the Studio

Structures for learning. Teachers addressed each of the habits of mind, individually and in many combinations or "clusters," not only in Students-at-Work sessions, but also in Demonstration–Lectures, Critiques, and Exhibitions. The next four chapters illustrate examples of how teachers emphasize each individual Studio Habit of Mind and how they interweave the Studio Habits of Mind within each of the structures by which studio instruction is organized. In Chapter 16 we present new research on how the integration of the Studio Habits of Mind across Studio Structures works to build student agency—their ability to form, refine and enact their artistic ideas in increasingly independent ways.

TWELVE

Demonstration–Lecture and the Studio Habits of Mind

The Demonstration–Lecture structure is used to introduce ideas, assignments, and the Studio Habits of Mind that will be developed in the Students-at-Work and Critique structures in the class (see Chapter 3). As the teacher deliberately models working, seeing, and thinking as an artist, all the Studio Habits of Mind occur naturally. By slowing down the processes of making, perceiving, and reflecting about art and artmaking for students in Demonstration–Lectures, teachers foster students' mindful attention to nuances that might otherwise pass by unnoticed.

FOSTERING PARTICULAR STUDIO HABITS OF MIND THROUGH DEMONSTRATION–LECTURES

In what follows, we illustrate how Demonstration–Lectures can promote the development of the different Studio Habits of Mind.

Develop Craft

Often, an assignment either requires or guides students to experiment with specific materials, tools, or procedures. Demonstration–Lectures, therefore, introduce students to particular features that are most likely to come up as opportunities and challenges as they work on Developing Craft.

For example, when Beth Balliro introduced clay to her 9th-grade students in her Sketching in Clay class (see Example 10.1), she showed them the practical realities of working with clay in their studio classroom. She showed them where tools and materials were kept, what was available, when they could use them, how they needed to care for them, and even how to clean clay off tables and prewash their hands in a bucket so the sink would not clog with clay. She assigned students the task of making a "chop," a traditional name-stamp used by potters. That provided further opportunities to clarify practical issues, such as the need to mark work for easy identification, to put work in progress and finished work on different shelves, and to treat unfired work delicately. She used the chop assignment as an opportunity to demonstrate the slab-roller, a large tool for flattening clay into slabs for a variety of hand-building and sculptural projects. Such practical, grounded demonstrations greatly ease the inconveniences and minimize the dangers of working in the studio with messy materials and sharp tools. Through the demonstrations, students develop clear images of what they need to do and how they need to do it.

Engage and Persist

Watching a skilled craftsperson at work is mesmerizing, and teachers often use Demonstration–Lectures to interest students in the potential of techniques, materials, or tools that they can learn to use at high levels of expertise. For instance, when Jason Green threw spouts "off the hump" (i.e., he stuck a large mound of clay to the wheel, then centered and formed only a small chunk of the top, a technique that facilitates creating many small pieces quickly), the students' focus was palpable as they watched in silent amazement.

In addition to engaging students' interests, teachers use Demonstration–Lectures to model ways to persist as they demonstrate some of the variety of techniques, tools, and materials that students might employ to address artistic challenges. For instance, Jason also demonstrated how to create spouts by extruding (i.e., using a metal pipe with a plunger, called an extruder, that can be fitted with different internal and external shapes, called dies, to make variously shaped tubes of clay), how to make spouts from slabs pressed in the slab-roller by wrapping them around cone-shaped wooden forms, and how to "pull" spouts off wooden dowels (a technique of repeatedly grasping and sliding a wet hand down a piece of clay to shape it). While no one student would use all of these techniques to create the pouring vessel required by the Ceramic Sets Project (see Examples 11.3 and 12.2), seeing such a broad range of possibilities encouraged persistence in finding and developing techniques that would serve students' particular creative intentions.

Envision

Demonstration–Lectures are a way for teachers to model a range of possibilities inherent in their assignments and help students open their imaginations to what could and might be done within the assignments' constraints. Recall Jason's spring Tile Project (see Examples 5.1 and 6.2), in which students were assigned to create low-relief sculptures of nine mold-pressed tiles. During the Demonstration–Lecture at the beginning of this class, Jason not only demonstrated techniques but also showed students a wide range of images of tiles from different cultures. Kathleen Marsh did a similar "tour" of possibilities with a slideshow of drawn self-portraits to introduce a self-portrait assignment to her seniors (in which students drew themselves wearing hats and vests they created themselves; see Example 13.4). By studying a wide range of examples that satisfy the challenges of an assignment in different ways, students are less likely to hold onto a mistaken belief that there is one "right" way to solve the problem.

In addition to helping students imagine possibilities for pattern, form, and color through multiple examples, teachers also help them envision the *process* of the assigned work. For example, Jason helped them envision making tiles by demonstrating step by step how to use tools and materials. He showed students how to build a mold box, how to press clay into it and how to get it out, how to arrange wooden shapes and other objects in the mold to create patterns, and how to consider common problems like direction of forms (e.g., letters come out backwards when they are pressed in this way).

Express

Teachers often gather a range of samples—of works, techniques, materials, tools, or ideas—to guide students' thinking about how to express personal meanings, feelings, or ideas in their work. Similar to the way Critiques let students see many possible solutions and hear many possible responses from their classmates, Demonstration–Lectures offer a chance to gain a wider view of the field of art, both from the present and the past. Such a broad and varied perspective encourages students to consider reasons for the variations that they observe, to think about what these variations "say," and what they themselves might "say" with a particular material, tool, or technique. For example, Jason often brought in artworks that he owned which were made by professionals (as well as a mud-wasps' nest that he had found in the clay studio and fired). Beth often copied packets of pictures for her students to achieve a similar objective. In Jim's opening class on contour drawing (see Example 14.1), he gathered descriptive words from the students onto a written list to describe the still life they'd been drawing.

> Just take a look at these words. Take a look at them and think about how this might relate to the way you're drawing. What we do in drawing, we express things by the way that we put lines down, by the way that we draw. These objects don't mean anything. It's just some old junk I piled up here. OK? But you're already making psychological, making emotional connections, making connections to other things by looking at this. We do this with everything. OK? So, [that's] what makes drawing interesting.

In Demonstration–Lectures, teachers point out meaningful characteristics of the works or processes of interest to students because of similarity to something they recently made (e.g., drawings of a still life, handles, spouts, glazes), or something they were about to use in a new assignment (e.g., expressive marks and lines, lips of a pouring vessel, coils, the mood or idea conveyed by a form or glaze, or the way a group of objects interrelates).

Observe

Demonstration–Lectures help students "see more" by exploiting their already developed interest in observation. Visual arts students are usually adept at learning from looking, and developing the disposition to do so is critical to their continued growth as thinking artists. For example, Guy Michel Telemaque opens his 9th-grade design class session by introducing students to the Viewfinder Project (see Example 8.1). He asked students to use a viewfinder to "see the world in a new way" so that they could begin to stand back from what they *knew* and start to see the world as design.

Often, the processes involved in using and caring for materials and tools, and working with techniques, are complex, multistep operations. Showing these steps in the context of preparing to make something is an effective way of giving students a great deal of information in a sort of visual–temporal "outline" form, which they can then use when they need to refine their understanding. In an early drawing class on perspective, for example, Jim followed up on a Students-at-Work session (when students drew still lifes of boxes) and a Critique of those drawings (when students identified and discussed what "bugged" them about their work), with a quick, efficient demonstration of one- and two-point perspective drawing (see Examples 3.3, 4.3, and 8.2). By showing how to create a horizon line and a vanishing point or points, he could model how to draw boxes from any angle—a task they had just completed without that insight and which they would revisit immediately after the demonstration. Jim could then take the lesson one step further, by showing, through removing the rectangular case of an old film projector, how nongeometric objects could be "seen" through their geometry, so that objects of any shape could be understood through these simple perspective rules. His demonstration simplified to its essence a technique that can be very complex.

Reflect

Question and Explain. Because Demonstration–Lectures are generally brief, teachers often do not dwell here on developing students' disposition to Question and Explain. However, the Question and Explain Studio Habit of Mind is sometimes fostered in Demonstration–Lectures. For example, as the teachers showed works of art, they often modeled the internal conversations that the creators of these works might have had while creating them. And as students become attuned to different features of particular types of work, they have a chance to practice raising questions and suggesting possible explanations for the forms, styles, appearances, or methods that they have noticed in their recent art-making efforts. For example, when examining a collection of vessels for the Ceramic Sets assignment (see Examples 11.3 and 12.2), Jason's students asked about techniques for making different vessel "feet," probably motivated by their efforts to trim the bottoms of vessels just before the Demonstration–Lecture. They also focused on variations in handles and lips, which had been their recent concern in throwing cups, and on glazes, since they had just gotten their first glazed pieces out of the kiln. Both teachers' "thinking aloud" and students' practicing raising and answering questions help develop the Question and Explain disposition.

Evaluate. Evaluation is a peripheral focus in Demonstration–Lectures, but it is there. This habit shows up as teachers point out common challenges and solutions that arise from techniques, as when Jason pointed out how he was using his arm on his leg to build a solid foundation to support his throwing hands while working on the wheel (see Examples 4.4 and 13.1). He sets his own performance as a standard against which students can evaluate their own wheel-throwing. In addition, examining a wide spectrum of examples related to a particular assignment offers chances for appreciation of what works, what individuals like, and what is possible. All contribute to students' understanding of quality and help them develop their habits of evaluation.

Stretch and Explore

Just as the variety of forms, techniques, and materials that teachers use in Demonstration–Lectures allows students to envision more and to consider possibilities for expression, that range of possibilities also reinforces the habit of deliberately stretching beyond a current level of ability and responding to "errors" as opportunities—because that is what is modeled in the objects and processes the teacher shows. For example, in Jason's Repeating Units Project (see Example 10.2), his Demonstration–Lecture kept raising new possibilities for what might count as a unit (a bottle, a brick, a plug of clay, a cell in a wasps' nest), and kept using "what if" questions about techniques (what if you ripped clay with your fingers, cut it with a needle tool or with knotted string, or pressed it with burlap or the bottom of a cup). All of these possibilities helped set students up to explore, push beyond the known, and observe accidents as opportunities and options for creation.

Understand Art Worlds

Domain. Demonstration–Lectures are a prime opportunity for teachers to inform students about the context of the culture of art in which they are working as artists. Jim showed students historical works that drew on the processes he was asking them to try. Guy Michel encouraged browsing through journals and magazines to find examples of design techniques students were exploring, such as fonts, layouts, and color schemes. Beth worked to expand students' attitudes about what counted as "art" by showing students the objects from African and Japanese cultures that they might otherwise see as "only utilitarian." Jason showed students books of tiles from contemporary and ancient Asian and Middle Eastern cultures. In each case, work by other artists (past and present) is used to expand students' thinking about what is possible, what has been done, and what they might try. The learning of *domain* in the art studio occurs in the context of work that students are currently doing, and not as an isolated "style" that they should simply learn "because it's important in art history."

Communities. Art history and contemporary artistic practice are sometimes taught in studio art classes through Demonstration–Lectures that focus on grounding students' own work in the contexts of the work of others. When teachers model processes, focus attention on the work of professional artists, or show students characteristics of particular art materials, these methods all emphasize the ways in which artists have worked in their own historical context, which includes the relationships to other artists as well as the relationship to their audience. While we only rarely saw teachers introduce assignments that required students to work in teams (Kathleen's Egg Drop Project is a notable exception; see Example 11.6), we frequently saw teachers remind students in explicit and implicit ways in Demonstration–Lectures that they were artists, and that artists were individuals who worked within communities.

We also saw teachers set up assignments that required sharing tools or materials. Recall that Jason's students created a library of molds that they shared for multiple projects (see Examples 3.2, 9.2, and 11.5).

INTEGRATING STUDIO HABITS OF MIND IN THE DEMONSTRATION–LECTURE

The next two examples show how a Demonstration–Lecture integrates several Studio Habits of Mind.

TEACHING THE THEORY AND PRACTICE OF COLOR: INVENTING COLORS PROJECT   (EXAMPLE 12.1)

In Beth Balliro's Inventing Colors Project (see Examples 4.1 and 6.1), which is taught near the midpoint of her second-semester 9th-grade course at the Boston Arts Academy, she uses a 20-minute Demonstration–Lecture to introduce three purposes for the painting unit that students are about to undertake:

- Developing a theoretical appreciation for color (Understand Art Worlds: Domain)
- Understanding how to work (Develop Craft: Technique and Studio Practice)
- Helping students develop the disposition to experiment with materials and take risks in low-stakes "sketch" paintings (Stretch and Explore).

As Beth outlines the basics of color theory with the color wheel she has drawn on the board, the focus is on Understand Art Worlds: Domain. She asks students to copy the wheel into their notebooks and refers to it throughout her short Demonstration–Lecture, which now changes focus to emphasize Develop Craft: Technique. "This is a magical wheel, because you can invent any color you want, if you understand how this wheel works." She explains that color is difficult to mix with acrylic paints, which they will be using (Develop Craft: Technique). When they begin to work, the focus will shift again to Stretch and Explore as students start to create a couple of "sketch" paintings. But, for now,

the Demonstration–Lecture focuses on Develop Craft: Technique and Understand Art Worlds: Domain.

Beth uses the wheel to introduce primary colors. "You can't really make them. If you were a cook, that's the first ingredients of your recipe, those colors." As is typical for Demonstration–Lectures, she introduces the information that students will use right away: "So the paints I'm going to have you use today. . . . Can you guess?" [*gesturing toward the board*]. The students respond: "Red, yellow, and blue. Plus white."

Next, Beth introduces secondary colors, again referring to the board so students see their relationship to the primaries—those colors mixed by combining the two primaries on either side. She suggests that the hue varies by the ratio of the primaries to each other in the mix and suggests that they experiment with that when they're working. "I want you to play today. You're really playing with mixing" (Stretch and Explore). Then she introduces the complementary colors, with reference to how they stand opposite the primaries on the color wheel and how they contrast with each other, and she closes with the neutrals: "A neutral color happens when you mix a color with its opposite."

As the time to paint approaches, Beth sets the students up to paint experimentally by telling them that the color wheel doesn't work perfectly.

> *My* teacher said, "If you mix red plus blue, you'll get purple." So I took red, like the color of his shirt red [*pointing to a student's shirt*], and I took blue, sort of the color of his shirt blue, and what did I get? Brown. And I thought, "I thought you said . . . ?" What would be the problem there? Well, this red has a little bit of orange in it. So it's not completely true, but it's something to guide you. That's why I'm going to give you two shades of blue, because sometimes blue acts differently [*holding up two cans of blue paint*] (Stretch and Explore).

With the theory taken care of, Beth concludes the Demonstration–Lecture by showing students the materials they need to do the assignment, where to get them, and how to set them up (Develop Craft: Studio Practice). She shows students their palettes (new white Frisbees), paints (fresh tubes of acrylic), and new brushes, which she reminds them to use and clean carefully. She shows them how to set up their palettes with the colors in the order of the color wheel, shows them gloss medium, to "make colors clearer" or "see-through," and shows them the paper they'll use. The students transition quickly to a Students-at-Work session in which they create two paintings of imaginary settings, one using complementary colors and one using neutral colors.

DESIGN INSPIRED BY OBJECTS: CERAMIC SETS PROJECT   (EXAMPLE 12.2)

The Demonstration–Lecture with which Jason introduces his Ceramic Sets Project (see Example 11.3), taught in the middle of the first semester of his year-long ceramics course, emphasizes the relationships among four goals:

- Looking carefully at objects to see how they were made (Observe).
- Planning ceramic design in a variety of ways (Envision).
- Making choices to convey ideas or feelings (Express).
- Synthesizing technical skills learned over the term (Develop Craft: Technique).

During this portion of his Demonstration–Lecture, Jason shows students a range of tools, techniques, and processes that they might employ to express meaning in the design and creation of their sets.

Goal 1: Observe

Jason shows students several tools and techniques to add to their repertoire of choices for this final assignment of the first term. He shows them new tools (e.g., the clay extruder for pressing spouts, dowels for pulling spouts) and new techniques (e.g., throwing small cups off a hump that, when cut in half vertically, become pitcher spouts). He also shows them new uses for old tools and techniques if they are combined with new ones (e.g., using slabs to roll spouts around dowels).

> You saw the spouts over on those other teapots, which are made in a way very similar to this. We can pull spouts on dowels [*beginning to form clay*]. Very similar to pulling handles. You want to put this through the middle as close as you can get to the middle [*pushing dowel through the clay*] and you want to get water on this [*removing the clay and dampening the dowel*] so it slides and just like you're pulling a handle, you can pull a spout [*beginning to form the spout over the dowel*] (Observe, Develop Craft: Technique).

Goal 2: Envision

As Jason demonstrates the tools and techniques, he emphasizes how students might think creatively about their use. The interplay between techniques and ideas, therefore, is modeled as seamless. He teaches his students how to make the leap between the concrete materials and tools and the aesthetic purposes to which they aspire.

> You can pretty dramatically change the form of something by cutting in and adjusting. Now all these connections I would score—slip and score—so they would stay together [*beginning to form and shape a spout and attaching the spout to the tube*]. But just to give you the idea, there's the spout. And ahh, something like this [*using the tube made in the extractor*], you could use [*beginning to cut the form*] and alter in some way to make some weird spout (Develop Craft: Technique, Stretch and Explore, Envision).

Goal 3: Express

In his initial interview, Jason was skeptical about the importance of teaching expression. On probing, it became clear that he worried that art was often trivialized by emphasizing its therapeutic uses as a way of "merely expressing feelings." However, using our expanded definition of Express, which includes the expression of concepts, personal meanings, *and* feelings, we observed Jason including Express as a goal in many classes that might appear on the surface to focus exclusively on skills. Jason shows that craft is necessary in order to express meaning.

As Jason begins to form the spout over the dowel, he explains:

> But as you pull, this will get tighter and tighter, so you have to keep adding water on this and making sure that it's loose and sliding. And then you may also put some sort of lines in [*forming lines in the clay*]. And you might do something like spin it [*spinning the clay, making a spiral shape*]. Then you can slide it off [*removing the clay from the dowel*]. Then if you really want to give it some shape, you might have to turn it on its side and let that get leather-hard and then come back and cut it, the exact shape that you want it (Develop Craft: Technique, Express, Stretch and Explore).

It may be difficult to understand why we label some of these examples as Express. Jason emphasized to us in interviews and to students in class that how artists touch clay leaves impressions that convey different meanings. A glaze applied with splashing "feels" more casual, so the object may feel more informal or convey a reference to the idea of movement, as Zen ceramics often do. A smooth surface feels more worked, so the object may convey more formality. For these reasons, we see Jason's references to different ways to touch or mark the clay as emphasizing Express.

Goal 4: Develop Craft: Technique

When Jason shows his students how to use a tool or technique, he almost always encourages them to think about the many possible ways they could use it in their own work. Thus, he uses a cluster of Observe–Express–Envision–Develop Craft: Technique to make sure that students are not only learning skills, but also understanding the artistic purpose and potential of artistic tools and techniques.

> So, now we need to score this with our scoring tool before we put it together. I'll score this side [*scoring the clay*]. And we can press this together [*pressing the seam*]. And I'm using this part of my hand [*pointing to the part of his hand he is using*] to try not to get too many fingerprints all over it.

And you might leave the seam. If you don't want the seam to show, you can also roll this [*rolling the tube on the table*] and later when it gets a bit harder you can come back with a rubber rib and go over that (Develop Craft: Technique, Express, Observe).

With this ceramic sets assignment, Jason has helped his students develop a variety of Studio Habits of Mind. They learn to Observe as they look carefully at ceramics; they learn to Envision as they plan their designs; they learn to Express as they think about conveying some kind of idea or feeling in their set; and all the while they are learning to acquire technical skills required for expertise in ceramics.

This chapter has illustrated the complexities and richness of Demonstration–Lectures and the role that they play in fostering Studio Habits of Mind. In the next chapter, we focus on the Students-at-Work structure, in which the assignments, concepts, processes, approaches, and attitudes introduced and modeled in Demonstration–Lectures are practiced by students as they create artworks under the personalized guidance of their artist–teachers.

Figure 12.1. Seeing Student Learning: Mykael Pushes the Figure

This in-class self-portrait assignment shows Mykael developing his mastery of observational drawing and facility with drawing tools and techniques (Observe, Develop Craft: Technique). Placing his mirror at a low angle adds interest to the drawing and adds challenge to the execution (Express, Stretch and Explore, Engage and Persist).

For homework, Mykael chose to work from a photograph in which Kayne West strikes an expressive pose that he accentuates by using extreme contrasts with black and white in the drawing (Develop Craft: Technique, Express, Understand Art Worlds: Domain). Mykael continues to develop accuracy in observation and ways to use drawing materials to interpret what he sees (Observe, Develop Craft: Technique, Express).

A reclining figured seen from this perspective is a challenge to depict (Express, Develop Craft: Technique). The accuracy of this drawing and use of materials—white for highlights, blue paper for midtones (Develop Craft: Technique)—shows Mykael applying what he learned in class and homework to his life drawing class (Observe, Express).

Mykael used this homework drawing to explore several colors for modeling the figure with a thin layer of color to create an atmospheric space (Develop Craft: Technique, Express, Stretch and Explore). According to Kathleen, Mykael sets goals for himself and likes to carefully plan his work (Envision, Engage and Persist). His classmates often ask him for feedback on their work (Reflect).

Here Mykael took risks (Stretch and Explore). Instead of a full-frontal view of the figure, he chose to compose a complex story within a story: An angled monitor shows a music video of Kayne West and Jay-Z within a larger composition of a room—demonstrating his appreciation that popular culture is a useful resource for subject matter (Envision, Express, Understand Art Worlds: Domain).

THIRTEEN

Students-at-Work and the Studio Habits of Mind

Teachers may emphasize any or all of the Studio Habits of Mind during Students-at-Work sessions. Because Students-at-Work sessions always involve working with art materials, Develop Craft: Technique is a central goal. But, as mentioned, this Studio Habit of Mind is rarely taught in isolation. In the individual consults with students, teachers often cluster Studio Habits of Mind to help students understand the connections among habits and how to integrate them into their working process. Certain clusters of Studio Habits of Mind occur together frequently in a single student–teacher interaction. (For instance, Develop Craft: Technique was often layered with Observe, Envision, and Reflect).

STUDIO HABITS OF MIND ARE TAUGHT IN CLUSTERS

The two examples that follow show how teachers, depending on their goals, emphasize differing clusters of Studio Habits in their interactions with students during a given studio work session.

INTRODUCING THROWING: CENTERING ON THE WHEEL PROJECT (EXAMPLE 13.1)

This example is taken from a Vase Project introduced in mid-October in Jason Green's introductory year-long ceramics course for 9th–12th-graders at Walnut Hill (see also Example 4.4). Looking at Jason's interactions with two students over the course of his centering lesson, we see how even the seemingly narrow technical issue of trimming a pot can become a vehicle for students to develop the disposition to think with a wide range of Studio Habits of Mind. Two students, one advanced, one a beginner, are having technical problems with trimming. Jason asks questions that help them verbalize their technical difficulties and see what in their working process led to these difficulties. He patiently demonstrates techniques, observes the students, and guides their hands as they try techniques. He looks with them at other finished pieces to get ideas for successfully solving their own problems. When a beginning student is discouraged and wants to

destroy the pieces she has built, Jason encourages her not to be too hasty in her evaluation, and to Stretch and Explore in her envisioning of the possibilities:

> You should save a lot of your stuff even if you think it's not working right now, because since these vases are going to be put together out of different parts, you might be able to use a lot of the parts, even if it doesn't come out exactly the way you want it. It might not matter, because you might cut it up and use it a whole new way.

Jason thus helps these students Engage and Persist through work they are finding very difficult. He frequently encourages them to keep trying and assures them that they will succeed. When the beginning student complains that she feels so far behind, Jason, shows that he understands her concern and responds in a reassuring and practical way

> Don't worry about that. Just [*laughing*] just don't worry about it, because your skills will catch up. You missed some classes so most everyone in here is two classes ahead of you, so they've had a lot more hours on the wheel. So it's easy to look around and see that everyone's making really tall things and you're not right now, but don't worry about it. It's still really early in the trimester so just keep practicing, and it'll come along OK.

When an advanced student feels frustrated with her lack of facility to achieve the delicate lip she envisions, he encourages her, saying she just needs to practice and showing her the precise skills necessary. He also makes sure to spend some time with her looking over her other work, pointing out its many strengths, and praising her on her progress so far, thus helping her Engage and Persist.

As these two students wrestle with trimming their vessels, Jason works with them to solve technical problems and thus Develop Craft: Technique. He also encourages them to look closely at their work and his demonstrations (Observe), consider their progress (Reflect: Evaluate), imagine new possibilities (Envision), move beyond their current capabilities (Stretch and Explore), and stick with it through difficulties (Engage and Persist).

CONNECTING WORLDS:
SECRET RITUAL VESSELS PROJECT (EXAMPLE 13.2)

During her Secret Ritual Vessels Project in the middle of her second-semester course for 9th-graders at the Boston Arts Academy, Beth Balliro's interactions with students focus on yet another cluster of Studio Habits of Mind. An ongoing theme in her 9th-grade class is to build connections between students' artmaking and their daily lives. In one homework assignment, each student is privately assigned a type of vessel (an heirloom, a container for holy water, a cat's water bowl) and asked to make a set of three while keeping the prompt secret.

The aim of the "secret assignment" is to help students connect with the project (Engage and Persist), think about the function of the objects (Reflect: Question and Explain), and create symbolic forms that the assigned function suggests (Envision, Express). Also, as is often the case in Beth's classes, her assignment ties into the school's humanities curriculum as she seeks to forge links between students' own work and artworks produced throughout other times and cultures (see also Examples 3.1 and 11.2). This class builds on earlier field trips to the nearby Museum of Fine Arts. Beth often provides packets of articles, images, and information that explore artists, mythologies, or religious cultures. She wants her students to find links between their works and those of recognized artists.

Beth also wants her students to be able to articulate the thought behind their work—the process they went through in creating the work, the decisions they made, and the relationship of the work to values of subcultures that they understand (Reflect: Question and Explain). It is not uncommon for students to spend part of the class thinking about a certain type of art, making written and/or drawn notes, and writing in their journals. Articulation is of particular importance to Beth, and she sees it as a central skill to help students gain recognition in the broader art world. In this class, the Students-at-Work session is followed by a Critique, where students look at each other's vessels set out on tables for display, write their observations about each vessel, and guess the type of "secret assignment" for one vessel.

As the Students-at-Work session starts, Beth directs energy to getting students excited about the project. The prompt of their assigned secret vessel serves to get them interested and focused (Engage and Persist), and to find ways to adapt their own ideas to their assigned form (Express). As students consult with Beth about their ideas, they do a lot of whispering of their ideas to keep their assigned form "top secret."

Early on, Beth consults with students on their ideas (Express), on how to think about their assigned form by imagining and planning possibilities (Envision), and on how to connect it to the idea of ritual (Express, Stretch and Explore, Understand Art Worlds). For instance, one girl aims to make hers look like a family heirloom wine glass. Beth talks with her about the idea of making it look "old." For students who have a hard time coming up with ideas, Beth asks them questions or helps them consider what the key functional aspects would be. She encourages their thinking of different possible ways to realize the form (Envision) while keeping true to the constraints of the assignment. Beth also reiterates the key idea of functionality in her interactions. For instance, for a student who is to create a vessel that transports something, she suggests thinking about making a lid for it because that would make moving its contents easier. To a student making a very small vessel, she reminds her, "Remember this is for a human, not a mouse. It's so cute. But try to see if you can actually use it, 'cause I'd love for you to have something that you can actually use" (Envision).

As students move further along in the development of their form, Beth works with them to think about what they are making (Reflect: Question and Explain). She talks with them about the strengths and weaknesses of their pieces. For instance, she tells one student, "You've got a solid form and an amazing idea. What I would say now is deal with craftsmanship. Try to make it clean, perfect, beautiful, solid." She also challenges students to think about what their vessel will communicate to others (Express). For a student who is making a water bowl for a cat, Beth asks, "How do we know that this isn't to feed a big cat?" The student thinks and asks if she could write the word "bath" on it. Beth challenges her, "See if you can do it without words" (Stretch and Explore). With this assignment, and in each of these brief interactions, Beth reiterates the challenge to make an object's form express its use, a key artistic concept in ceramics. This project challenges students to move beyond their usual concepts of vessels and their uses (Stretch and Explore, Understand Art Worlds: Domain).

INDIVIDUALIZING DURING
STUDENTS-AT-WORK SESSIONS

The examples from Jason and Beth show how teachers' goals for a given class or assignment permeate the casual, impromptu interactions during Students-at-Work sessions. However, another powerful aspect of the Students-at-Work structure is that it allows teachers to differentiate instruction without upsetting the general flow of work for the group. The two examples that follow show different ways in which teachers use the work session to individualize the curriculum.

DIFFERENTIATING FOR STUDENTS OF VARIOUS ABILITY/EXPERIENCE LEVELS: ABSTRACTION PROJECT (EXAMPLE 13.3)

It's the second semester in Jim Woodside's multi-age drawing class at Walnut Hill. Some of the advanced students are taking this course for the second or even third year. All the students have had at least a full semester of drawing, experimenting with different materials and drawing from the figure and from still life. With this foundation, Jim's students are ready to move on to abstract drawing. Jim creates assignments that engage the wide range of abilities and experiences of his students and then adjusts his instruction to individual needs during the Students-at-Work sessions.

Today Jim has set up a massive tower of twisted paper stretching from ceiling to floor with lighting accentuating the abstract forms present in this still life. Students have positioned their easels around the structure, and, charcoal in hand, they prepare to draw. As they look at the still life and begin to set up their compositions, Jim tells the students to think in terms of dark and light shapes on the paper and says, "You can't look at it and get it wrong, so feel at ease." Over the next 3 hours, students draw multiple studies on newsprint. Ultimately, each chooses one of their sketches to develop into a larger finished drawing.

Over the course of this working session, Jim brings the class together several times for Critiques. He punctuates the Students-at-Work sessions with mini-Demonstration–Lectures about how to observe and draw shapes and the still life. Jim balances the need to develop less-experienced students' observational skills and techniques with challenging students with stronger backgrounds in drawing to enhance their more developed skills.

Jim has designed a project that will accommodate this wide range of learners. Considering their drawing experiences from the first semester and the technical skills they developed, he now wants to challenge students to explore the concept of abstraction—a concept that Jim recognizes may be difficult for his students. In an interview, he tells us:

> Abstract art, to a lot of people, is sort of fringe and something that eccentrics and intellectuals talk about. I mean, these are stereotypes about, caricatures of it. And I'm not saying to them that

> I understand it all myself, you know. Or that I like it all. But I want them to know that it really grows out of the same stuff that all art grows out of. And they can learn to evaluate it, and they can learn to understand it themselves. And the best way for them to do it is to begin to do it themselves. And that's what I mean. And so what I'm doing here is a little bit artificial and forced, setting up a way for that to happen for them.

The large still life in the center of the room is not an uncommon setup in Jim's class. Observing a still life, choosing compositions from different points in the room, creating multiple sketches with various materials, and working toward a more finished piece over the course of several weeks are all familiar activities by this point in the year. Jim deliberately decided to design an assignment similar in scope and feel to the representational drawing with which students had become comfortable earlier in the semester. He wants students to see the link between representational and abstract drawing. Briefly explaining that abstraction is an important art world concept (students are well aware of this but hesitant nonetheless), Jim gently encourages students to do what they always do when looking at a still life. "Draw what you see," he tells them. By now this phrase is a familiar mantra in the class, so students can easily prepare for this otherwise novel task of observing and trying to make sense of the crumpled paper still life. Over the course of the afternoon, students begin to see connections to the drawings they made earlier in the year: They see that they are still working with shapes and lines and value.

Helping students build a bridge between representational drawing and abstraction is the primary goal of the class. However, Jim adjusts how he talks to students according to their individual needs. In what follows, Jim works with two beginning students, one who is struggling with the assignment, and one who has more confidence, excitement, and skills.

At five separate times throughout the working session, Jim consults with a 9th-grader new to the school who has limited English skills. About a half hour into the class, Jim notices that this student's page is sparse and that he looks confused. Jim takes the student aside and spreads another student's work out on the floor. He asks him to observe the series of sketches and notice how each drawing is different. By looking at the work, he could see how his peer deliberately changed the way she thought about each drawing, purposely using different lines and patterns each time. During this mini-Critique, Jim not only supports the beginning student in overcoming his initial obstacles with the assignment (Engage and

Persist), but also helps him refine his observational habits (Observe). Jim encourages the student to move beyond his current abilities and try new ways of seeing the still life (Stretch and Explore). As Jim explains to us later:

> I want him to throw himself into the act of drawing. Have fun with it. He really needs to loosen up and really put forms down and manipulate them on the page, and in a big bold way. So I'm always trying to get him to do that, because he doesn't. He's always watching himself. There are all the other kids in the room. And he doesn't have as much experience. But what I was really doing there was showing him an example of a kid from the previous day who I would say is in a somewhat similar situation. And I think giving him a real clue to how to go about it. That helps artistically for him. And also language, you know, he needs to see something. So I was trying to explain that in as simple terms as I could, but I know he didn't understand the whole of it. So giving him an example I thought helped.

A little later, Jim briefly checks in with the student again and encourages him to use the viewfinder, a tool for designing compositions that Jim has frequently employed and discussed in earlier observational drawing sessions (see Examples 3.3, 4.3, and 8.2). Returning to him later, Jim watches the student working and notices that he is looking at too small an area of the paper still life and is not attending to the larger shapes that would help him make the bridge between observation and abstraction. He sits at the student's drawing easel and demonstrates looking too closely at the paper and how it keeps him from seeing the structural forms in the twisted paper. By explicitly demonstrating both technical drawing skills and the *process* of observing, Jim encourages the student to develop new habits of looking. By drawing on his sketch and then referring to the still life, Jim shows the student how to see the large shapes and learn to improve his own technical drawing skills (Observe, Reflect, Develop Craft: Technique).

It's now halfway through the class, and the beginning student has made some progress in identifying and drawing large shapes. In his next consult, Jim encourages him to go even further in pushing the lights and darks by using a kneaded eraser on his drawing, a new technique for the student (Stretch and Explore). Jim demonstrates this process right on the drawing, so the student can see clearly how to juxtapose a white surface with a dark black shading to make the forms on his page look like the crumpled paper he is trying to draw (Develop Craft: Technique, Observe).

In the last few minutes of the class, Jim compliments the student's work (Engage and Persist) and gives him some final bits of technical advice, demonstrating how to use white charcoal to make his contrast even stronger (Develop Craft: Technique, Stretch and Explore).

Jim works quite differently with a more confident beginner. With the first student, Jim needed to help him engage with the assignment, use visual techniques to work around the student's limited English proficiency, develop basic drawing techniques, and start to develop a way of observing the structure of the still life that would help him eventually bridge to ideas of abstraction. This next student, on the other hand, starts off excitedly, with a clear plan of what he wants to do. For his first study, he has darkened his whole page and is using an eraser to depict where the light falls on the paper. Jim supports this idea but also encourages him to explore more of the central ideas of the abstraction in this phase by doing multiple studies rather than focusing so much on technique:

> That's really good. That's a good idea, and it would be good for you, and I don't want to discourage that. But I also don't want in this drawing for you to get too much into refining that technique. I want you to think about how those shapes relate to the four sides of the paper. So on your next one, let your approach be a little more with that in mind (Stretch and Explore).

When Jim next returns to this student, he encourages him to explore abstraction further. He tells him to depart from drawing strictly what he observes and become more logical about what he puts on the paper. "I think you should proceed almost like it's a math problem. Like very logically." He shows him how he can develop a "system" for thinking about which lines should be dark and which should be light (Envision). He gives him some tools to do this. He tells him to develop a plan, such as making all the larger forms darker. When the student seems a bit hesitant ("Outline it?"), Jim explains a core idea of abstraction: "That way there's a purpose for what you're doing. It's not just decorating your drawing. And that logic is really important, especially in an abstract drawing. It gives you a sense of purpose and relationship to what you're doing" (Stretch and Explore, Understand Art Worlds: Domain).

After students have done several studies, Jim breaks up the working session with a Critique in which he discusses each student's work. When he discusses one student's work, he comments that it seems to be the one that has gone furthest to abstraction, where you no longer easily connect it

Figure 13.1. Seeing Student Learning: Transformation Over Four Years

Over 4 years, we watched this student progress from minimal engagement in school with limited craft except in his graffiti repertoire to a student who developed beyond his initial style into a reflective and engaged artist.

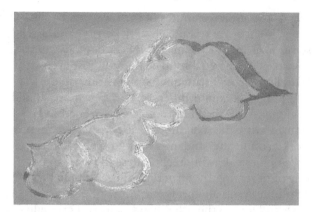

He begins as relatively weak in the habits of mind of Engage and Persist and Express: He proudly states that he did his familiar graffiti lettering for this 9th-grade logo painting in less than 5 minutes. He did the minimum, saying: "So I made my name, because he wanted us to make a name. And I made up some name just so I could get done with it." Later in the year, he notes its design flaws: "I kinda' used like the wrong colors, because it's not really dramatic, and you can't really see the outline of the letters." (Reflect, Develop Craft: Technique) Looking at it again 2 years later, he's more blunt: "That is garbage. I don't know what the heck I was thinking . . . I was just BS-ing." (Observe, Reflect: Evaluate)

This 3rd-year self-portrait weaves together skills he's developing in school with his graffiti style, giving his work "more originality, more flavor" (Engage and Persist, Express, Reflect). He captures a considerable likeness and chooses to draw from a difficult angle to give a sense of the king looking down on the viewer. He views the drawing as expressing sorrow and frustration: "I'm king, but I've gotten nowhere" (Develop Craft: Technique, Engage and Persist, Express, Observe, Reflect).

By the end of 9th grade, he moves beyond doing *only* graffiti: "Say, all right a year ago, I would not be drawing mountains from nothing. I would not be drawing mountains. I don't think I would be doing basically any of the stuff I'm doing now." (Engage and Persist, Stretch and Explore) In addition to learning skills of manipulating paint and planning a gray-scale under-painting (Develop Craft: Technique), he analyzes the composition and thinks in terms of the viewer, saying "He's [the turtle] trying to draw the viewer's attention. Like basically the viewer feels like he's in the painting, like he can interact with that figure, like 'look at me, I'm in your face. Like what do you want?'" (Observe, Express, Reflect)

His senior exhibition is filled with expressive self-portraits and large-scale layered graffiti landscaped worlds. This self-portrait reflects his interest in exploring his African heritage through studying African masks, a move he says was inspired by learning about Picasso's use of African art (Develop Craft: Technique, Express, Observe, Reflect, Understand Art Worlds: Domain).

to its original source of the still life. He uses the student's piece to reiterate a central idea of abstract drawing. "It's a texture on a piece of paper, and it's a way of organizing a piece of paper. That's what abstract art is. You're taking references from the world and you're organizing them into a two-dimensional world of your own." Following this group Critique, the second student walks up to Jim and talks with him about his piece, saying that he's not really pleased with how the lines are working, mentioning his ideas for further work. Jim offers suggestions and supports the student's ideas. Jim reiterates the idea that the goal is to explore options, reminding him, "This is just a learning process here" (Stretch and Explore).

INDIVIDUALIZING FOR MULTIPLE AGENDAS: CREATING HAT AND VEST PROJECT   (EXAMPLE 13.4)

While Jim's example is about individualizing for a range of experience and ability levels, Kathleen Marsh's story in this Students-at-Work session with seniors at the Boston Arts Academy, is one of a teacher multitasking to keep students on track with the assignment at hand and to help individual students with their outside work.

It's the first day of the final semester for Kathleen's 12th-graders. There's a lot going on, and Kathleen must prepare her students for the final push of their high school art careers. They are in the process of applying to colleges and art schools or preparing for jobs upon graduation. Not only do they need to have their professional portfolios in order, they also need to meet their graduation requirements, which include showing and defending their work in a senior exhibition. The students are somewhat distracted by all these outside events and battling a case of spring semester "senioritis."

Kathleen has much to accomplish in this class session. She introduces students to the current assignment of a self-portrait wearing a hat and vest that they have designed and created out of paper. She also introduces them to what they will be doing over the course of the semester, as well as going over what, as seniors, they will be doing outside of the class. She gives an introduction to the course requirements and reviews the syllabus. Kathleen discusses the defense process and her plans for curating the show and taking slides of finished work. Since students are putting together their final portfolios, she reminds them of this by introducing a several-week self-portrait assignment that will result in a finished value drawing that can be a "showcase piece" in their portfolios.

Today is the first installment of this self-portrait assignment. In this class, students create wearable paper hats and vests from oaktag that express something about their identity. In later sessions, they will make charcoal value drawings of themselves wearing the paper clothing. Today's portion of the assignment challenges students to both Envision and Express something about themselves, as they must imagine what the hats and vests they make now will convey about themselves, and how they will look as they wear them for their value drawings. As seniors, the students are accustomed to working independently. However, Kathleen monitors their progress on this assignment, including instructing and getting materials for students who are proceeding ahead of others to the next phase of the assignment.

While students create the hats and vests, Kathleen consults with each student about the progress of their portfolio and completion of tasks for the senior exhibition. This is in part an administrative task to make sure the students are on target in their application process, but it can also be a chance to model an important process of evaluation. For instance, Kathleen spends time with one student, looking over each piece of his portfolio, discussing ways of finishing some of the pieces, and identifying which ones he should include in the senior show. She later explained that this is one of the strongest students in the class, but he had initially only selected two pieces to include in the show. Kathleen discussed working over the course of several years with this student on his tendency toward perfectionism and being overly self-critical.

The flexibility of the Students-at-Work session allows Kathleen to keep the group focused on their work, while also adapting to students' varying work paces on a multiphase assignment. In addition, she has many chances to address crucial issues with each student that are not tied explicitly to this class assignment. In a single working session, Kathleen is able to keep the class as a whole engaged in working (Engage and Persist), while connecting with individual students on issues central to their development as artists, such as the preparation of their portfolios (Reflect, Develop Craft: Technique) and progress in applying to college or art school (Understand Art Worlds: Communities).

This chapter has illustrated how teachers use Students-at-Work sessions to keep their artmaking goals at the center of the learning process while personalizing instruction to suit a range of student needs. The Studio Habits of Mind emphasized by an assignment sometimes take a back seat to habits of importance to a particular student at a given time. In the Critique structure, described in the chapter that follows, both general and personal goals become the focus.

FOURTEEN

Critique and the Studio Habits of Mind

Critiques, by their very nature, foster the Studio Habits of Mind of Reflect: Question and Explain and, especially, Evaluate—learning how to judge what makes one work better or more effective than another. However, in the Critiques we observed, learning to evaluate works was only one of many goals. In every Critique we analyzed, teachers intended to teach at least five of the Studio Habits of Mind.

TEACHING STUDIO HABITS OF MIND THROUGH CRITIQUE

Develop Craft

Looking at students' work collectively often provides illustrations of how particular techniques can function differently in different works, which can help students expand their ideas about craft. In addition, techniques are often offered as solutions to problems that students identify in works. For instance, in one of Jim Woodside's Critiques, he asked students to identify errors in perspective in their own work, and they worked together to figure out how to correct them.

Engage and Persist

Critiques can be highly motivating. Knowing that everyone is going to look at and comment on their work can spur students to put their full effort into it. In addition, the critique process can engage students by giving them new insights into their work. For instance, Jim often uses Critiques at the early stage of a drawing to help students identify the potential of a piece and to get them excited about its possibilities. Mid-process Critiques can also help students work through difficulties in a piece, either by identifying unrecognized strengths in their work, or by offering specific advice on aspects that they could change. In Critiques, the current piece is treated as an opportunity for deeper commitment to work and learn. For instance, Jason Green tells a student, "The glaze is transparent because you put it on thin. But you can try re-firing that and put the same glaze on thicker."

Envision

As students stand before their work, they are encouraged to think about what would have happened if they had done it another way. For instance, Kathleen Marsh asks a student to think about how much white space he intended to leave in his self-portrait. Jim Woodside asks students to imagine how one student's drawing would look if she had fully drawn the leg rather than leaving it unfinished. Guy Michel Telemaque asks students to think of ways a given photo could heighten its focus on light as the subject. Frequently, in Critiques, teachers also ask students to envision how they will finish a piece, or what they envision working on next. Even without direction, as students look at and discuss each other's work, they envision different possibilities for how the work could look. In a senior Critique session, students' comments frequently involve envisioning their own and other students' pieces differently.

Express

Critiques offer an important chance for students to step back and recognize aspects of their work that they might have missed while immersed in the process of making. In addition, Critiques offer a chance for students to hear how others interpret their work. One of Guy Michel's design students described finding out that while her intention in a flag design was to celebrate her native Puerto Rico by showing that it was so hot, other students interpreted it as an image of burning the Puerto Rican flag. Students learn that artists' intended meanings are not always matched by the messages received by viewers. This can lead them to revise their works or simply to recognize that works have multiple interpretations. Critiques offer a testing ground for finding out how one's work communicates.

Observe

The type of observation most particular to Critiques is that of observing works in comparison to one another. During the process of making works, most of the observation involves students looking carefully at their own work, and in the case of observational drawing, looking at the relationship between the work and the referent. In Critiques, the focus often shifts to looking at your work in the context of others' works, or by comparing multiple works of your own. Teachers often encourage specific observational comparisons, as when Jim asked students to compare the expressive effects of different qualities of line.

Reflect

Question and Explain. More than at any other time in the studio class, reflecting about student work is highlighted during Critiques. Teachers strive to draw students into a discussion that moves beyond just noting what they like and dislike and into observing in the context of particular artistic concepts. Critiques are often framed around a set of targeted questions, such as when Guy Michel asked his photography students, "Why is this a photograph about light? All photographs depend on light; how are these [for the light assignment] different from every other photograph?" Another example is when Beth Balliro asked students to guess the intended function of their fellow students' clay vessels and to start thinking about the relationship between the vessels' forms and their ritual functions.

Evaluate. Critiques offer an important chance for students to evaluate their own and peers' work. Sometimes an evaluative process precedes the Critique; students might be asked to choose their best work to put up for critique. Critiques often begin with discussions about what "works" in varied pieces. Evaluation in Critiques is often analytical. Rather than merely sorting "good" from "bad" work, students learn to identify which aspects of a work are most effective and which may detract from the effect of a piece. As Jason explains, "I really try not to say something's good or bad. I just say, this is what it is communicating."

Stretch and Explore

Just seeing the range of work produced by the group may push individual students to expand their thinking about their own work. To foster the Stretch and Explore aspect of Critique, teachers assign projects that are likely to yield diverse results. For example, Jason Green spoke about deliberately choosing glazes that produce widely varying results in order to promote more student exploration. During Critiques, he invited students to analyze the results of their explorations of materials much as they would analyze a scientific experiment. Critiques offer suggestions for how to think about what can be seen in the work and how the student artist might explore other possibilities.

Understand Art Worlds

Domain. Teachers draw connections between student art and professional art, and they make allusions to historical and contemporary art references as they point out features in students' work. They may tell students that their work reminds them of a particular artist, sometimes showing them an image or two. This informs students about the larger culture of art and art history, but its greater purpose appears to be to emphasize students' connections to the historical and current community of working artists. For instance, during a Critique, Jim Woodside commented on one student's developing a certain "electric line quality" and use of space in his work:

He's really finding a way to draw, a kind of language that's his own, that will succeed for him as he approaches different kinds of problems. But that's something that he came up with really on his own, playing around with this project [*pointing to a self-portrait from a previous class*]. And I certainly think it's something that he can take into the way that he draws something like this [*holding up a sketch that the student is currently working on*]. It reminds me of a Dubuffet painting.

In this Critique, Jim identified aspects of a student's emerging style and tied it to the larger art world.

Teachers present Critiques as reflective processes, including evaluation, that happen in professional arts communities, and not merely as isolated elements of an art class. As Beth prepares 9th-graders for a Critique, for example, she explains that Critiques are part of being an artist and that some Critiques are meant to be about evaluation, while others focus more on other aspects of reflection.

Communities. The social aspect of Critique is one of its defining features. Teachers focus on how students learn to value responses from peers and on ways to offer respectful and constructive criticism to their peers. Critiques reinforce the idea that artmaking is a communal process, not only a private activity. Art is made to be shown to others and discussed, and that can be learned through the social process of Critique.

INTEGRATING STUDIO HABITS OF MIND THROUGH CRITIQUE

The eight Studio Habits of Mind fostered by Critiques are usually not discussed separately, but rather are integrated flexibly during Critique sessions. This integration is illustrated by the following examples of Critiques from Jim Woodside's drawing class at Walnut Hill.

COMPARING WORKS:
CONTOUR DRAWING PROJECT   (EXAMPLE 14.1)

While each teacher we observed held a Critique at least once, Jim held multiple Critiques in nearly every class session of his multi-age drawing class. These Critiques were not necessarily formal, lengthy discussions; sometimes they lasted only a few minutes. However, Jim's consistent use of Critiques stresses the importance he places on coming together as a group to look at and discuss the work that has been done.

In the first class session of the year in Jim's drawing course, he introduces Critiques as a central but informal part of the routine:

> What we'll do is, we'll draw for a while. Then we'll put some drawings up on the wall, and we'll start to look at them and talk about them. And that's something we'll do a lot in this class. Those of you that have had me before, we, we always do that—we draw, put the drawings up, talk about them.

After the students do a few quick drawings, some blind contour (in which students do not look at the paper but only at the referent) and some in which students look at both the still life and the drawing, Jim asks each student to hang a blind and nonblind drawing next to each other. Before beginning the discussion, Jim guides their observation and reflection: "Everybody take a look at their two drawings, and just think in your mind how to compare the two. Just to describe the difference between your two drawings." This task helps students integrate learning how to Observe with learning to Reflect. Jim encourages them to evaluate their works, asking which they preferred and why.

As students make comments, Jim acknowledges and expands on their responses in a positive and encouraging way. For instance, one student says of a blind drawing, "Notice all her details are not . . . it's detailed but it's not." Jim affirms her evaluation and draws this comment into its fuller meaning:

> It's detailed but it's not. Yeah, that's really good. I couldn't have said it that well. That's very true. I mean, we have all the information here [*pointing to a section of the drawing*], we know it's there, yet it doesn't seem like it's overly precise, or overly worked.

In this first class session, he wants to ensure that students feel comfortable talking in the group, and his comments help them to Engage and Persist in the Critique process.

While Jim uses this Critique to create a positive social atmosphere, it also works to build students' understanding of key aspects of the assignment. Through discussion, students come to recognize characteristic differences between blind and nonblind drawings. A few minutes into the Critique, Jim moves a pair of drawings that reflect this distinction well to the center of the wall and asks students to focus on them. Building on students' comments, Jim introduces the idea that while the nonblind drawings may have been more technically accurate, the blind drawings have a more direct expressive quality to them:

> Even though this might, there's a certain accuracy that's stronger here [*pointing to a nonblind drawing*]. These things are placed more in position. But there's a kind of believability here [*pointing to a blind drawing*], and that's a word that I'll use a lot throughout the year, *believability*. What makes drawing interesting is how direct your relationship is to what you're looking at, OK? And here, the relationship is in a way very direct, very honest. There's not other things in the way. Like your perception of how it should look.

While students talk frequently in this Critique, Jim carefully guides the discussion to center on this key point. Thus, through a process involving the Studio Habits of Observe and Reflect, Jim helps students explore a key intended lesson about the relationship between Develop Craft: Technique and Express. Jim also pushes students to see how they could use what they learned in the blind drawings in the rest of their work:

> Now obviously we don't do every drawing in the world covered up and sort of scribbling. But there's a really important lesson here in that—how can you bring some of this state of mind, in a way, to this [*pointing at a nonblind drawing*]? How can you bring this kind of freedom or lack of inhibition into your work?

In this very first Critique of the year, Jim explicitly sets up the expectation that what you learn through Critique of a given assignment should be applied to your work more broadly: Jim challenges students to use the lessons from this assignment and Critique to Stretch and Explore beyond their usual habits of artmaking.

As shown, Jim's Critiques help students integrate various Studio Habits of Mind. By encouraging students to Engage and Persist in the Critique, Jim fosters an iterative process in which students practice Observing and Reflecting, while they also explore the relationship between Express and Develop Craft: Technique. In addition, he encourages students to Envision how they might use what they learned to Stretch and Explore beyond their usual drawing habits.

CRITIQUING THROUGHOUT THE PROCESS: FIGURES IN EVOCATIVE SPACE PROJECT   (EXAMPLE 14.2)

Jim often uses Critiques to guide a class and punctuate a working session. (See Figure 14.1). In this midsemester figure-drawing session, students were meant to focus on the expressive potential of light and of the space between figures (Express, Develop Craft: Technique; see Examples 7.1 and 11.1). Jim has set up dramatic lighting and shows examples of professional artworks (reproductions of paintings by Hopper and Diebenkorn) that have the evocative sense of space and light that he emphasizes in the class assignment. Throughout the 3-hour class, Jim repeatedly holds short Critiques to keep students on track with this focus and also to help them make explicit what they are learning about expression.

Opening Critique

Jim begins the class with a Critique focusing on high-contrast figure drawings from the previous session. This quick Critique has no student discussion; Jim's goal is to get students quickly into the mindframe of working and to help them build connections between what they have done in the last session and what they will do today.

Jim notes the effectiveness of the drawings, commenting on how students were building on their previous experiences. This encourages students and reinforces the idea that assignments in the class connect to each other. With

Figure 14.1. Jim holds multiple Critiques in a class session.

a long wooden pointer, Jim draws students' attention to different areas of each drawing as he comments on how the high-contrast technique helps students organize space, separate shapes, reduce a complex scene, and maintain the focus on light.

Jim says, "I want to put you mentally to where you were last week." He emphasizes the thought process that went into making their drawings: "This shape may have been a lighter gray or toward the lighter end of the spectrum, but you make that decision to go black or white with every gray you see and what you end up with is an abstract composition." In this, as in all his Critiques, Jim moves beyond discussing technique while simultaneously staying grounded in the work.

Jim chooses to focus on aspects of the drawings such as expression and light that will be central to the next assignment: a drawing that focuses on the expressive, evocative properties of the space between two figures. Thus, this Critique, while seemingly a reflection on completed work, prepares students mentally for the coming work session and primes them for key ideas to come.

Critique of Sketches

After students complete quick sketches of two figures, Jim gathers the class around the array of sketches on the floor for a few minutes. In an interview, Jim explains that this Critique aimed to help students envision their final drawings from the sketches. "It was to make sure that they had the maps before the journey starts." He also uses Critique to build inclination, to get students "excited about possibilities of this little assignment by seeing that emotional things are already being said in the pictures."

Jim begins by integrating Observe, Envision, Reflect: Question and Explain, and Evaluate. As he surveys the drawings, he says, "I see plans starting to form in your brains about how you are going to approach this." The group looks at and evaluates the sketches in terms of what they reveal about how students envision the final drawings.

Jim chooses two students' drawings and asks the class to compare their different approaches. One student has exaggerated the distance between the figures and another has made the figures small relative to the space in the room. After talking about the expressive aspects of each piece, he focuses students' attention on the makers' choices to treat space differently. This Critique helps students learn to observe their sketches for the purpose of envisioning a more finished drawing. Jim wants them to Reflect on the expressive potential of choices they made in their sketches and to Envision ways of stretching to heighten this expression.

Figure 14.2. Seeing Student Learning: Min Finds Her Voice

Min, a senior starting her third year at Walnut Hill, says, "I think I haven't changed much technically, but I am more comfortable and free when I draw than before. I think I'm finding my own style in these drawings. I don't know what it is yet, but I'm starting." Jim Woodside explains that expanding artistic voice (Express) from a base of high-level technical skill (Develop Craft: Technique) is one common developmental path for some students at Walnut Hill.

This drawing shows Min's technical skill when she arrived at Walnut Hill. She describes focusing closely on the model (Observe) and her challenge to draw "reversely" using white and color on a black surface, with oil stick, a new material (Stretch and Explore, Develop Craft: Technique).

"I wanted to have the feeling of a book and remind you of books" (Express), Min says of her goal for this collage, which was inspired by a still life of stacked books. Prior to the collage, Min drew a light and shade version of the same still life on pink paper and a collaged drawing on brown cardboard in which she pushed herself to try something new: "I started by observing closely. It seemed boring so I did collage on it. I didn't want to put a lot of effort into it. I wanted to do it intuitively" (Envision, Observe, Stretch and Explore).

This is Min's first attempt to use only abstract shapes and lines to translate what she observes into an image (Observe, Envision). She describes this as "a big change in my drawing history." Her teacher also saw it as a leap for her and says: "I think she learned that implying things is often more effective than showing them fully" (Express, Envision, Stretch and Explore, Reflect).

For this observational drawing, students drew on an unfamiliar surface: maps. Min's drawing creates an abstract mix in which neither figure nor environment dominates. She describes her intent in this way: "This drawing was a big challenge for me. I also tried to imply things and merge the figure by using color and shared lines" (Develop Craft: Technique, Envision, Express, Stretch and Explore).

Final Critique

After the working session, Jim holds a longer Critique that involves more student discussion. In this Critique, each student's work is carefully discussed. This Critique focuses on giving students a chance to Observe and Reflect what they have done in their work and to practice talking about work. After listening to students' general observations about the works, Jim focuses the questioning on which pieces have the strongest sense of dramatic, evocative light, a central focus of the assignment. When students comment on a dramatic piece, Jim often expands on their comments. For instance, he talks about how one piece has the feel of a big movie set in which only a small area is lit up, and that area is where the action is. He ties this to a "pretty strong decision" the student has made in leaving much of the drawing empty. In this way, he models how to connect observations about Express with Develop Craft: Technique. For another student, he holds up a Hopper print for comparison of the dramatic power of light. When students comment that the drawing has an "outside feel" even though it is inside, Jim ties this observation about an expressive property to a more technical idea, showing how this effect results from how the student has highlighted multiple light sources. Again, Jim connects students' learning to the central idea of the assignment, which is to link technique and expression. His use of the Hopper print is intended to help students begin to connect their own artmaking to other artists' work (Understand Art Worlds: Domain).

This Critique proceeds one by one through each piece, with students making observations and evaluating their own work and working process, and then listening to comments about it from Jim and the rest of the students. Suggestions for further work involve noticing an interesting aspect nascent in the work (Observe and Reflect) and figuring out ways it could be taken further (Engage and Persist, Envision, and Stretch and Explore). For instance, Jim tells one student that she can work on hers without the models so that she can focus on heightening the contrasts. This suggestion connects to her other recent work (discussed in the opening Critique) that involved building up abstract compositions. This final Critique integrates all eight Studio Habits of Mind.

Critiques have a variety of structures and functions, but they consistently aim to help students integrate their learning and development of Studio Habits of Mind. Students are meant to learn how asking questions and explaining ideas can support evaluation, to connect their work to that produced by others in their class and throughout history, to observe how different techniques can produce different expressive effects, and to stretch beyond their usual habits to envision new possibilities and sustain engagement. Teachers can guide Critiques flexibly so that they highlight the integration of different habits at different times. For instance, in the planning stage of a drawing, Critiques may focus more on tying Observe to Stretch and Explore and Envision. Students are meant to open up and explore a range of possibilities for their work. After the work is complete, the Critique may focus on tying Observe with Reflect. Students are meant to figure out and describe what aspects of a work function well, which do not, and why.

FIFTEEN

Exhibition and the Studio Habits of Mind

With Exhibition, in which students display their projects to the public, any of the Studio Habits of Mind can be developed as students and teachers together work through the stages of Exhibition outlined in Chapter 3. Each phase of Exhibition—planning, installation, public, aftermath—may employ any of the basic Studio Structures, and the Studio Habits can be developed within any structure, as discussed in Chapters 12, 13, and 14. In what follows, we offer examples of how each Studio Habit might be developed in an exhibition.

USING EXHIBITION TO TEACH STUDIO HABITS OF MIND

Develop Craft

Technique. Numerous aspects of Develop Craft: Technique are called for in all phases of Exhibition. Installing a physical exhibition is an opportunity for training in a slate of special skills. Installation involves preparing pieces so that attaching them to walls or pedestals doesn't harm them, determining the placement of each work, leveling each piece exactly, attaching pieces to the wall or floor securely, allowing for viewers to flow around pedestals and sculptures, and making sure that how the work is hung does not distract from the work itself. A wide variety of tools needs to be used, including drills, hammers, pliers, wire cutters, attachment hardware, sanders, levels, tape measures, putty knives, paint rollers and brushes, tape, ladders, and dollies for organizing and moving heavy walls and pedestals. Similarly, an online exhibition requires attention to the technical requirements of an exhibition space (e.g., protocols for posting material and procedures for testing how the exhibition will be seen in different web browsers and on different size screens).

Studio Practice. During installation, the exhibition space becomes a studio workshop. That calls for Develop Craft: Studio Practice—arranging the tools so that they can be readily found and shared, keeping everything organized, making sure there are enough pins, that drills are charged, and that the exhibition space is left clean, spackled and repainted, swept, organized, and ready for the next show. Parallel issues of maintenance arise in online forums as well, such as the need for organization of digital files and coherent naming conventions.

Engage and Persist

Engage. When students are involved in preparing work for public audiences, engagement tends to be high. Exhibition lends a sense of seriousness and purpose that helps students become fully committed to displaying work so that each piece is honored. Such engaged commitment helps students to sustain the attention to detail required by installation.

Persist. Because an exhibit is a public display, students are motivated to strive for excellence. Anything that is shown will be read as meaningful; thus, fingerprints cannot be on gallery walls unless they are there intentionally, labels must be applied straight, and signage or text must be interwoven harmoniously with images. Persistence is critical. Students work long hours on all four phases of an exhibition.

Envision

Whether planning an exhibition online or in a physical space, a student, a group of students, or students and teachers together must curate: envision a plan and convey that vision to others.

As an exhibition space is set up, curators have to continuously envision how the exhibit will look to an imagined audience. For a traditional gallery exhibition: Where should walls, pedestals, or shelves be? What should viewers see first so that they are drawn into the exhibition space? What works should be close to one another or spaced farther away? Where should the show's title be displayed? Similar decisions need to be made for a virtual site: How should texts and images interrelate? How should the virtual exhibition space be introduced? How will the display look on different sizes of screens?

Express

Exhibition expresses meaning in ways that are similar to how works of art convey meaning, only here through a collection of works. Meaning is conveyed by the selection and arrangement of the works, and decisions are guided by the theme and style of the exhibition. Like curators in museums and galleries, students choose work to include in an exhibition and, by doing so, learn to attend closely to the expressive content of work so that each selection contributes to the meaning of the whole.

The habit of Express is also developed as students learn to curate thematically. When Exhibition is thematically structured, students must select works that, together, express something about the theme. The narratives at the end of this chapter offer examples of themes.

One theme explored by educators is how to display student work to reveal learning—a practice influenced by the Reggio Emilia preschools in Italy, where the art of documenting learning to make it visible has been perfected (Giudici, Rinaldi, & Krechevsky, 2001). By selecting works that show change over time and/or including written reflections or transcribed oral comments that speak about the work's development, a display can show the thinking behind the artistic process.

Observe

The habit of Observe is called upon notably during the planning phase, when students select the works that they want to display, whether those works are their own or belong to other artists, and whether the exhibition is physical or virtual. It is helpful to see all the work at the same time; a common strategy is to lay everything out, look closely, then choose those works that best represent the artist and the focus of the exhibition. This winnowing requires careful observation: there is no formula. Student curators also must observe works and groupings of works closely enough to be able to choose which works "go together," either because of their similarity or because together they create a desired meaning or contrast. The entire display must be coherent to the eye as well as the mind, and thus students must keep looking until they deem that all of the parts interrelate.

Reflect

Question and Explain. Whether talking about their work at a reception, writing artist statements, responding to their own or others' works in online forums, or explaining works to viewers in gallery talks or formal defenses, students need to interpret their works, process, and thinking in words, formally and/or extemporaneously, to public audiences, reviewers, and critics. Because of this, students use and can develop the habit of Question and Explain through mounting or discussing an exhibition, whether online or in a physical space.

Evaluate. When students select works to show, they rely on their disposition to Evaluate. They must look critically at their works and determine which ones are most successful and worthy of display. They also need to judge the quality of the exhibit itself, considering each individual work and the collection together. Are labels or captions error-free and grammatically correct? Does the work cohere and make a strong impression as a whole? Just as rests are critical to musical compositions, so the spaces—between works, between captions, signage, or labels and works—are important in an exhibition, whether it is online or in a gallery or hallway.

Stretch and Explore

Exhibition can be set up in experimental ways. When students come up with innovative approaches to showing their work (e.g., Figure 15.1), they are flexing their Stretch and Explore muscles. Professionals in art worlds are continually exploring new definitions of Exhibition, stretching them out to the street, onto the web, or, as with artist Jenny Holtzer's work, projected onto the faces of buildings.

Understand Art Worlds

Domain. Learning how to set up an Exhibition requires paying attention to how professional artists display their work, by attending professional exhibitions, observing documentation of exhibitions, or participating in online forums. Attention to expert models allows students to learn varied ways of setting up exhibitions. As the exhibition world expands from gallery to street to virtual, students need to continue developing familiarity with the evolving formats used to display artworks.

Communities. Exhibition calls upon and builds communities. Students installing a gallery or website have to work together as a community, selecting and/or hanging their works at the same time, because they need to see and adjust responsively, for example, to how well or poorly a work or group of works resonates with other works, how the space feels between them, and what unexpected meanings emerge from the juxtapositions. Exhibition also teaches students about the division of labor needed for complex collaborative tasks. Because Exhibition is the

Figure 15.1. Exhibition: "A Feast for Your A-muse-ment"

Mónika Aldarondo's high school junior students mounted an Exhibition that explored the idea of "muse." Through individual and collaborative works installed in the student gallery space, students created a gallery-as-dining room "feast" for their artistic muses (Develop Craft, Envision, Express, Understand Art Worlds, Stretch and Explore).

1. Welcome

Students collaboratively generated the exhibition title, *A Feast for Your A-MUSE-ment* and their teacher made and posted a title sign together with photographs that documented students' learning process as they cooperated to complete all phases of the Exhibition (Engage and Persist, Understand Art Worlds).

2. Preparing the space

Students prepared the gallery space by selecting and painting the wall a color that conveyed the feeling of a dining room (Develop Craft, Express). Students installed shelves and positioned and secured individual 2D and 3D "mini-muses" and the works they inspired onto shelves, the wall, and the ceiling. They made decisions about how to arrange works throughout the Exhibition (Envision, Reflect: Evaluate).

3. The Muses

Collaborative groups created five "muse" sculptures representing "what inspires you to create your work." Here, the *Muse for Creative Process and Memory* sits at one end of the dining room table. A seat built into the sculpture invites viewers to sit inside the hooded Creativity Chamber where fragments of mirrors guide them to reflect on their past experiences to inspire their creative endeavors (Envision, Express, Reflect: Question and Explain).

The *Muse of Mysterious Creatures from Urban Legends* (left)— "part fish, frog, and octopus"—joined the other muses for dinner. The table is set to suggest a formal dining experience and "what feeds our muses" fills plates and adorns the table (Envision, Express, Stretch and Explore). "Foods" include a suspended moon, whose "light cast on dark nights feeds the *Muse of Mythical Characters and Tales*." The small white figures on the plate at lower right, "whose heads are filled by what's on TV and the internet so they can't think for themselves," feed a *Muse Against Mass-Media Brainwashing and For Counter-Cultural Voices* (outside the picture frame) (Reflect, Stretch and Explore, Express).

4. The opening

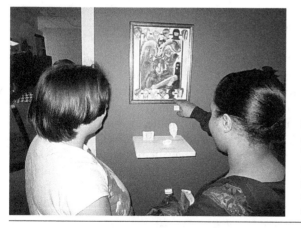

Students invited peers, families, teachers, administrators, and visiting guests to an afterschool opening reception (Understand Art Worlds). The artists "schmoozed" about the work and making the Exhibition, and they listened to responses from their guests (Reflect). Later, students returned the gallery to its original condition and discussed strengths and weaknesses of the experience (Develop Craft, Understand Art World: Communities, Reflect: Evaluate).

structure in which art is made public, students also need to think about the community that will be an audience for their work. How can they install work so that the display draws in and speaks to the viewers they anticipate? They need to consider who their audience will be; an adolescent student might choose to show an edgy work in an exhibition to be viewed by her peers but something less provocative in an exhibition that she expects her grandparents and younger siblings to attend.

INTEGRATING STUDIO HABITS OF MIND IN THE EXHIBITION

Examples from Boston Arts Academy

Kathleen Marsh Reflects on Exhibition. Kathleen believes it is important that, by graduation, Boston Arts Academy (BAA) students learn to do the work of mounting a show themselves. For some students, that is part of their training as an artist. But for all, it builds understanding of how artists take their work out of the privacy of the studio and into the public, whoever their "public" may be. It also develops important dispositions through attending to the many dimensions of creating a successful show. To support that goal, BAA's visual art department teaches a 4-year series of courses on Exhibition where students learn to write artist statements, to create installations for all kinds of art media, to curate works for display, to experiment with exhibition formats, to build a web presence, to "schmooze" with audiences. Students engage in all phases of Exhibition.

Kathleen says, "We haven't figured this all out entirely; we run into problems all the time." It's difficult for students to switch from artist to curator mode. But Kathleen told us that the hallways are always filled with varied artworks displayed by students, from inflatable sculpture to performance art, ranging from simplistic to profound. Because they've had many shows, including junior shows where students all work toward one theme, the senior exhibitions have improved steadily over the years.

The next set of examples reveal Studio Habits of Mind within learning experiences centered on understanding Exhibition.

A First Show   (Example 15.1)

In 2011–2012, BAA 9th-graders collaborated with seniors, who curated the 9th-graders' work in a show focusing on the theme of line (Understand Art Worlds: Communities, Express). The first-year and senior classes were taught by the same teacher, who facilitated coordination between the

groups. The work consisted of classic contour line drawings in different colors of markers that were then translated into wire sculpture. The senior students wallpapered the school's 3rd-floor hallway, leaving no space between drawings and creating a great wave of color with the wire pieces layered in front of the drawings. Track lighting created shadows on the visual presentation (Develop Craft: Technique, Envision, Express). In the show description, the seniors wrote that they recalled what it was like to hate your work and be embarrassed by taking risks and trying something new. They said to the first-years, "We get it that you won't like it now, because that was us, too. But looking back, we can tell you, this is good work" (Reflect: Evaluate). They affirmed the 9th-graders and pushed them a little bit (Stretch and Explore; Engage and Persist). The message was: "Get tough—the work needs to go up." Kathleen concluded: "Tough love, empathy. It was cool."

A Sophomore Show   (Example 15.2)

In 2011, Exhibitions 1, taught by Guy Michel Telemaque, was designed to encourage exploration and to help students "feel free to experiment" (Stretch and Explore). Students visited and wrote reflections about local exhibitions—at colleges, community galleries, and alternative exhibition spaces—in order to observe the "conversation between the form of the space and the artwork" (Observe; Reflect, Understand Art Worlds). Guy Michel asked them to transform one of the exhibitions they had seen, without any constraints—they had limitless (imaginary) money, time, help, even no gravity (Envision; Stretch and Explore). Their designs varied from making minimal adjustments to the existing exhibition to "some very inventive stuff" (Stretch and Explore). Meanwhile, the students were also making collaborative artworks they would actually exhibit. Through group brainstorming, students came up with the idea of a circus: The works were large and they wanted to hang them like circus banners (Envision). As the group played with titles, Cirque du Soleil was mentioned. Since the theme of the works was dreams, this led them to title their exhibition, Circus of Dreams—or, in French, "Cirque du Reve" (Reflect: Question and Explain; Express).

In the first draft of the exhibition, students were experimental: They hung the pieces back to back—so viewers could see both pieces—and from the ceiling (Envision; Stretch and Explore). Once installed, the students and Guy Michel held a Critique in the exhibition and students decided the final exhibition should be more formal: four walls of two-dimensional works, with one wall of "bad" dreams and three walls of "good" dreams. The students covered the windows with colored tissue paper, an innovation that made the light softer and more dreamlike (Stretch and Explore; Express; Understand Art Worlds).

JUNIOR SHOWS   (EXAMPLE 15.3)

Every year, the juniors at BAA create a cafeteria show which lasts only as long as a lunch period. Mónika Aldarondo developed this idea, and it has endured. For instance, one year students made an inflatable sculpture—a giant fort made of plastic and packing tape inflated with fans with rooms and connecting tunnels their fellow students could enter and explore (Develop Craft: Technique; Stretch and Explore); in another they did a performance piece where artists ate "dirt" (i.e., pudding and mashed Oreos) from flower pots they had placed on the lunch tables.

Juniors often conduct additional exhibitions outside of school. Kathleen shared an example of a less than successful student-led public exhibition. BAA students curated a show at a farmer's market in an upper-middle class area, with the theme of neighborhood. Students meant for the show to reveal the qualities of the students' often much less well-off neighborhoods (Express; Understand Art Worlds: Communities). However, they did not adequately study the space and envision the show, so when the work was hung, the space did not feel activated. The signage was inadequate and the works seemed to just hang there without context, so the market shoppers did not get a sense of their theme (Develop Craft: Technique, Express; Reflect, Understand Art Worlds). Kathleen told us that while it is difficult for a teacher to let an exhibition fail because it is so public, it is important to resist the impulse to rush in and fix it. She firmly believes that the work has to stand in all its nakedness in order for students to grow (Stretch and Explore, Understand Art Worlds, Reflect: Evaluate).

A SENIOR SHOW   (EXAMPLE 15.4)

For senior shows, Boston Arts Academy students, in collaboration with their teachers, select their work to be shown, organize the display, and collectively hang their work. Students write artists' statements that are posted on their school blogs. Artists and art educators from outside the school are invited to a solo review for each senior (Understand Art Worlds: Communities). Faculty select external reviewers for their expertise in art and art education (Reflect: Evaluate; Understand Art Worlds: Community). Reviews are held in the gallery in front of the students' displays, and reviewers have familiarized themselves with the students and their work before the review begins. During reviews, students give a short, prepared presentation that addresses themes, process,

formal elements, and connections to contemporary and historical art. Reviewers comment, challenge, and raise provocations. Reviewers hold the students to a high, professional standard. They write comments on a form designed to be general enough to embrace the wide diversity of presentations and work while still ensuring that students address the fundamentals for this graduation requirement (Understand Art Worlds: Communities; Reflect: Evaluate).

Examples from Walnut Hill

Jim Woodside Reflects on Exhibition at Walnut Hill. Exhibition is an important part of the culture and rhythm of the Walnut Hill School (WH). Jim describes their exhibitions as more like a studio visit than a museum show. Exhibition is a way for students to see their work in relation to the work of others and a way to share their work with the school community. Regular exhibitions contribute to a school culture focused on the arts.

Jim believes that it is important for students to see that their teachers are working artists who produce art. Every fall a faculty exhibition of new work is the first exhibition of the year. The faculty show is an opportunity for students to view their teachers' most recent work and a chance to see examples of formal gallery installations.

Students learn how to create exhibitions themselves by working side by side with their teachers to select and mount their own work. Learning is through mentorship rather than through explicit courses, a model Jim describes as "organic," with an emphasis on process that "ties in with the way things are done at the school." Jim believes that students who are at the school for 3–4 years "learn by seeing." New students quickly catch on: "They just pick it up by experiencing it and by the January show they have a good sense of how the show works. They just know this is something artists do: They exhibit their work."

By the time students are seniors they select work to be exhibited, install the exhibit, and handle publicity and the reception. Jim believes students learn by working with someone who knows the process: "Students have to learn what works. It's not a science. We're not at all bashful about telling them we like everything, but they really should change that piece. Students learn from their mistakes."

END-OF-TERM EXHIBITIONS   (EXAMPLE 15.5)

Every term at Walnut Hill there is an exhibition of work created during that term. Jim describes this as an "open house festival." He tells students that the show is an opportunity to show off their work and show off the department: "The show is 100% an extension of what we do during the term and the icing on the cake is a party to celebrate students' achievements." Even if he had a huge gallery space, Jim says, he would not want to make this show more formal.

The selection process is shared between teacher and students. With each student, Jim goes through the portfolio of their work, and together they choose five to seven pieces from which Jim then chooses final selections for the show. To start the conversation, Jim asks students to choose which pieces are weak and which they really like. He says the two or three pieces students pick for each usually coincide with what he would pick, but if not, they talk about it and what to do: "Sometimes all it takes is to crop the drawing a bit." As the conversation unfolds, Jim reflects with each student on the quality of individual pieces, the student's progress for the term, and the process of choosing work for exhibition.

Some students may have more work in the show than others. Jim tells students, "This is not a scorecard. Some of you will have more pieces in the show and some fewer." He tries to explain, "This is not only about showing individual pieces. It's showing off the art department as a whole to the community, other departments, and outsiders."

Installation of the student shows helps students learn more about Exhibition. Teachers direct installation of the show and students help with the physical installation. While installing work, teachers and students talk about what it takes to arrange and hang a show. Jim describes installation as an opportunity for students to learn from their teachers: "Students don't have a good understanding of what this takes, so they learn in the process." Every piece has a label so students all know who did what work. Jim stresses to students that they have to be willing to talk about their work.

Student work hangs in the gallery and throughout all the studios. Work in the show varies according to what the class worked on during the term. Teachers often group together work that responds to a particular assignment, sometimes writing an explanatory paragraph about that assignment. For some assignments this is really important. For example, without a label explaining that the work was from a class in which Jim asked students to draw with markers and crayons, a viewer might think the work was done by young children. In fact, Jim was encouraging students to think back to when they were children and to think of their drawings as play. In this case, then, the grouping was a demonstration of how Jim taught the process of making.

On the evening of the opening, there is a reception for the show that is attended by the entire school community and by parents who live locally. The show is advertised on all school calendars. A parent organization that raises money during the year arranges for refreshments. Every student is given a card when entering and is required to write something about a piece in the show. As students leave the show, they are required to turn in the card. After the opening, the cards are distributed to each exhibiting student as responses about their work. Comments vary, ranging from the useful and thoughtful to the cursory "I like it."

Jim gave the following summary of the show at the end of each term:

> It's a big, kind of goofy festival and not like going to a museum. It's as close to a performance atmosphere as we can get it. Kids who see it think "Wow! This is great!" and the student artists take pride in their work. It's a good way to complete the semester. It's not about the preciousness of the art work. It's about being able to see everything uncluttered, the work that stands out. The context is conducive to viewing.

A SENIOR SHOW   (EXAMPLE 15.6)

Every spring at WH, students in the Senior Studio Class show their work. Each show features 2–3 students, so the number of shows varies depending on the size of the Senior Studio Class. Like the End-of-Term shows, Senior shows are also part of the school culture and an event eagerly awaited on campus. Work is installed in the art building gallery, a setting with pristine white walls and track lighting. Each show has a formal opening attended by large crowds. Jim describes these shows as more like a formal gallery show: "Everyone knows the opening is like a happening. The opening, which includes music, is much more like a gallery opening than are the end-of-term exhibitions."

The work is only up for a short time, typically going up on a Monday or Tuesday and coming down at the end of the week. The students do all the work for their show—they select work, install and deinstall it, write labels, create advertising flyers that they hang around campus and in town, and get the information to the office to be included in the calendar. Jim notes that by senior year, teachers have solid relationships with students and students have had a great deal of experience working with their teachers on shows.

KOREAN STUDENT SHOW IN KOREA   (EXAMPLE 15.7)

Every spring when they return home for spring break, the many Korean students who attend WH show their work in Korea. One month before the show, Jim ships two to four pieces per student to a framer in Korea. Parents pay for the framing. The show is only for two-dimensional work (to keep shipping expenses down). Choosing work for this show is done in the same way as for the end-of-term student shows—Jim and a student reflect together while looking through the student's portfolio, and they select a group of work from which Jim makes the final selections. However, there is one difference: Jim finds it's sometimes hard to present a variety of work, because students are very concerned about what they want their parents to see.

Like the end-of-term student shows at the school, the Korean show is a big event with a festival-like atmosphere. Both the show and opening draw large crowds of parents, friends, and former graduates. For the Korean community, the show is a celebration of the students and their work.

These examples of Exhibition from Walnut Hill and Boston Arts Academy share many features, yet they are also different in a number of important ways. There are certainly many more possible ways to teach Exhibition to students, and each school will develop its own culture around public display of student work. But the examples are meant to catalyze readers' thinking about how Exhibition is an essential component of artistic learning. While Exhibition trains all of the Studio Habits of Mind, each habit is fostered somewhat differently though Exhibition than through other classroom experiences. When students learn about Develop Craft (or any of the other habits) in the context of an Exhibition, they learn something different from what they typically learn in other studio classroom experiences, something that expands their artistic minds. Whether students go on to careers as professional artists or to non-art careers, the Exhibition structure offers a context for understanding more about what art is and is for, what it takes to do it well, and how to convey its meaning effectively to broader publics. When the Exhibition structure is under-taught, as it is in many schools, educators miss an opportunity to teach the rich facets of the Studio Habits of Mind.

SIXTEEN

Students as Contemporary Artists

Building Agency in the Studio

Making art involves using the Studio Habits of Mind in seamless combination with one another, and this means using a complex way of thinking. Even in a quick observational sketch, students may Observe, Envision, and Stretch & Explore as they make decisions about which vantage point to take. They may Observe, Develop Craft, and Engage and Persist as they work through the sketch. As they Envision next steps and Reflect their sketch, they might attend to a feeling or association (Express) that they want to amplify. They may also connect their observational exercises to what they know about how artists routinely hone their skills (Understand Art World). This integrative, layered use of the Studio Habits of Mind is even more evident when students develop complex works (and bodies of work) that involve multiple drafts, research into social issues, research into the work of other artists, and mining of their personal histories.

In Chapters 12 through 15, we have shown how teachers support learning by weaving Studio Habits of Mind within and across the Studio Structures. Though it is occasionally helpful to highlight a particular habit of mind, we consider the Studio Thinking framework as primarily an *integrative* tool. In this chapter, we argue that as students use the habits in an integrated fashion, they are building their agency as artists: developing their capacity to engage in creative processes where they find problems, form and refine *their* ideas, and learn to use techniques, tools, and materials to create increasingly self-directed artworks. That is, they take ownership of their artmaking and think and act like the contemporary artists they are.

HOW TEACHERS SUPPORT STUDENT AGENCY

With support of a National Endowment of the Arts Grant in 2018–2020, Kim Sheridan revisited the original Studio Thinking data to examine how the teachers profiled thus far in this book support students' agency. Here are some of the findings (for further details on the study, analyses, and findings, see Sheridan et al., 2022).

First, we found that studio art teachers use the strategies that researchers tell us support learner agency in non-arts classrooms. Reeve (2016) labels this body of research as "autonomy-supportive pedagogy," meaning the things teachers do to help students work more independently. Autonomy support does not allow pure freedom; rather, it balances freedom with sufficient support for the student to build the competency necessary to work on their own. The strategies Reeve and many other researchers have identified make intuitive sense: Teachers support students' autonomy when they provide meaningful choices, explain their rationale for decisions, take the students' perspectives into account, encourage intrinsic motivation, allow students to work at their own pace, and express a range of opinions and affect.

Comparing our subjects' teaching with the autonomy-supporting characteristics Reeves identifies, we found that the studio arts classes described in this book are highly autonomy-supportive. Over three-quarters of the studied interactions (n = 741) used autonomy-supportive strategies, and the teachers employed the full range of strategies. Across the Studio Structures, the three most frequent autonomy-supportive strategies seen in teachers' interactions with students were the following:

(1) *Taking the students' perspectives.* Teachers sought to understand what students thought and felt by observing and asking questions. Teachers supported students' autonomy by trying first to understand them and the ideas guiding their work.
(2) *Inspiring intrinsic motivation.* Teachers did not just assume students would come to art class inspired, but, rather, sought ways to tap their motivation (Engage and Persist) by providing opportunities to follow their interests and become intrigued by a prompt or a new way of working.
(3) *Providing rationale.* Teachers regularly explained the "why" of their directions, decisions and advice. This supports agency in two ways. First, teachers are not just

123

giving orders but are providing information so students can opt in. Second, this shows students how to decide when to use a given tool, technique, or approach so they can take control over their work. (Sheridan et al., 2022)

Building Artistic Agency in the Studio

Though studio arts teachers use many of the same pedagogical strategies that teachers in any discipline or area of study use, we found that supporting artistic agency was more deeply tied to studio teaching practices. The enacted studio curriculum—the day-in, day-out experience of students working on the complex activity of art as teachers watch and periodically encourage reflection, individually in Students-at-Work or collectively in Critique—builds students' agency as artists. And when we analyze these interactions, we find that they involve integrating past resources to inform present actions towards future goals—what can be called a *temporal view* of agency (Emirbayer & Mische, 1998; Holland et al., 1998). We think of this as a kind of time-traveling.

Agency in Art as Time-Traveling

If you look at an artist's action on an artwork at any given moment, you usually see some kind of mark-making (whether it's a mark on paper, a keystroke in a digital file, or a touch that shapes a 3D form). But to make a mark competently at any given moment, artists draw on all sorts of past resources: their prior knowledge and skills, the way they have chosen to focus their attention in this current work, the problem they have posed to themselves. They are also looking toward the future—envisioning and playing with possible directions for the piece, constructing possible narratives (visual and verbal) for their ideas. Even with something as simple as an observational drawing exercise, artists may draw on *past* resources as they begin to sketch: They know they have done this before, and they know they need to look from different vantage points and think about size and scale. As they make their marks, they are also looking to the *future*, imagining moods, making free associations, mentally playing out what would happen if they made one part darker, larger, or smoother. Each *present* moment of artmaking involves this kind of time travel to the past and the future, whether we are consciously aware of it or not. Each present action on an artwork shifts what past resources become relevant and inspires new future imaginings.

Holding all this together on their own is challenging for students (for anyone, really!). One pedagogical

approach to this challenge could be to keep assignments very structured and simple, tiny exercises to teach students step-by-step and slowly build competence, hoping that the steps eventually add up to an agentive, artistic practice. Or, teachers could give up artmaking altogether and just have students learn to appreciate what other artists have done. But neither of these is what we see happening in studio art classes. Instead, teachers help students launch into the full artmaking time travel process, and then they strategically support students' attention to *past* resources, and co-imagine with them *future* possible trajectories, all with the goal of keeping students engaged with their artwork in the *present*. Thus, to support students' agency, teachers strike a balance between open-endedness and structure, guided by their insights into students' perspectives. Teachers remind students of past resources they can use, encourage them to pause periodically to reorient, and co-envision future possibilities for their work with them.

Dynamically balancing open-endedness and structure. To build artistic agency, students need enough freedom to make decisions and shape their own artwork, but enough structure so that they can find a problem to work on and learn how to use a range of tools, concepts, and other resources in art to solve problems they pose (Sawyer, 2017). In Demonstration–Lectures, we see how teachers often provide just enough structure so students can begin working productively. They may pose a prompt or assignment that identifies the terrain to travel, introduce new resources (concepts, skills, techniques, tools), and point to past resources that might be relevant. Then, as students take the assignment in different directions, with different levels of understanding, confidence, and engagement (or, at times, sputter and fail to start at all), teachers dynamically adapt the degree of structure in their interactions as needed with individual students. In Chapters 12–14, we see many examples of teachers' dynamic adaptations.

Deeply taking the student perspective. A teacher's dynamic adaptation to the right level of structure often involves watching how students are approaching a project, seeing how it connects to what they have done in the past, and asking them questions about what they are doing and where they are thinking about going. To support artistic agency, teachers try to get inside students' thinking about their work before making suggestions. If you look back through the quotations in this book, you frequently see teachers asking questions that surface a student's thinking so that teachers can understand the student's perspective. We have focused on how these questions encourage students to Reflect: Question and Explain, but from a

BOX 16.1. TEACHERS SCAFFOLD STUDENTS' "TIME-TRAVEL" PROCESS

For a repeating unit sculpture, Jason pauses a student's making process to focus her attention on a *past* decision—to make the unit of a wing—that has a lot of potential. He invites her to imagine a wider range of possible futures for its use in her work. Earlier, we linked this to building the habit of Stretch & Explore (Chapter 10, Figure 10.1), but Jason is also supporting her disposition to pause to mine her *past* decisions and to envision a range of possible *future* trajectories to inform her *present* action of the next mark she makes on the clay—what we see as helping

her build artistic agency. She has initial ideas; Jason supports her ideation process in these moment-by-moment ways as she works. Teachers scaffold students' thinking dozens of times each class session, thousands of times each year. As Jason explains, agency is the goal: "What I don't want to do is give them the recipe for making art, because there is no real recipe. I want to give them the tools so that they can be innovators and come up with *their own* problems and *their own* solutions and *their own* questions."

 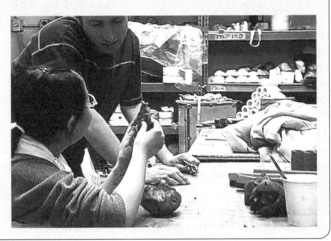

perspective of supporting students' artistic agency, this insight into students' thinking helps teachers support them without controlling their work.

Reminding about past resources. As students are working, teachers regularly remind individuals and the group about relevant past resources—things they have already learned that they can draw upon. These resources can be physical (e.g., tools or materials they have learned to use), relational (e.g., a prior conversation, a regular practice in the studio community), or ideational (e.g., a concept or idea, a skill) (Nasir & Cooks, 2009). As students work on the complex time-travel process that is artmaking, teachers point their attention to what they already have in their toolkit, the habits of mind, skills, techniques, ideas, tools, and interests that will help solve the problems of the moment. Teachers don't load up a full packing list of resources in advance, because it is through students' own actions and decisions that particular past resources become relevant or useful. Suggesting resources "just in time" in response to students' actions and choices helps students become alert to which resources are relevant when, building both the

dispositional aspects of the habits of mind and their artistic agency. (See Box 16.1 for an example.)

Pausing the Present. During artmaking time-travel, it is important to periodically press pause to reorient. Students might pause and ask for help when they have lost track of where they are going in a piece or don't know what resources will help them get to where they envision. Teachers might initiate this pause if they think the student would benefit from reflection. In both individual consults in Students-at-Work and mid-process Critiques, teachers and students regularly interrupt their present work to Reflect. As we have discussed in earlier accounts of Students-at-Work, teachers show care in whether, when, and how to interrupt a student's work process. Often, if a student is engaged in work, teachers just observe, discern the direction they are going, and let them keep at it. But these interruptions help build agency; they encourage students to take periodic moments to assess what they have just done (past resources in the work) and consider what else they might do (envisioning future possibilities). Students become more mindful in their artmaking. We have shown how students and teachers draw on a range of habits of mind in these consults, but learning to pause is, itself, an important learned practice. Students eventually internalize this practice of periodically reorienting in their artistic process, which is central to building their agency as artists.

Co-envisioning future possibilities. Artmaking involves continually reimagining the future. Each mark reorganizes the future possibilities for a work. When teachers pause the students' artmaking process, they often join in with them in a sort of improvisational imagining, envisioning together future directions the work could go. Sometimes this is playful: When Beth helped students imagine how to approach their assigned ritual vessels (e.g., cup to drink from the fountain of youth, container of milk for a wild beast), they had light conversations about possibilities for how to show what the cup was for, how to tempt a wild beast. This imagining future directions is rarely prescriptive. Both teachers and students use a lot of "maybes" and "I wonders" to express their ideas. The conversation is about the important process of pausing to *consider* future possibilities, not an attempt to lay a precise course.

Sometimes, however, teachers take a more directive stance. For example, when a student is feeling lost or disoriented, teachers suggest the next few things they should do to get back on track in their work. Though this teacher directiveness might seem to (and possibly could) undermine student agency, the students are still the makers of the work; they interpret and choose whether and how to use and enact the teacher's directions. Directions that help move a student from frustrated, confused inactivity back to the creative process can at times support agency, just as leaving confused students to find their way on their own can undermine agency. Each time studio teachers intervene in students' artmaking, they need to be mindful of whether their directions are supporting students' artistic agency—their capacity to form, refine, and enact their ideas—or whether their directions are inhibiting students from being able to express their own vision.

Language and Agency

Art teachers have to manage many students, tools, materials, and activities. Given this pressure, it is easy to become controlling. Studio teachers regularly use controlling language, such as *commands*, "Take out your paper and sketch three ideas"; what linguists call *modals of obligation*, "You have to step back and look"; or a little more gently, *requests*, "I want you to think about lines." This sort of controlling language may often be the clearest, most direct way to communicate, or it may be necessary to

keep a whole class functioning in a smooth way. However, to support students' agency, language that frames students as agentive should predominate over controlling language (Reeve, 2016). Agency is embedded not only in *what* we say, but even in the grammatical structure of how we frame ideas (Konopasky & Sheridan, 2016). We discussed above how teachers' language supports agency when they explain their rationale for directions and decisions and ask students questions about their thoughts and ideas to gain insight into their perspective. We also found two other ways in which teachers' language supports students' agency as artists: speaking as an artist and narrating students' agency.

Speaking as an artist. When teachers issue commands, they implicitly draw on the authority in their role; when they make requests, they draw on their relationship with students. But when teachers frame advice in terms of their own thinking, they subtly affirm that they, too, are artists forming ideas about a student's work or work processes. When a teacher frames their advice to students with "I think," "I wonder," "I notice," or "If this were my work, I might . . ." they indicate that they are a fellow artist, engaged in an artistic thought process, drawing on their own artistic experiences to make meaning of the student's work. Teachers may have expertise from a longer period of artmaking, but the student has the expertise of being the creator of the work being considered. The teacher becomes a partner in thought (Tabak & Baumgartner, 2004). When teachers use this framing language, they subtly reinforce the idea that art is about thinking, decisions, and possibilities, and not about getting it right or pleasing an authority.

Narrating students' agency. Teachers support students' agency by regularly narrating them as agentive. Throughout this book we see how teachers describe students' artworks as records of their thoughts, ideas, opinions, interests, actions, and decisions. They say things like, I see powerful decisions being made, or you figured out how to mold that idea, or you're finding a way to draw here that's your own. Artwork is not inert. It is a record of students' thoughts and actions, and it is an arena to think about the artists' future directions (Sheridan, 2020). Teachers link properties and concepts they notice—the "believability" of a figure, expressiveness of a space, power of a work—to the actions and decisions students made, the thoughts and interests they had. In contrast, when teachers talk about the work as an isolated, apparently self-generating object, they reduce the students' sense of themselves as active artists. Teachers narrate the student's agency most fully when they link the properties of the artwork to the thoughts and actions

of the student who made it and to the effects that it has on the viewer: "I feel a sense of tension from your decision to put this figure so large in the foreground," narrates student agency more than, "The large figures in the foreground create tension."

When teachers' language acknowledges the agency embedded in any work, they also highlight that what has come to be in the artwork is a result of many moments of students using such habits as Express, Envision, Observe, Reflect, and Stretch and Explore. Language that supports artistic agency highlights the kinds of thinking—the habits of mind—that students use. (See Box 16.2.)

STUDENTS ARE CONTEMPORARY ARTISTS

We have focused on how teachers support and students build agency *in* the studio classroom, but as shown in the discussion of Exhibition in Chapters 3 and 15, students also learn to put their work out to a larger world. Exhibiting one's work connects to the habit Understand Art World, and it is also a manifestation of agency. We develop and express agency within domains and through

participation in communities (Holland et al., 1998; Lave & Wenger, 1991). Students express their agency when they take on active roles in particular communities (Sheridan et al., 2013). Agency is not simply the freedom and competency to act independently; rather, we develop and express agency through relating to others doing similar work (Ryan & Deci, 2000). Understanding Art Worlds includes understanding yourself as an artist in that world.

Your students are contemporary artists: They are experiencing, thinking about, living in, and working in a particular time and place as they make their art. Your students' works will reflect their age and skill, of course, but their works confront the same issues as that of other contemporary artists.

All artists are aware of the same broad social issues—racism, immigration, climate change, political polarization, pandemics, globalization, economic inequality. These issues inform and motivate much artwork today. Students and established contemporary artists are encountering and experimenting with the same new technologies and using the same social media tools for sharing their work. Students' experiences of these social issues and new

BOX 16.3. *STUDENTS ARE INCREASINGLY SELF-DIRECTED*

By senior year, students are working on self-directed bodies of work in consultation with teachers. As this Walnut Hill senior describes her large-scale sculptures, she recounts decisions in particular works and patterns in what she has noticed about her style and her artistic process (e.g., "I love repetition"; "I pick ways of building things that are very tedious, very meticulous"). When she compares the body of work in her senior show with her earlier art, she frames it in terms of agency: "It has more of me and more of my thought process in it."

When this BAA senior describes his series of work, *Representation of My Life,* his love of painting process comes through—he notes how he uses texture, layering, and transparency to get varying effects. He explains: "Some of it was done intentionally and some of it not. It was unintentional at first, but then once it happened, it became intentional. I saw the effect and tried to repeat it, use it, refine it." That is, he paused his *present* making to reflect on *past* actions and to envision possible futures. In doing so, he enacted his agency as artist.

  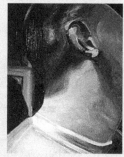

technologies are shaped by their adolescent contexts and personal concerns, and of course they bring this lens to their forms of contemporary art.

The art world and art education have changed since we first began studying the teachers profiled in this book, and they will continue to evolve. The resources the teachers used then to help students build their agency through connecting to a broader art world are different from those currently being used. Students now have far more access to contemporary artists and art practices. They can follow artists they like on social media and see not just their works in the museum but their day-to-day thoughts and responses to the world. Resources such as Art21 have built up an impressive collection of videos of artists working and talking about their work. This wealth of resources on artists' current practices and approaches

is transforming art education practices and helping to forge students' connections to contemporary art (Gude, 2004; Marshall et al., 2021).

We have argued that the Studio Habits of Mind are general dispositions, ways of thinking that characterize the artmaking of preschoolers all the way up to adult professionals. These habits are therefore good tools to help students see connections between their own ways of working and the ways of contemporary artists. To support agency, contemporary art cannot be considered as inert, distanced examples. Rather, contemporary art can be presented to students as ways to get the inside view on how other artists think about their work and engage in their creative processes. In short, contemporary artists become models for what it means to think like and be an artist in the current world.

Part IV

STUDIO THINKING IN CONTEMPORARY PRACTICE

So far you have been reading primarily about the practices of five artist-teachers from two high schools that formed the original research of this book. In the years since our original study, artist-teachers, researchers, and others have built upon this work by using the framework in distinctive ways and in diverse contexts. In the next three chapters, we share the experiences and perspectives of just a few of the people and organizations who are using the framework in varying ways. We outline who they are, what they are doing, and how we are learning from collaborating, observing, and talking with them. Our hope is that these stories of contemporary practices with the Studio Thinking Framework help readers to envision how you might use the framework in your own art, teaching, and research.

Looking across practices, we are first struck by how Studio Thinking is both a frame for thinking about art and a frame for thinking about teaching and learning. For instance, Steve Locke, Professor at Pratt Institute in Brooklyn, New York, describes the Studio Thinking Framework as the window that makes apparent the connection between his art practice and his teaching. Building on this idea, we spoke with seven artist-teachers working in different contexts about how the Studio Thinking Framework informs their artistic

practice and their teaching practice. In Chapter 17, we share their stories, which focus on how they have evolved as artists and as teachers and how they use the Studio Thinking Framework to inform and reflect on the intersections between their teaching and art practices.

Next, in Chapter 18, we look at how artist-teachers grapple with a topic that is often vexing in the arts: assessment. Formative assessment has been an underpinning theme throughout this book—studio teachers engage in continual ongoing assessment of students' learning as they observe what their students do, make, and say or write. This chapter delves more explicitly into ways that the Studio Thinking Framework helps artist-teachers think about assessment of learning in the arts. We focus on the perspectives of four artist-teachers who have thought deeply about how to create assessment practices that are fair and that honor the complexity of thinking and learning in the arts.

In our closing chapter, we look more broadly at how the Studio Thinking Framework is used by a range of educators and researchers in visual art classes, across other art forms, and in contexts beyond studio classrooms. We reflect on how these different uses have shaped our understanding of the framework and how we envision its future.

Art by Danielle DeVellis's middle school students (top) and David Ardito's high school students (bottom)

SEVENTEEN

Artist-Teachers

Using Studio Thinking to Connect Artistic and Teaching Practices

Artist-teachers have two practices: artistic and teaching. We interviewed seven artist-teachers to learn how Studio Thinking might have influenced their teaching practices, expecting that we would also learn more about how they understood the relationship between their artistic and teaching practices. To this end, we posed two questions: Are there ways your artistic practice informs your teaching? Are there ways your teaching practice informs your artistic practice

ARTISTIC PRACTICE INFORMS TEACHING

All artist-teachers said their artistic practice informs their teaching. Responses from Danielle DeVellis ("I want to practice what I preach") and Jaimee Taborda ("I think the two are hard to separate") convey what is central to many answers: empathy, an implicit, felt equality of the student's and teacher's experience. David Ardito describes the relationship in this way:

> When you're a working artist, you have empathy toward the making process, toward that student's making process. You can feel it. You can feel what that student's going through, because you've just been through it. So you just know it, and that helps you know how to help that student. (David Ardito)

Bryce Johnson based his teaching on his artistic practice:

> I was making that work at the same time I was developing curricula, so the curriculum actually mirrors the steps that I went through. It was really powerful to create curriculum in that way, because I would go through a step in my art practice and would then write steps to help students go through that process. (Bryce Johnson)

Kimberley D'Adamo saw her artistic practice as a way to help students see art as a conveyer of meaning:

For me, I use art as a way of making complexity visible and providing an entryway for people who are new to the conversation. What I want kids to learn if they're interested in art, or even if they're interested in medicine or in engineering, is that art can be a way that they can explore ideas and then make those ideas and their thoughts accessible to other people outside their head. (Kimberley D'Adamo).

TEACHING PRACTICE INFORMS ARTISTIC PRACTICE

All the teachers thought their teaching practice also informed their artistic practice. Some answers were general, like David Ardito's: "I really believe teachers learn as much from students as students learn from them, maybe even more." Others recalled a specific example:

> This year one of my kids suggested using translucent rice paper and thin bamboo sticks in a project. I had been using chicken wire when I was in college for these big 3D wall installations I'd been doing. And I was, "Wow! I wish I'd known about this when I was trying to bend and cutting myself on chicken wire. I could have tried this out with the bamboo and rice paper." (Danielle DeVellis).

Sometimes, the sheer multiplicity of ideas that students generate feeds the teacher:

> I feel like when you make something, there are tons of choices you can make. Having students go through a similar process, invariably, they make different choices about what they decide to turn the camera on. They've all made different choices, so you start to think: What choices could I make? And it's really kind of fun, because you get to see the power of potential outcomes. It's like shopping with someone else's money. It's really a lot of fun. (Bryce Johnson).

Or a teacher can position herself directly as a member of the students' Art Worlds, with her own practice benefitting:

> Occasionally I'll share my work with my students, or I'll sit down and work on something at the same time they're working on something, so they can see that I'm not just their teacher—I'm an artist, too. I might ask them for feedback, so I feel that being a part of this community of artists is part of what impacts my practice. (Jaimee Taborda).

TWO PRACTICES: NURTURING THE RELATIONSHIP

The artist-teachers' answers made us wonder how the connection between artistic and teaching practices can be nurtured and whether Studio Thinking might support that. Their answers emphasized the dispositional elements of *inclination* and *alertness*. To make a mode of thinking habitual, you must practice, which means you need the inclination to stick to making art and the alertness to recognize when to use a particular mode of thinking.

One way to practice nurturing both artist and teaching practices might be to look intentionally for opportunities to have one practice inform the other: Can investigating different media for teaching or remembering something that happened in class open up ideas for one's work? Or can one's work suggest new ideas for teaching? Some artist-teachers described opportunities to apply the Studio Habits of Mind as support for that, and two did so in contexts outside what is commonly considered art.

> When I'm out there in my garden, I'm looking and watching it every day and observing to understand how to respond. I'm reflecting to understand what it looked like a week ago and what needs to happen. And you're stretching and exploring when you're trying to clip things here and clip things there—it's just that engaging and persisting in trying to grow things is a huge tool that comes

into play and also understanding the world of plant life. (Trena Noval)

> I think my art practice is a living practice, just living my every day through creativity and with an artistic eye. I've been able to create a life and a life style that is truly artistic and authentic to what I am in every aspect. With my mother, I've created a beautiful paradise in my backyard that's just gorgeous. It's a living art piece that's constantly growing and evolving, and all the Studio Habits of Mind go into it. Sometimes I just sit there and observe there's more sun here or more shade, so when I get a plant I have to make sure it's a plant that fits this location. (Natalia Dominguez)

Trena and Natalia's comments suggest that everyday contexts such as gardening, decorating a home, and cooking could be places to practice the habits of mind. If teaching full-time time makes it hard to seamlessly continue making art (which it often does), might an "everyday practice" be another place to work on what is central to artistic thinking? We think so. There is no one way to nurture artistic thinking, and what is important is to be alert to opportunities, in or out of the studio, to practice studio habits of mind and to engage with them to build one's artistic thinking toolbox.

This next section describes how the seven artist-teachers we interviewed believe Studio Thinking influenced their teaching practice. The seven featured here differ in backgrounds, teaching practice, and geographic location. Their years of experience differ, too, from recent graduate Danielle DeVellis, who used Studio Thinking to set up her classroom as a studio, to teachers with many years in schools. Their relationships to Studio Thinking vary. For some it is foundational, laying a groundwork for artistic thinking in the classroom. Others use it explicitly in planning, teaching, and reflection. And one experienced teacher has not embraced it fully, but sees parallels to her focus on her students' thinking and the language she uses when talking with them.

(Continued on page 135.)

David Ardito

David is the K–12 Director of Visual Art for Arlington Public Schools, Arlington, Massachusetts. His position includes supervising 14 K–12 art teachers in their teaching practices and curriculum development. He also advises high school juniors and seniors on portfolio development and college admissions. Prior to becoming K–12 Visual Arts Director, David taught at the high school and middle school levels for many years. His artistic practice includes sculpting in a variety of materials including wood, metals, and found objects.

Kimberley D'Adamo

Kimberley taught in California public schools for 22 years, first at Frick Middle School in Oakland and then at Berkeley High School. She is currently a lecturer and doctoral student at the University of Nebraska, Lincoln, where she is charged with integrating creative thinking across the curriculum for pre-service teachers. Kimberley conceives of her own art practice as a means of inquiry and social practice. Her website, Teaching Thinking, is at artasresearch.org.

Danielle DeVellis

Danielle teaches grades 6–8 at Olive Vista Middle School, Sylmar, California. She is a recent graduate of a master's program in which she intentionally combined two areas, art education and painting; by the end, she had moved into sculpture and carpentry. Her last piece was a 5′ × 5′ box, for which she made a series of many interior boxes to fit the roughly 80 objects she collected from family members. She describes the piece as a "deep dive" into families: an estranged family, a close family, a family you barely see.

Natalia Dominguez

Natalia is a grades K–5 art teacher at South Hills Elementary School, Fort Worth, Texas. She describes her art practice as "a living practice, just living my every day through creativity and with an artistic eye." "I've been able to create a life and a lifestyle that is truly artistic and authentic to what I am in every aspect—from my cooking, to organizing, to flower arranging, to baking." Recently, Natalia turned her backyard into an installation that started with paintings on fence panels and grew to include an intimate patio, table, and plantings—a space that she envisions will continue to grow and evolve. She continues to work with media including performance and photography, her media of choice while in college.

Bryce Johnson

Bryce teaches Digital Storytelling in the Digital Arts and Technology Academy at Cathedral City High School, Cathedral City, California. In California, academies are public schools within a school. Seventy-five percent of his students are minority, at-risk students. Prior to teaching, Bryce started his own photography and videography business. Bryce is currently making short autobiographical films and oral stories investigating heritage and family to answer some personal questions, some of which deal with love and belonging within the context of the Black community.

Trena Noval

Trena describes herself as an educator, researcher, and artist who is interested in how learning theories become creative practices that solve problems and surface voices that aren't traditionally heard. Currently she is working on a public art commission for the City of San Jose that poses the question: How does a city move toward change? At California College of the Arts, Trena teaches a course in interdisciplinary studio practice. She is also co-founder of Integrated Design for Education, Arts and Leadership (IDEAL), an organization that engages artists, teachers, and educational leaders in co-designing transformative learning spaces and communities.

Jaimee Taborda

Jaimee is a grade 8–12 art teacher at Oxford High School, Oxford, Massachusetts. She teaches two semester-long courses (Art Introduction and Ceramics) and two year-long courses (Art Studio and Advanced Placement Art). A recent body of work grows out of personal reflections as a White mother and wife to a family that is not White, in which she explores race, racism, and bias. She is working with encaustic painting (where colors are mixed with hot liquid wax). She eventually expects to include mixed media, combining encaustic painting on paper with sculpture using molds and casts.

DAVID ARDITO: MISTAKES AS PORTALS OF DISCOVERY

Students frequently complain that what they're working on isn't turning out as envisioned or that they have made a mistake. They don't know what to do next. They're stuck! David Ardito knows this feeling well: "When I'm making art, I can feel the studio habits raging through my process. Am I really stretching and exploring, am I taking chances and risks, am I using mistakes to my advantage—to me that's a big one. Just keep going."

We all would do well to heed David's favorite James Joyce quotation: "Mistakes are the portals of discovery." But seeing opportunities in mistakes is often hard; it's tempting to give up. As students work, David is alert to opportunities to help them learn to stay committed and keep going.

> To me, Engage & Persist is one of the most important habits. How many times do we as artists fall into getting stuck, not knowing where to go next? And how many times do we see students at that place? Teaching students to get unstuck, like you would in your own practice, is essential. Like saying, "What if you were to do this and this?"

Learning to reflect goes hand in hand with learning to sustain interest and effort toward one's work. As students work, David encourages them to take time to reflect, a habit he practices in his own work.

> One of the big things in my own work is to remember to always stand back and reflect, which is a

huge habit in my view. So when I see a student with their head buried in their work, getting too close, I feel that they're not reflecting enough about it; that's where they may be getting stuck or repetitive.

Often David draws on his own experience as an artist to help him understand what he sees, so he can respond to students. He describes this as "getting into the creative mind of students and figuring out where they are in their process."

To help students learn to reflect, David encourages them to think about their work from different viewpoints. Sometimes this is as simple as physically changing where they stand or putting work in a drawer, taking it out later to see it anew: "So I tell them, 'Stand up,'—first of all, stand up as much as you can when you work—and then 'Stand back,' walk 5 or 10 feet back from your work. 'Whether it's 3D or 2D, look at it from all sides.'"

Considering work from a different point of view need not always include a physical change of location. Using four pieces of cardboard to frame parts of a painting can suggest ideas, as can considering different perspectives on an event to suggest different ways to tell a story in a documentary or narrative work. The point is to look closely at the work and stretch to consider other possibilities—to observe with new eyes.

Just as teachers use conversation as a route to understanding a student's thinking, David uses questions and suggestions to encourage students to envision possibilities:

> So what I do with a student is take the student and their work out into the hall, away from all the

distractions of the classroom, and I have them look at their work from five feet away and ask, "What do you notice now? What's different about seeing it here?" And wow! Suddenly they get all kinds of ideas about what to do next. And I can back away, which is your goal, right? Get out of the student's head and let them make the decisions.

As an artist, David finds comments he calls "false praise" unhelpful. He believes that to be useful, what he says to students must be specific.

> Everyone wants to be positive, but I really believe that's not helpful at all. It may build some positive reinforcement, but saying something specific about the work is far better, never offering just one option, giving students a number of options so they can get unstuck. So that's critical to me both as an artist and as a teacher.

Envisioning different options is an important part of navigating James Joyce's portals of discovery. Students who complain that what they're working on is not turning out as envisioned have to learn to figure out on their own what to do to continue. They have to learn to think like an artist.

KIMBERLEY D'ADAMO: FINDING A FIT

Kimberley D'Adamo wants her students to think of themselves as contemporary makers using arts and imagery as a method of research to put together ideas and come to conclusions about important interdisciplinary questions. Prior to learning about Studio Thinking, Kimberley spent 12 years developing a structured approach that weaves together parts of several art education pedagogies and puts thinking at the center of the creative process

When Kimberley first learned about Studio Thinking, she didn't think it could contribute effectively to the learning goals she has for her students: "When I first became aware of the Studio Habits of Mind, it was through watching other teachers use them in their classrooms with their kids, and the way that they were using them didn't feel like it was a tool that would help with my pedagogy."

But with teachers in her school using Studio Thinking, Kimberley started to try on some of the language of the habits in her classes for structuring responses to students:

> I would use it almost like synonyms for other things. I would say that indicates a relationship there and that it helps widen the way kids can think

about what artists do. But I'm not exactly sure how it fits into my practice other than that I was starting to use some of the words in my probing questions.

So what might be next for Kimberley? She is interested: "I do find that I am starting to understand the Studio Habits of Mind in a different way and am attracted to the emphasis on artistic thinking." Over time she has also come to see the habits as a tool to use in structuring probing questions for students and encouraging dialogue during critiques.

How might the habits help Kimberley focus students on the thinking involved in using art making to research interdisciplinary questions and express their findings? Since Kimberley already has a well-developed approach, she initially may want to consider where the habits align with her existing goals and projects: How might the habits help her to more clearly focus students on their thinking? Where might she want to re-envision what she already does?

Kimberley enjoys coming up with different ways to teach the same thing: "I basically run experiments. I teach one way to one class and another way to another class. Then I look at the student work and their feedback, and think, 'What happened because of the different teaching moves that I made, and how does that help inform me?'" Trying out her ideas would be the next step, followed by reflection on how her experiment went with each class.

Reflection is a particularly helpful part of what Kimberley describes as a "really deep diving into a bunch of student work at any stage in the process, whether that be exit tickets, or reflections, or a project plan, or a finished product, or even a close observation of how they critique and why they talk about the things they do."

> That piece of taking time to reflect on student work and what is embedded in student work, and how that demonstrates something you did in your teaching or didn't do, is super important. So looking back at a project, I might be able to see in that project, "Oh, I forgot to do this with them," or, "They needed me to do this, but I didn't know it," because it was my first time and, as a result, I got a different set of results from my kids than I expected. I can look back at the work and see where the gap was.

Kimberley poses reflection as "core" to good teaching. She sees reflection as both a way of looking back and looking ahead to next steps.

> I think that cycle of reflection to me is one of the cores of good teaching, and one of the things

I love most about it. I love looking at student products or process and digging deep into that and seeing what I can learn about my own teaching to get better as a teacher. I think that's what teachers always do: We're always somewhere in that cycle of reflection.

DANIELLE DEVELLIS: MAKING A ROOM INTO A STUDIO

Recent graduate Danielle DeVellis faced challenges when she began teaching middle school: "You're by yourself and there's no one to help." The first few weeks were particularly difficult.

I had just started, and I had a list of IEPs [Individualized Education Plans] this thick. They give you massive packets, and I didn't know what I was looking for really. But I knew I had to read the accommodations. So I was going through all of them and making a chart just to make it a little easier. But no one tells you how to do that.

Classroom management was also a learning curve. While student teaching, her mentor teacher gave Danielle lots of freedom and purposely stepped back if things weren't going well. But this was different—there was no one to step in if needed.

Danielle did have a room to use for her classes; however, other than some materials shoved in a closet, there was no evidence of the room having been an art room. Nor was there a program on which to build, because there had been a series of 1-year art teachers.

I would say that I started to frame my understanding of what Studio Thinking and the Studio Habits were going to look like first by how I was going to set up my room. We spent a lot of time the first week talking about what we wanted it to look like, sound like, and operate. I wanted it to operate as closely as possible to a real studio.

As part of learning studio practice, students prepared their materials, cleaned up and stored their materials at the end of class, and helped students who needed assistance.

I wanted it to be someplace where students had a lot more autonomy in what they did and what they wanted to learn. I think the Studio Habits were particularly helpful, because they are about how you think and how you go about making your artwork.

Converting a classroom into a studio also meant helping students learn what artists do in a studio, how they work, the tools they use, and the things they think about. Danielle invited artists to visit, including a floral designer, a storyboard artist, an illustrator, and a cosplay artist who uses costumes and makeup to represent characters. Artists already scheduled for next year include a photographer and a muralist.

I think sometimes parents and kids are so, "I'm not going to be an artist, why am I doing this?" Or "I can't paint and I can't draw—I don't like art." So I tried to bring in outside people that would show them there are so many things you can do with art beyond school. And then we tie it back to the studio habits—what you're learning in an art classroom means you can do any number of these professions.

Prior to each class visit, Danielle talked to the guest artists about their presentations and sent a template for their slideshow. During visits, Danielle also asks questions and makes comments that tie the presentation to the studio habits.

I don't say what the studio habits are to the guest, but when I'm asking them to share certain things, they [the habits] are in the talking points that I ask them to address. When the floral designer came in, I wanted her to talk about the names of the tools that she uses. I wanted her to talk about an instance where she had a big mistake or some obstacle she had.

At the start of her presentation, the designer asked what students thought it meant to be a floral designer. Their response: "You pick flowers." She then showed images intended to show pieces very different from the table arrangements the students envisioned, including giant hanging wall installations and one designed for the Grammy awards: "'No, it's not as simple as just cutting them and sticking them in. I had to learn all these new tools. I had to use chicken wire, special foam, anchoring devices, and how to use this versus that.'"

Sometimes students also try to envision other aspects of the guest's life—"Is this what you wanted to do since you were little? Did your parents fully support you in this? How do you support yourself financially?"—all questions that Danielle hopes will help students to envision life beyond school.

NATALIA DOMINGUEZ: WORDS MATTER

Natalia Dominguez's students (whom she refers to as "artists-in-training") are learning to think and work like artists. For Natalia, the Studio Habits of Mind were "the light at the end of the tunnel" that gave her the language to help students develop the types of thinking they would need to truly take over their own creative process:

> A lot of people think that with little kids, they can't handle Studio Habits of Mind or they're not mentally there. Or their brains are not developed enough for them to handle it. But from working with little kids, I know that they can. I guess I'm going back to "words matter," and once you know the word to describe something, it's empowering. So the Studio Habits of Mind are a way to empower the abstract thinker.

For the past 3 years, Natalia's classes have been full student choice art studios organized around stations. Each station has visual instructions, written instructions, and suggestions.

> People think choice is a free-for-all. But it has to be structural. The Studio Habits of Mind are the structure to bring the abstract into something that we can hold, grasp, mold, and present. So for me, it wasn't intimidating—it was what I've been looking for. There is room for them to explore, to make mistakes, and learn from their mistakes, but there's a structure holding them and guiding them, and the way I have it is as if we're having a conversation, but it's in writing.

Stations for students in grades K–2 have a paper "passport" for going from station to station. The passport includes which stations are open and "I Can" statements based on the Studio Habits of Mind. Resources at centers are designed for a variety of learners. Natalia also designs presentations to help students understand the meaning of each habit. Additionally, Natalia talks with her students about their thinking and models reflection. Conversations with younger students often include gestures and acting: "We would come up with hand symbols for the habits like *I observe* [forms "glasses" with hands]."

Stations for students in grades 3, 4, and 5 are more complex and include an "Artistic Habits Guide." Students use this planning sheet to Envision their next project by sketching their idea and filling in the blank about their idea in words: "For the next six weeks my original art project will be [students fill this in]. . . ." They also decide

whether the project will be a drawing, a painting, mixed media, sculpture, or collage. In addition to envisioning, the planning guide includes questions focused on other habits of mind and checkpoints for students to use to decide on their own when their art is finished.

To be clear about the structure and learning goals of her classes, Natalia uses a spreadsheet to keep track of what works and doesn't. Each year she refines the spreadsheet in collaboration with her students. The spreadsheet includes the TEKS (Texas Essential Knowledge Skills) that are required by the state and the Studio Habits of Mind, the thinking she intends students to learn. Natalia describes the spreadsheet as "connecting the dots" to show how the two systems relate.

> Here in Texas, TEKS are a priority, so everything you're teaching to is, "What are the TEKS in it?" "What do the TEKS say?" I have to show my administrators that I am doing TEKS. I tell them I'm using Studio Habits of Mind in their projects, but, yes, TEKS are being covered. So everything I do, I point out, "This is a habit of mind; this is the TEKS that we're using." I also added the national standards in there as well.

The structure Natalia has developed is helping her K–5 "artists-in-training" become better able to connect the choices they make to their thinking, an important step in shifting control from the teacher to the students and allowing students to develop their own artistic voice. Next steps? Natalia has some ideas:

> In the curriculum, we're often still telling the kids which habit of mind we're using instead of the student saying, This is the habit of mind that I'm using. Where I'd like to be is that they say, "Today in art these are the studio habits I used," or as they're talking about their process they're able to say which studio habits they used without me putting that on them.

BRYCE JOHNSON: BALANCING CRAFT AND EXPRESSION

The vocational program where Bryce Johnson teaches digital storytelling provides students with professional or close-to-professional industry-level equipment that teachers must help them learn to use. Bryce Johnson is well-positioned to do this: He has a Career and Technical Education (CTE) teaching credential, which means he has industry experience in the area in which he teaches.

Initially, Bryce felt that he had to front-load craft heavily in his teaching: "You have high school students and you have all this expensive equipment. Your brain just goes to 'teach them how to use it so they don't break it.'"

Bryce learned about Studio Thinking while creating a new curriculum for his digital storytelling course. Although he does not usually use the language of Studio Thinking directly, the Framework confirmed for him the importance of students learning a process for thinking and working. He also came to trust the studio process more and reflect on the balance of craft and expression in his teaching and the value of in-process, just-in-time, informal Critique:

> I think oftentimes we artists just think about the big critique at the end when you sit down and all that. But what about walking around and looking over a student's shoulder and you say a little something—just recognizing the power in that, not just waiting for the big critique at the end but purposely putting in points where the work isn't done to speak to it.

When Bryce began to teach the reworked digital storytelling course, he had to adapt his curriculum to the constraints of remote learning during the COVID-19 pandemic. The limited availability of professional equipment meant that most of his students used free software and their phones, even the ones who had cameras. With his classes remote, his curriculum was "flipped on its head."

What initially seemed a loss turned out to be an opportunity for Bryce to reconsider how to teach craft in a way that focused more on expression and process: "It really pushed me as a teacher, because my program is well-funded—I usually have everything I need—but I had to say 'Hey, however you can make this, make it.' Now I know there are certain things I will do differently when I go back to the classroom."

Bryce's students produce a 2- to 4-minute autobiographical documentary film and a 3- to 6-minute podcast investigating some aspect of their self-care practice—e.g., eating better, working out more, getting more sleep. The goal of both projects is to use video and audio production toward expressive ends—creating products that are positive narratives around self-care:

> We know that when we make art about different issues in society it brings awareness to it. So if we make art in our own life about areas that we want to bring awareness to on a personal level, can that help make any significant change? If they

were to do this, if we were to, say, make a video about working out more, could that help them do it more?

After writing an initial "process paper" about ideas for films, students create storyboards, shoot their films, edit, critique, and re-edit to refine their stories. Bryce describes this process of envisioning, reflecting, and critiquing as "writing and then rewriting and writing even after the film is shot."

While the process he teaches is specific to making a film, Bryce intends students to learn "a methodology of learning and of doing artmaking they can apply to working in any medium." For the 10% of his students who go directly to film school and others interested in learning more about the technical side of film, Bryce imagines perhaps having an after-school or summer program. But for everyone else, Bryce is convinced that learning to develop a story will benefit students in whatever career they pursue.

Upon returning to in-person teaching, Bryce has some ideas for how to keep his students' attention on developing stories while at the same time making sure they have the necessary technical production skills:

> I feel it's not that the technical stuff is not important, but I think I'd rather start with the story and the content, and as we go, introduce the technical camera and editing skills. I'd like to create an environment where students can be more self-driven, and we spend more time on process, developing the idea, and writing and sharing.

TRENA NOVAL: USING THE STUDIO HABITS AS PROCESS

Trena Noval started using the Studio Habits of Mind while working with students and teachers around 2005. She soon saw the habits would be useful when working with groups in her community-based artistic practice. Can the Studio Habits of Mind inform the work of artists interacting with or in dialogue with communities? For Trena Noval, the answer is, "Yes."

> When I first learned about them, it was really exhilarating for me, because I felt it really does bring language to things that you see but you don't necessarily identify with language. And so it was a way to talk about how we were learning and understanding certain processes and practices. As I started to use them as an educator, they became deeply embedded in my mind, and now I see them everywhere in everything I do.

Trena describes herself as a guide using the habits to help students and adults craft futures for themselves, envisioning where they see themselves later in life and supporting them with the tools to get there. Trena includes listening as an important part of observation: "It's like developing a very deep observational practice—not only looking but also listening to voices."

In her work with communities outside of schools, Trena uses the habits to structure a process for members of groups as they talk together to figure out shared understandings going forward:

> It is a community process if we're all talking about what we're observing, and this is allowing us to reflect and envision new possibilities. When we're doing that together, it creates a common language and identifies things that are often not said or talked about. I think that when you can create a common language around an experience together, it deepens the experience, and it helps to see a pathway through to the next place.

"The Land and Me" (2017–2019), a collaborative project with Carol Mancke, illustrates how Trena uses the habits as a process of listening and observation during community discussions. The project was one of four chosen by the City of Santa Rosa as part of a Public Art Program seeking temporary art installations addressing the 2017 northern California wildfires that had destroyed much of the city. Trena describes Santa Rosa as "a city that was in mourning trying to figure out how to go forward, with the threat still lingering." Installations were to be in public places or within public view for one day or up to 3 months.

The Studio Habits were a way for the community to analyze and structure the process they wanted to take people through.

> One of the important things about the Studio Habits is that it's a way for us to move ourselves forward, to move learning forward. When you're teaching or working with others, or collaborating, having tools that move you through a process is a way of creating community and a process around it.

Publicity for the culminating engagement events describes "The Land and Me" as a traveling neighborhood-scaled public conversation and community performance. One invitation read, "Bring along your families, neighbors, and friends to note and celebrate some of the ways that the richly diverse Santa Rosa community has responded to the 2017 fires through renewed connections to the land." Many people did.

In reflecting on the series of public conversations and the final events, Trena describes ways that the habits were embedded in the process:

- We wondered how we could get people to turn back to land when it was the thing that took away everything. We used the studio habits as a research frame to understand how people were processing what had happened.
- We used reflection and observation to turn their gaze back to the land. Observe, envision, stretch & explore, engage & persist came into play as people were grappling with something that was really challenging and the many things that were lost.
- When you're looking at a place that is empty but once held something, you're remembering and observing at the same time. You're also engaging & persisting just to get to the place where you can confront the memory.
- It was also all envisioning—in the end we did three creative engagement events where people walked through a process that included a culminating event in which people could express what they were thinking and envision a new world, envision a new community.

JAIMEE TABORDA: NURTURING A COMMUNITY OF ARTISTS

Jaimee Taborda learned about Studio Thinking when she began to use Teaching for Artistic Behavior (https://teachingforartisticbehavior.org/), an approach (referred to as TAB) in which students come up with their own projects, just as artists do. Teachers using this approach often use the language of the Studio Habits of Mind as they consult with students. Jaimee describes the language of the Studio Habits of Mind as woven into the fabric of her classroom. "I feel that it's just a part of all of the things that we do all the time."

TAB teachers strive to nurture a community focused on thinking and creating like artists. In choosing work to show, Jaimee tries to include artists representing the 20% of her school who are not White: "I think it's important that we open up the narrative—that it's not just dead, old, White men who create art. It's way more than that." Jaimee found the habit Understand Art Worlds particularly helpful when researching artists, because giving students the opportunity to see artists who look like them is one way to do this:

I try to decenter the stereotypical White European "masters" and help expand the idea of what art is, because a lot of my students think art has to be a pretty painting of flowers or landscape or something like that. If you're not good at drawing realistically, then you're not an artist, and you're not good at art. I want to dismantle that idea.

To encourage digging more deeply into what she presents, Jaimee asks her students to reflect and connect their observations to expression. "What do you notice? What do you wonder? What do you think this piece is about?" Students write their responses in their sketchbooks and then pair up to share their responses. Students have learned to think about the habits when talking with each other in what Jaimee describes as "artist-to-artist conversations." Whether reflecting on work or responding to others, Jaimee encourages students to go beyond "I like it" or simply describing what they did.

To encourage helpful feedback, Jaimee models *actionable* feedback, responses on which students can draw for ideas as they continue the whole process of drawing, reflecting, and asking for feedback again. Her feedback often includes asking questions instead of making suggestions:

If the student is trying to make an abstract artwork about their feelings and I say, "I can't tell what it is," that's not helpful. That's where I might say, "Can you tell me what you're hoping for this piece? Oh, you want to create a work about your feelings. How important is it to you that the audience understands the feeling?" "Really important." "Have you considered what colors you might choose to make sure that people understand?"

Sometimes Jaimee pushes students to persist by asking them to consider other possibilities, as she did with a student who did something that took 5 minutes and called it a day:

I've noticed that a lot of your artwork has this small subject in the middle and then lots of empty space outside of it. I wonder what it would look like if you tried to fill up more of the space with the subject.

The simple phrase "I wonder" encourages students to envision possibilities and helps Jaimee not be seen as the sole person who has skills and experience. The resulting conversations are "more like I would talk with an artist friend."

For Jaimee, the explicit language of the studio habits has helped to make students aware of how they can grow as artists:

When I introduce the habits to students, I say these are all things that you already do. You might not do all of them well, you don't do all of them all of the time, but these are things that artists do. And having that awareness of them can help you to notice, "Oh, I haven't been stretching and exploring lately. Maybe I should try to do something different for my next piece."

The language of the habits has been particularly helpful talking with students about their own work:

I keep coming back to the language [of the Studio Habits]. It helps me to provide feedback and have conversations knowing that there are these eight habits that are universal for artists. It helps me to highlight them for students, so they can also become more aware of them as they work.

SEEING STUDIO THINKING ACROSS THE ARTIST-TEACHERS' STORIES

Looking across these seven artist-teachers' stories, we found several commonalities. Often, the teachers make connections among making, thinking, and understanding, as, for example, Bryce Johnson's students' uses of video to understand some aspect of their self-care practice with his goal of increasing their awareness and nurturing more commitment to better self-care.

We continue to see how important the language of the Studio Thinking Framework is to many. It helps students reflect on their thinking and learning. The Studio Habits of Mind language also can describe to others what it means for students to learn to think as artists, as Natalia Dominguez demonstrates for administrators concerned to see the relationship of the habits to the Texas state standards.

These artist-teachers' accounts show how learning to think like an artist can help students become more independent in their art practices. In describing a conversation with a student about his work, David Ardito says that the teacher's goal is being able to "back away." As described in Chapter 16, studio teachers support learners' agency as artists.

Several of the artist-teachers make connections between habits and contemporary concerns, as for example

Jaimee Taborda's selection of work by other than the traditionally valued "masters," and her inclusion of work representative of her students' cultures or communities. Additionally, these artist-teachers use an expanded meaning of some habits; for example, Trena Noval emphasized listening as a form of observation when working with students and communities, much as music educators do.

Finally, Kimberley's story is a good example of how, even for a very experienced teacher, it sometimes takes time to find the right fit with the studio habits. Kimberley sums up the importance of reflection in a teacher's journey: "I think that cycle of reflection to me is one of the cores of good teaching and one of the things I love most about it. We're always somewhere in that cycle of reflection."

EIGHTEEN

Assessment Is a Conversation

I am the ultimate arbiter of its success. I will look at my work and find that it either does or does not succeed in showing (according to my terms and understanding) how things really are, or how I need or want them to be, in order to express what I am after. Usually—nine times out of ten—my work falls short, which keeps me going to the next painting, and to the next.

—Christopher Chippendale

Assessment in the visual arts is complicated, and how to do it well is not obvious. Artists, as exemplified in the words of painter Christopher Chippendale (Groff, 2015), are always in the process of self-assessment. Students and teachers need to follow suit.

Assessment should reflect how well students are achieving the goals of learning, so let's start with what we see as the fundamental goal of arts education: teaching students to think as artists do.

Two questions arise from this perspective on assessment.

First, *how* do artists think?

And second, *why* should students, most of whom will not become artists, be assessed on how well they can think like artists?

The Studio Habits of Mind help with the first question. We believe that they are a "good enough" representation of how artists think to guide decisions about teaching, learning, and assessment. As revealed by practitioners later in this chapter, Studio Habits can support students while they are learning; they guide student self-assessment; and they can steer teachers' curriculum design and revision, especially when teachers reflect on the quality of curriculum by considering their students' learning. Assessing with the Studio Habits reminds both students and teachers to think more like artists.

To address the second question, consider that contemporary schooling has to prepare students for a world that is rapidly changing, that is threatened by a host of urgent social and environmental crises, and that offers access to more information of varied quality than at any other time in human history. An education that prepares students for such a world needs assessment that rewards disciplinary thinking and understanding, regardless of the area of study.

Visual art is, of course, one of the disciplines that helps us make sense of our world—the past, the present, and the possible futures. Just as schools help students who will not become mathematicians learn to appreciate mathematical approaches to understanding, history classes should get students thinking like contemporary historians who use history to face what is happening in the present, and science classes should ask students to think like contemporary scientists who address the world's current challenges, so should visual arts classes invite students to think like contemporary artists who grapple with perspectives about our current existence. Why? Because students need to understand the varied ways of thinking that the disciplines offer. Students need to appreciate how the arts are tools that can help us unravel the complex knots that are tightening across the world today. In a mathematics class, we should be assessing mathematical thinking. And in an art class, it is artistic thinking that needs to be assessed.

ASSESSING VISUAL ART

To assess how well students can think like artists and why that's important for every student, we need to use the clues students offer about what's going on in their minds—what they say, do, and make—and check these throughout the process of artmaking. We do so by using "ongoing" or "formative" assessment.

For every age of student, assessment needs to probe how well students understand the kind of thinking used by professionals in that domain, adjusted for student level. At the earliest stages, as David Perkins says in *Making Learning Whole*, students need to use "junior versions" to absorb the structure of each discipline, its "whole game" (Perkins, 2010). Assessment will be different for different domains, because teachers need to judge student understanding of each discipline's basic structures.

In 2007, the Council of Arts Accrediting Associations published *Achievement and Quality: Higher Education in the Arts*, laying out implications for assessment based on the aims, values, and practices around quality in postsecondary arts education. The report states that visual art needs its own form of assessment, not one borrowed from other disciplines, and we agree that each domain should assess students based on the particular focus of that domain:

> [Assessment in arts] must be based on a particular mode of thought and work used in the arts. Though deeply intellectual, artmaking works differently than research or scholarship in the sciences, humanities, or social sciences. (CAAA, 2007, p. 5)

The CAAA paper suggests three principles to keep in mind when thinking about assessing visual art.

1. Art is a mode of thought.
2. Assessment of quality must focus on individuals' uniqueness as artists, and the uniqueness of their artworks.
3. Both process and product should be assessed.

Studio Habits are a set of lenses for taking these three principles seriously. In *Studio Thinking from the Start: The K–8 Art Educator's Guide* (Hogan et al., 2018), we addressed assessment for K–8 teachers. There, we offered robust examples of formative assessment by tracking younger students over several years to show how assessment with Studio Habits track and support growth over time. The Council of Arts Accrediting Associations asserts for preprofessional education the same qualities that apply to assessment at primary and secondary levels. Studio habits support assessment aimed at the CAAA principles in at least four ways.

1. **The Habits Describe What to Assess: The Artistic Mode of Thought (Principle 1).**
   Taken together, the Studio Habits describe the ways artists think. Artists have developed *skill* in all eight habits, have the *inclination* (drive, passion, or motivation) to use the habits, and have the *alertness* (sensitivity to opportunities) to know when to employ any particular habit. The Studio Habits help teachers meet students where they are in their artistic development, guide them toward

increasingly sophisticated uses of each habit, and encourage combining multiple habits.

2. **Assessing with the Habits Addresses Uniqueness (Principle 2).**
   The Studio Habits offer enough structure to guide assessment, enough roominess to allow individuals to flourish, and a context against which to perceive what is unique. Because the Studio Habits have what David Perkins calls "optimal ambiguity" (Perkins, 1999, personal communication), assessing with them is less likely to "impose detailed rules [that] usually stifle art" (CAAA, p. 5). Defining what to assess *within each habit* is best left to individual teachers, who can support the uniqueness of each developing student and work.

3. **Assessing with the Habits Addresses Process (Principle 3).**
   Assessing final works alone, like assessing technique alone, is not enough. Assessment needs to address students' drafts, what they say or write about their work in journal reflections, critiques, and conversation, and how they act throughout the process of making; for example, how much autonomy they demonstrate, how they respond to "errors," or how they collaborate.

4. **Assessing with the Habits Supports Investigation (Principles 1, 2, and 3).**
   The Studio Thinking Framework supports an investigative form of learning where students, peers, and teachers use them to check learning, and teachers use them to refine curriculum. There is no one right way to use Studio Habits for assessment: Teachers assess with them in a wide range of ways, and how they do that is likely to shift over time. In fact, teachers often disagree about how others choose to employ the habits in assessment, and that is as it should be. Teachers can and do put their personal stamps on how they assess.

In the next sections, we focus on how four high school artist-teachers have each developed their own assessment practice using Studio Thinking. The notion that assessment is a conversation runs through all four examples in this chapter. The three principles from the CAAA paper and the four ways that Studio Habits support these principles are vividly evident in the examples from these teachers. Below we describe how they manage formative and summative assessment, including assessment of self, assessment by peers, and assessment by the teacher.

ASSESSMENT DEFANGED:
LEARNING AND ASSESSMENT IN THE ARTS
AS A FORM OF CONVERSATION

WITH TODD ELKIN

Todd Elkin's artmaking is a hybrid of text, drawing, and printmaking with digital and analog tools. He is an artist-teacher at Washington High School in Fremont, California, who has used Studio Thinking since the early 2000s. His high school students help him refine methods of reflection as they conduct self- and peer assessment. For over a decade, from around 2009 to 2020, he designed and taught the assessment module, one course in a three-course certificate program sponsored by the Alameda County, CA, Office of Education, called the Integrated Learning Specialist Program (ILSP). Three frameworks developed at Harvard's Project Zero were foundational in the program: Teaching for Understanding (Blythe et al.,1998; Wiske, 1998), Making Learning Visible (Giudici et al., 2001), and Studio Thinking (Hetland et al., 2007, 2013).

Artist-teachers in high schools are almost always required to grade their students. Unfortunately, reporting systems rarely match the ways artists assess art. "The natures of the arts disciplines and the ways work is done in them dictate the basic principles and approaches necessary for . . . evaluation" (CAAA, p. 6). Artists move toward quality through *conversations*—with materials, artworks, and themselves in self-reflection; in portfolios, studios, salons, critiques, and reviews; around exhibitions and artist talks. Over his career teaching art in public schools, Todd has found ways to transform the school system's requirements for assessment so that his assessment meets school criteria while also supporting the artistic goals of student learning. Todd sums it up: "People get hives when they think about assessment, and I think it doesn't have to be that way."

Studio Habits Guide Ongoing Conversations About Quality and Artistic Process. Todd talks with students, other teachers, other artists, and scholars, helping them be alert to "how the world talks to them," explore, dig in, and stay grounded. For him, the Studio Habits are entry points and guides to continuous conversations about quality and moments of artistic engagement. "It's so great that we have them. We might get there if we didn't have them, but it would take longer, and it might not be certain that you got there. They're a kind of quality control to ensure you have deeper conversations about arts learning."

Todd's classroom is a collaborative space for sustained exploration that includes assessment. In his classroom, assessment is a constant back and forth that integrates making and learning. Todd assesses artistic learning through conversation, reflecting internally on his own artwork and with others about theirs. His teaching braids a playful, improvisational mind with an intentional, planning mind.

> First you realize that you are having a deeper experience or engagement with life, and then you make that visible and document it. A lot of what I do is trying to design different kinds of dialogues that students can have around their learning. They need to become visually literate in talking about qualities of artwork. Then they can talk about what they're aiming for, or what emerged that they weren't aiming for.

Supporting students' self-assessment. For Todd, the Studio Habits are an ongoing reflection tool that illuminate particular moments emerging around what he calls "extreme noticing": "When you've done a playful thing, just messing around, and then you're like, oh, I like what's happening here. How can I do more of this?"

Todd front-loads the SHoM as artistic lenses by teaching them to his students in the first days of each term; then he asks that they use them as self-assessment.

> I introduce the SHoM early on by saying, "This is going to help us talk about our learning. It mirrors what actual artists do in their studios. It's going to help you be more transparent about your learning."

He asks his students,

> "What was happening when you did that thing?" The SHoM are useful lenses to talk about what

happened in those moments, and they're pretty comprehensive—many moments of learning can be seen though those lenses. They are tools to see what was happening in that process.

After that, the SHoM become part of the class vocabulary. "They become a skeleton or armature, they're a bedrock, underground." In particular, he sees Observe and Reflect in all conversations. Todd uses simple protocols iteratively to look with students at artworks that combine these two habits.

We use modified thinking routines. What do you notice? What do you think is successful? The protocol is similar whether we're looking at student work or practicing artists. From the beginning of the year, they're looking at each other's work as well as at the pros.

The simplicity of the protocols is what makes them powerful and also helps build links to other habits, often in students' own words and framing.

First, they look—it's a prolonged time for "What do you notice?" Then "What is successful? Be specific and concrete." Then, what could they do to make it even more successful? If you want, you can go to "What makes it great? How could it be even greater?" Ninety-eight percent of my students can latch on and contribute.

Defanging assessment for teachers. Todd also facilitates professional development for teachers around assessment, and he is aware that the topic can trigger negative feelings that seem at odds with the purposes of art. The teachers would come in, and I'd say the word *assessment*, and it was like a dark cloud entered the space. Assessment was being done to them because of various imposed systems of evaluation, and they had to do it to their students. In conversations, together, we unpacked thoughts, feelings, and attitudes the teachers had around assessment. We talked about "What do you think or feel when assessment comes up?" They'd say, "I have an idea it could be better," but they weren't sure how. So I made it my mission to take the cloud and turn it

into a rainbow or a unicorn—we needed to have a transformation about assessment.

Todd uses the Studio Thinking Framework to reframe teachers' thinking about assessment to make it into a thoughtful reflection on what matters in art rather than a mandated requirement. Todd and the teachers collaborate to develop assessments by using them to emphasize (1) talking about art as artists talk about art and (2) making assessment a dialogue about learning. Teachers select the qualities they want to be assessed, develop annotation strategies for commenting on their own and peers' work, and make tables with more casual language, like levels such as, "I nailed it," "It's almost there," or "It's not there at all." Teachers in turn give these strategies to students who use them to take charge of their own artistic learning.

I want them to understand that assessment, primarily, needs to benefit the learner—it's for the learner, and it's a gift, as my former colleague, Mariah Landers says. Giving thoughtful feedback to your peer is a huge gift. Having the space for self-reflection is a huge gift.

Grading as Collaboration. For Todd, grading is a collaboration with his students, built upon their reflections and written self-assessments, their self-chosen criteria for evaluation, and his own "observations based on students' engagement, progress, and growing understandings." He does not grade students directly on the Studio Habits of Mind, which he sees as, in some ways, "antithetical to grading." Instead, he asks students to reflect on their work, which includes reflecting on how the Studio Habits of Mind show up in their process.

My goal is to create a system in which assessment is an ongoing dialogue, not an inflexible ranking machine, which is all too often the case in my students' other classes. Assessment, in my experience, is more an art than a science, and my approach is something I've been working on for the past 23 years. At the end of the day, I want something that both my students and I can live with and feels fair to everyone. It has taken a while to get there, and I am still continually looking for ways to improve.

ASSESSMENT MOMENTS THAT SUPPORT INDIVIDUAL DEVELOPMENT

WITH KIMBERLEY D'ADAMO

Kimberley D'Adamo brings learners into her classroom to explore and solve interdisciplinary problems in the world. Over 12 years of action research, she and her students developed and refined a curriculum that supports students in learning to think as contemporary artists (Marshall & D'Adamo, 2011; 2018). She continues this work now as a lecturer and doctoral student at the University of Nebraska, Lincoln, where she is facilitating a Department of Education grant on teacher professional development. While she did not use the Studio Habits of Mind in developing her approach to assessment, she is considering how they intertwine with her curriculum.

Every teacher faces the dilemma of how to assess individuals fairly while holding high standards of quality. Artistic process results in unique expressions, and because "quality is individual, it is extremely problematic to assume that what works in one case will work automatically in another (CAAA, p. 10). Kimberley addressed this challenge by guiding students to document and self-assess their personal artmaking journeys through what she calls the *Creative Research Process* (Marshall & D'Adamo, 2011).

A key part of Kimberley's Creative Research Process is the use of protocols that students document in research journals, which are blank books for students to record and assess stages in their artmaking processes. Students use these books to document their non-linear, iterative learning trails. In many ways, these journals are similar to the "processfolios" described by Project Zero's ArtsPROPEL (http://www.pz.harvard.edu/projects/arts-propel) in the 1980s and 1990s, which also include documentation and process pieces (Winner & Simmons, 1992). As they construct works for exhibition, Kimberley's students refer to a Student Guide that illustrates and outlines these protocols for each stage of creative research. The guide offers descriptions, objectives, examples, guiding questions, and sentence frames that support both learning and assessment at each stage, developing student agency in ways similar to those discussed in Chapter 16.

Students use protocols about topics, planning, and reflection; several of these are illustrated in Figure 18.1:

1. **Topics**: Protocols for topic selection, refinement, and research include Curiosities/20 Questions, Sub-topics/Deepening, and Research for investigating Content, Artists, Artworks, and Materials
2. **Planning:** Protocols for planning include Creative Strategies and Project Plans
3. **Reflection**: Protocols for reflection include Free Association, Process Stage, Process Critique Notes, and Synthesis

Kimberley says:

Students decide how many of each protocol to complete, when to do them, and what to include in them. So each student's notebook is unique. Students also decide when a protocol is complete. Sometimes, however, during informal conversations, I notice that students have skipped a stage, or that the ideas in a protocol aren't fully developed yet; the stage seems thin. When that happens, I help students figure out what they really care about and dig into it.

Kimberley's guidance happens mainly during these informal reviews and conversations. "Because students need a safe space to develop their own voices, I do not grade their notebooks. Instead, I use my gradebook as a checklist for what students have completed. Because documentation is self-directed and exhibited as artwork, kids are motivated to do it well."

Assessing "Watershed Moments." Kimberley inserts a few "watershed moments" for more formal review into the otherwise student-directed process.

Figure 18.1. Abril uses the creative research stages developed in Kimberley's classroom to document her artistic process.

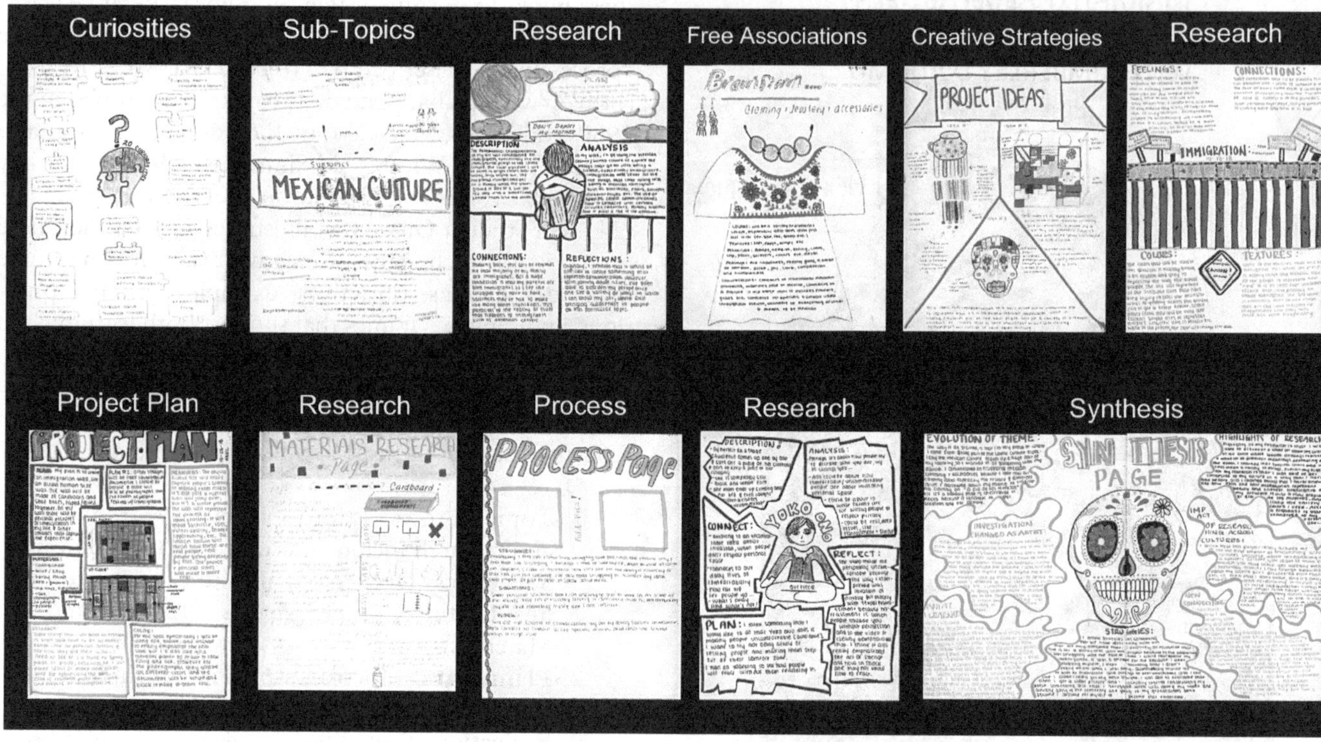

1. *Project Plan Stage*. Each student's Project Plan is a critical step that separates initial topic exploration and research from making works for exhibition. Kimberley pauses every student's forward movement on their exhibition artworks for this review. "If they haven't done certain steps well, it shows in their Planning protocol. For example, if they skip the Free Association stage, I can tell, because their projects are too predictable and don't show their personal experiences and ideas. When I see that in a Project Plan, I send them back to particular steps so they can expand their thinking."

2. *Synthesis Stages*. At midterm, students review their documentation from the first half of the course and summarize their learning trail. Peers review these summaries and offer comments, suggestions, and a score. Kimberley reads these carefully and adds her suggestions. Students can improve their scores if they incorporate advice in a revised synthesis, which becomes their final review.

Reviewing a page from another student's journal (Figure 18.2), Kimberley comments:

This is an example of a project plan not yet resolved. The fairy lights are my first clue—whenever I see fairy lights in a plan, I know the student has not owned the materials as her own expression. I suspect that she hasn't fleshed out the Free Association stage, where students discover personal connections to their topics, because her interest in brains doesn't show in unique symbols, images, or materials. Even though I know Magda is a very sophisticated thinker, this Project stage is underdeveloped, because she hasn't explored the free associations stage thoroughly yet. My review showed that I needed to talk with her about how to develop her personal vocabulary of materials, symbols, processes, for her investigation. This is common; pushing students into associations results in works that are fresher. After the conversation, Magda developed a more sophisticated and novel project by melting acrylic brain scans into sculptures that showed neural generation or degeneration, depending on the viewer's perspective.

Kimberley is describing qualities that are readily expressed by Studio Habits. When she recognizes that the

Assessment Is a Conversation

Figure 18.2. Planning Page Example from Magda Gourinchas's Workbook, 2019

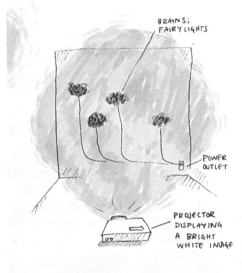

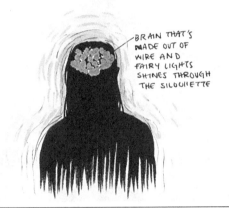

page is unresolved, she is seeing that Magda's Envisioning is incomplete. Her thoughts about the fairy lights are about Develop Craft: Technique. Magda had not yet imagined how to use materials in her own way. As a strategy for developing a personal voice with materials, Kimberley recommends the Free Association stage. That requires Magda to Stretch and Explore. By playing with the associations, Magda begins to use materials as expressive vocabulary for personal meaning. Doing so helps her Engage with her topic, which allows her to Persist in its full development at a higher level.

What does this translation into Studio Habits language offer Kimberley and her students?

> The Studio Habits would have been a good common vocabulary to convey the behaviors I wanted to see. They could help me depersonalize critique. You have to be really careful when you're talking to students about their tender work, feelings, and ideas. Making the criticism more objective by referring to Studio Habits as "what artists do" would allow them to stand back and consider their own artistry. Students often hear my critique as "just what Ms. D likes." But framing it with Studio Habits would let us talk about how artists communicate.

Because the Creative Research Process is authentic to the practices of contemporary artists, and because the Studio Habits are a vocabulary for describing and talking about the categories that artists think in, the two systems mesh easily. The creative research process offers open-ended structure that scaffolds creative thinking, which the Studio Habits name. Moving back and forth between the two languages offers students more ways to understand their own artistic thought: "Using the SHoM could allow students to see their granular, making-specific skills and actions in the context of the broader habits that artists use as they make art."

As far as grading goes, Kimberley's stance parallels Todd's in many ways, where assessment is a collaborative conversation that leads to a joint decision about grades:

> I do not have much tolerance for the factory aspects of school, like traditional grading. Assessments should be conversations, because assessing creative learning is complex and can be counterproductive and hurt students. No grading scheme is perfect, and I am always tweaking grades and adjusting expectations for each individual, but I do that in conversation with kids, not as a punishment. This approach keeps practice at the center of the studio and allows us to push grades aside and relate more as real artists.

ASSESSING THE THINKING PROCESS WITH STUDIO HABITS

WITH JOE DOUILLETTE

JoE Douillette, a film artist who works with single channel non-narrative videos and multi-channel installation work with choreographers, is an artist-teacher of media arts in Swampscott Public High School in Massachusetts. Prior to teaching in Swampscott, he taught new media in the teen program at the Institute of Contemporary Art in Boston for 12 years. That work did not require him to assess student learning, but when he began teaching in a public school and was required to grade his students, he wanted to assess in a way consistent with his own artistry and beliefs about teaching. During his master's program in 2017, he undertook a year-long independent study with Lois Hetland to create an assessment system using the Studio Habits of Mind. Here, we describe his design, use, and refinement of that system for grading and revision of his teaching practice.

Figure 18.3 shows what JoE Douillette's students saw on their report cards before his independent study: Projects are named across the top with a grade for each assignment and an average term grade at the far right. The form looks similar to what many high schools require of teachers for reporting achievement. It is not designed to reveal an ongoing assessment conversation between an artist-teacher and a student-artist developing a disciplinary mind. Rather, it computes how much and how well work was completed. Teachers in all disciplines know how to work around required forms like this one. But few of them attempt to redesign their assessment to use the required form for communicating what they truly value.

JoE teaches artistry in his Introduction to Film/Video elective, but artistry was invisible in the grades and report. That frustrated him. Where could students see what they'd learned about expression, craft, or teamwork? Rather than emphasize what art actually teaches, the disconnect seemed to reinforce a negative cultural stereotype of art courses: Kids expect a "fun art class" (or "f-art" class). A student told him, "No disrespect, Mr. Douillette, but students don't really take this course seriously." JoE wondered, "How can I assess film/video in ways that show it's worthwhile to be here and learn to be creative film makers?"

Students were creating films. I was using rubrics. The rubrics seemed to make sense to people who looked at them. But every five weeks, which is how often I have to post grades, I dreaded it and didn't feel like the assessment system I was building did what I wanted, for me or the student.

JoE undertook the challenge of redesigning his assessment to correspond to the artistry he helps students develop. He wrote a new grading policy for his syllabus: "Assignments are not given discrete grades. All assignments are broken down by the Studio Habits of Mind reflected in each assignment, with each habit graded using a 3-point rubric. The philosophy of this practice is to allow you to understand your own strengths as artists, to identify areas of growth, and to ultimately apply this self-knowledge beyond this art form."

Figure 18.3. JoE Douillette's Original Report Card

09/15 Aural PRE PR	09/30 Aural AUD PR	11/04 Class Part CP	11/04 Aural VID PR	11/18 1x1x1 Pre PR	11/18 1x1x1 PRO PR	11/18 Aur - POST PR	12/09 2x2x2 Pre PR	01/06 2x2x2 Pro PR	01/20 2x2x2 Post PR	Q1	Q2
90	88	95	90	95	95	95	95	90	95	90.1429	94.1667
90.0 90	88.0 88	95.0 A	90.0 90	95.0 95	95.0 95	95.0 95	95.0 95	90.0 90	95.0 95	90.1429	94.1667

Table 18.1. Generic and Film/Video Specific Definitions of Envision and Express

Envision	Using mental imagery in both the process and the work itself. Thinking in images.	Describing characters, stories, shots, and synopsis verbally, in written format (screenplays, concepts), and in storyboards.
Express	Learning how to create a work that goes beyond craft to convey meaning and feeling, literal and metaphorical.	Generating characters and stories that have literal and metaphorical meaning. Creating specific emotions and meaning through camera shots, pacing of editing, juxtaposition, and layering of imagery and sound.

Figure 18.4. JoE's Revised Report Card

11/09 E & P SHoM	11/09 DC-SP SHoM	11/09 DC-T SHoM	11/09 UAW-C SHoM	11/09 EXP SHoM	11/09 ~~Cell Phone~~ CP	11/09 S & E SHoM	11/09 ENV SHoM	11/09 UAW-D SHoM	11/09 REFL-QE SHoM
A-	B+	A-	B+	A-		A-	A-	C	B+

As JoE began to roll out the new system, he showed students a chart that described each habit next to a second column titled "Film/Video Specific Description." Two examples from the chart, Envision and Express, are shown in Table 18.1.

JoE used this chart to introduce the new system to his students. "This is where we'll think about the habits of being an artist," JoE told his students. He then worked with his students to develop and refine the film/video-specific definitions for each habit.

To help students see the reasoning behind their grades, JoE uses a simple but explicit three-point scale to score the habits emphasized in each scaffolded assignment in the sequence that leads to the final video: 1 (didn't demonstrate what I taught), 2 (demonstrated what I taught), or 3 (demonstrated beyond what I taught). By doing so, he was grading each project as a studio habit process. He still grades each assignment, but now the grade is based on how students use their minds during that project, with the work produced serving as one piece of evidence. This deemphasizes "finishing work" as the main criterion for success, which is a limitation of so many grading systems. Finishing matters, but it is not all that matters.

JoE's report card still uses the form his district requires (Figure 18.3). But it now reveals artistic development, because he grades the students' uses of the Studio Habits of Mind (Figure 18.4). Taking this approach surprised both of us, since, as Todd Elkin says, the SHoM seem almost "antithetical to grading." But the qualities of the habits were what JoE was teaching, so he decided to try assessing them and see what happened. He was tentative, but optimistic.

Both students and their parents were satisfied with the new system. When one parent raised a concern about his son's grade, JoE explained that while the student came in with films every day, he hadn't done the reflective self-assessments. Doing these would improve his grade. The parent appreciated the specific observation which let him see how he could help his son; the system allowed clear communication that provided support.

The students began to internalize the Studio Habits and to be able to identify instances of them in what they were doing. In written reflections—one completed after the first project and another at the end of the 5-week term—they conversed with JoE about which of the SHoMs were easy and which challenged them. The system led to dialogue with every student about their metacognition: How were they thinking about their thinking? How could they think better? JoE said, "That gives them a lot of power." An example of one student's initial reflection follows (we added the italics).

Student Initial Reflection: For me personally, I found *envisioning and expressing* the idea the easiest part of the process. I come up with movie ideas on a regular basis, so thinking of a scene to explore within the constraints of a high school in the middle of the day was no problem. The scene I am writing about is semiautobiographical, since I have reached out to friends about their thoughts on stuff I have written. The major difference would have to be the reactions to the scripts. The hardest part of the process so far would have to be *engaging and persisting*. In the moment of working on different projects, I have a tough time seeing the problems in it. In due time, I do find leaps in logic and rushed character arcs but while writing I am blind to any errors. (In the monthly meetings JoE had with his mentor, Lois Hetland, Lois reviewed these assessments. Here, she noticed the student has not identified Reflect: Evaluate in his last two sentences, a point JoE could address with him in a follow-up conversation.)

A story about another student, JT, is also revealing. JT was used to getting failing grades in school, and he told JoE, "I know I'm going to fail your course, Mr. Douillette. I didn't finish anything." That was true. But JT had come to every class, was an active team member throughout shooting, and was a highly creative and inventive editor; he had learned a lot and enjoyed making videos. JoE showed him that the Persist habit of completing work was only part of his grade. "He had put in a lot of work, and I was able to assess his other habits. His Express and Understand Art Worlds: Community habits were really strong. When we averaged the scores, he'd earned a B-, and he started to feel better about himself and his role in the class."

Making such a system takes time and effort to start. But JoE told us that once he had developed this system, the scoring was straightforward; "Assigning the 1, 2, or 3 is pretty simple. It has to be, since I grade eight times in 40 weeks and use this in three of five courses."

So far, we have discussed JoE's summative assessment and grading, but he also uses Studio Habits to support both formative assessment of student learning and assessment of his own teaching practice.

Formative Assessment of Student Learning: Students use the SHoM in self-reflections (Reflect), in one-on-one discussions around screenplays, storyboards, organization, and edits (Reflect), and to complete ungraded quizzes on technical understanding (Develop Craft: Technique).

> I test, but not for grading. "I'm not grading your technique—I'm just making sure you're learning it so you can support your expression." The test is a self-assessment; students finish when they get it all right. So they read the manual and learn the stuff they need to learn to get to the good stuff. They do have to develop their craft, so they learn to use the camera and demonstrate their understanding as they're in production.

Assessment of Teaching Practice: JoE also uses the assessment process to improve his teaching practice. He reflects on which habits he emphasizes in assignments and how well that matches his intentions. He mentioned a time when he noticed that five habits—Stretch and Explore, Develop Craft: Studio Practice, Understand Art Worlds: Domain, Observe, and Reflect: Evaluate—showed up less often than the others. He wondered why. "Is that right? Are these habits really less emphasized in film production? Or am I missing something that's actually there? If so, I need to look for it. Maybe I haven't personally developed that habit, so I don't prioritize it?"

These are the kinds of questions a thoughtful, reflective practitioner asks to improve his own professional practice, and they have led him to adjust his teaching practice. For example, he recognized that one of the less-emphasized habits, Develop Craft: Studio Practice, was essential for beginners. "If they're not using Studio Practice well, they are so disorganized that they can't keep track of their work and lose their way." He added a day-long project that teaches students to use Google Drive and Google Folders to keep their work organized and accessible. And that project is part of students' grades.

Working with JoE on an independent study focusing on using Studio Thinking as an assessment framework also provided Lois with an extended opportunity to reflect.

- The system reflects JoE's disciplinary expertise; he's a professional, and he's scaffolded a sequence of "junior versions" of expert practice that lead students thoughtfully through the process of film production while developing their artistic thinking.
- His system reflects the non-linear nature and development of artistry, for both students and teachers.
- Naming the SHoMs that are emphasized in assignments makes them a tool for reflecting on the artmaking process, guides students in formative assessment, reveals to students how to use their minds in artmaking, and gives students a metacognitive support system.
- The system helps all students understand how to engage with the work of artmaking better. Students like JT are much more likely to take another art class because they did not fail. JT did not deserve to fail; he simply did not have it all together yet. The grade told him: "You're getting there," rather than, "Nice that you had fun, but too bad, you lose."
- JoE's summative assessment—his grading—assesses students' learning, not just how much work they do or how accomplished it is. That's unusual in any discipline; grades too often reward being a "good student," which is code for complying, neatly and on time, with what teachers ask. Not here.
- The system communicates clearly to the primary audience, students, as well as to parents, colleagues, and administrators.
- JoE's system is flexible and can grow and change as issues emerge and institutional mandates change.

JoE thinks the experiment was a success.

> I feel like such a newbie at this, but students are more aware of their own process and how that relates to their being an artist. They realize that they engage

in many of these habits, just like artists do. And I feel better about my assessment. It'll change, but my comfort has already increased. This system makes it hard for a student to fail, and that's important in art. It matters less if I'd prefer to watch this or that student's film—that's not what we're doing here. I'm trying to get this kid to feel confident about how he uses his mind, with these habits, regardless of the outcome. Sure, we'll talk about the outcome, the editing, the timing, and the sophistication of the sound mix. But we'll do it so the quality of the product is motivation to do the work, just like for practicing artists.

Remember to Start With What You Can Do

Whatever kind of assessment you use, you have to streamline—you don't want a cumbersome, time-consuming system. It needs to be elegant and serve something you're trying to do. If you're creating more work for yourself and your students, you're probably going in the wrong direction.

—Todd Elkin

Todd, Kimberley, and JoE have been refining their assessment for years. They developed their systems gradually, making mistakes, talking with students, reflecting on what worked and what didn't, and streamlining over time. No system emerges full-blown, nor is any system likely ever to be finished. We hope that teachers just start however they can.

To show how effective and elegant a simple assessment process can be, Shirley Veenema offers an example of a form she used for *Found Stories* (Table 18.2), a culminating project for a one-trimester, 9th-grade, 2D foundation course. The form reflects Shirley's focus on artistic thinking and process. In fact, members of one class eventually began to joke at the start of a project, "She's messing with our thinking again!"

Shirley kept Develop Craft as a separate category from the other Studio Habits that she assessed. Separating technique from the other habits helped to sustain engagement among those who found it difficult to execute their craft skillfully; they realized that their thinking could be strong, even if their technical craft might need work. That simple move addressed the common misconception that well-executed craft is all that matters in art.

The form always followed the same format for each project, and it always included a space for comments to personalize responses. Shirley refined the text of the form many times to match the learning goals of each project and the assessment criteria for the project's content. She also adapted the form for specific classes and available technologies.

Table 18.2. Shirley Veenema's Assessment Rubric

Name: Found Stories			
Concepts: *Use previously learned concepts in a complex project inspired by chance; convey a narrative in a three-panel composition*	(1) Shapes form a clear abstract structure in single panels and across all panels.	Panel and sequence composition would benefit from more attention to abstract structure.	Composition of panels or sequence lacks sufficient attention to abstraction.
	(2) Panels show careful observation of source material.	Panels would benefit from more attention to source material.	Panels are generalized and important observed details lost.
Habits: *Stretch beyond comfort zone; connect media choice and technique to expression*	(1) Working process shows attention to possibilities.	Process shows attention to possibilities but could go further.	Don't be afraid to find inspiration in chance or accident.
	(2) Expression & content are enhanced by chosen media & technique.	Choice of media & technique could contribute more to expression.	Other choices of media & techniques would enhance expression.
Craft: *Technique & execution*	Panels show well-executed technique & execution.	Technique & execution need a bit more attention.	Better technique & execution would make panels more successful.

Comments:

For most classes, Shirley found filling out this form by hand and circling choices the easiest way to use it, because she and students could do it anywhere while sitting with a portfolio of work. Sometimes Shirley chose descriptors and left comments, later discussing these decisions with her students. At other times, students used the form to assess themselves. Students kept all completed forms in their portfolios to revisit periodically when writing reflections about their work and growth over time.

CONCLUSION

Good assessment supports learning, whether it is formative or summative. Assessment in art should be an ongoing conversation that takes many forms, celebrates and accommodates individual uniqueness, uses both product and process as clues to how students think, and aims to understand and support students in learning to think like artists. The same can be said about assessment in any area of the curriculum: The goal of assessment is to foster learning by documenting how students think. Well-facilitated assessment connects people in the "studio hive" to each other's ideas. Through ongoing, collaborative, and supportive approaches to assessment, students learn to open up and take responsibility for their work. They learn to listen to what others say about their work, to accept criticism without giving up on themselves and their own ideas, and to provide criticism to others in a compassionate and supportive way. Conversational assessment can help students learn to understand themselves and improve their work. That's powerful potential!

If one purpose of schooling is for students to become good and able citizens of the world, then quality assessment—the ongoing conversation about learning—can be a vehicle to that end. Imagine a world in which every person did work that mattered to them personally, where they wrestled with it seriously over sustained periods of time, took in what others thought of it, responded openly and critically, and used their efforts as springboards to next efforts. An art classroom can model such a world. The Studio Habits bring the artistic mode of thought to the fore as the goal of teaching and learning, and hence as the "what" that needs to be assessed. Good assessment takes students on a journey toward better understanding of the visual arts as a discipline and of the place of the arts in their lives and the world.

NINETEEN

Studio Thinking

The Studio Thinking Framework is not a recipe for teaching studio classes, but rather a set of lenses for observing and thinking about teaching and learning in the visual arts and beyond. The artist-teachers profiled in Chapters 17 and 18 show us varied ways of looking through these lenses to reflect on and refine their individual teaching practices and to confront the challenges of assessment. Their inventive and thoughtful uses of Studio Thinking, along with those of many other educators, administrators, policymakers, and researchers, have expanded our understanding of the framework and what it means to think, work, and learn in studios. Our initial research, which began with the study of five high school visual art teachers in two schools, has been broadened considerably by the collective work of many people. People have carried this work into their worlds, made it their own, and transformed it in the process. We have collaborated with many of them. In this chapter, we share some of these efforts and reflect on how they inform our understanding of what the framework has become and how they help us envision its future.

A COMMON LANGUAGE IN THE ARTS

Conversations about how artists think and what students learn can be nebulous or filled with art-specific terms unfamiliar to those not versed in an art form. The Studio Thinking Framework has been used as a shared conceptual language to support conversations about art for teachers, students, administrators, parents, researchers, policymakers, and broader communities. Looking across examples, we see how the framework provides grounding for conversation within and between art forms and with disciplines and stakeholders outside the arts.

Using the Framework in Visual Arts

The Studio Thinking Framework was built from observation of visual arts teaching, and it has been most frequently used since in visual arts domains. Chapter 17 profiled artist-teachers who have used the framework in different ways and settings, and Chapter 18 dives deep into how Studio Thinking has informed assessment practices. Here, we focus on how educators have used the framework to emphasize the complex thinking involved in visual art, in conversations with students, colleagues, and other stakeholders as they plan and refine their curriculum.

Focusing art education conversations on thinking. The Studio Thinking Framework works as a common language for students and teachers to talk about learning in art. Lucinda Daly, a photography teacher at Berkeley High in California, noted that the quality of student critiques improved dramatically after she asked students to make notes in the Studio Habits categories when they selected photos to discuss in their critiques. "I think that breaking apart the way we see in terms of the language of the Studio Habits of Mind is useful to get the kids to slow down and think about what they are looking at and take more time to really focus." Todd Elkin, a visual arts teacher at Washington High School in Fremont, California, who is featured in Chapter 18, introduced his students to the Studio Habits and asked them to paraphrase them in their own words. Engage and Persist, for example, became something like, "Find what you want to work on and then work as hard as you can and never stop." These redefined habits guide students' ongoing self-assessment as they reflect on their own efforts in sketchbooks and blogs. Teachers have developed visible, collaborative reflection tools around the Studio Habits of Mind, such as large pie charts with eight wedges labeled for each Studio Habit, where students place work, reflections, and photos to show that they connect that material to a particular habit. These efforts place *thinking* at the center of conversations among students and teachers in art classes.

Lenses on curriculum. The Studio Thinking Framework has proved useful in curriculum planning. Teachers use the lenses to develop and refine goals for how they want students to grow as artistic thinkers, contrasting with goals that describe only what they want students to do. The framework provides coherence within and across grade levels: While techniques, media, tools, concepts, and contexts change from the preschool to postgraduate levels, the same eight habits of mind persist.

The Studio Habits of Mind can help align curriculum with mandated standards. For instance, teachers map the habits onto state and national standards in visual and performing arts. In particular, the National Visual Arts Standards (NCCAS, 2014) identify a range of artistic processes in which art students engage (e.g., generating ideas, developing concepts, connecting to other artworks) that dovetail well with the Studio Habits of Mind. These standards represent an important shift in art education to a focus on the complex and creative thought processes involved in arts learning. Teachers can highlight how habits of mind support ways of going about these creative processes—for example, showing how idea generation could be started primarily with Observe (e.g., collect images that visually intrigue you before planning an artwork), Envision (e.g., sketch out ideas for an artwork and then collect visual resources), or Stretch and Explore (e.g., randomly pick images and imagine how they might contribute to your initial ideas).

Similarly, the Studio Habits of Mind can guide how teachers select and frame resources to engage students. The wealth of online resources, including images of art and videos of artists talking about their practices, can be overwhelming when trying to choose samples that align with a particular curricular theme. Viewing the clips through the lenses of the Studio Habits offers ways to see connections across diverse media and practices so teachers can curate their classes around a theme, as teachers in the Art21 Educators' Program learn to do, rather than merely mimicking an artist's process or material use. The framework has also helped teachers to select resources for the teaching of specific Studio Habits. For example, artist Gwendolyn Huskens's project *Medic Esthetic* uses medical materials such as bandages, plaster, and steel to make designer shoes that resemble orthopedic braces. While teaching a course in Fashion and Fibers at MassArt, Marie Smith decided that using images of this artist's work would help to develop the habits of Stretch and Explore (the materials are novel for shoes), Express (the images convey a social message about women's health), and Understand Art Worlds (the contemporary art world uses humor and juxtaposition to communicate).

Building community conversations on thinking and learning in art. Teachers have been innovative in supporting conversations about studio thinking with their colleagues and broader communities. Teachers in Alameda County, California, set up Thinking Walls, following a model built on documentation practices used in the Reggio Emilia preschools in Northern Italy. These informal, temporary, public panels display learning goals, student artwork, captions, and commentary by students and teachers, including labels naming the Studio Habits in use. They open a space for making connections (individually, in small groups, or in large-group reflection conversations) between what students do and what they're meant to learn (Hetland et al., 2010).

Teachers also report using the Studio Thinking Framework as a tool to explain the learning in arts classes to their principals and other administrators who have less familiarity with the structure and approaches of art studios. The habits help administrators to understand learning and teaching in the arts, and they provide guidance for observations and evaluations of artist-teachers.

The Singapore Teachers' Academy for the aRts (STAR), an organization that provides professional development for art and music teachers in Singapore, has been informed by the Studio Thinking Framework. Lim Kok Boon, a Master Teacher (Art) with the Academy, sees studio thinking as aligning well with an general focus on inquiry-based learning in the arts and their efforts to support students' self-regulated learning. He shares that the framework can help teachers, parents, and school administrators understand the thinking and learning in art lessons, noting, "The Studio Thinking Framework gives structure and meaning to actions we see in the art classroom that might otherwise be bewildering." STAR's most recent efforts involve designing a poster that outlines the Studio Habits of Mind along with strategies to engage students in complex thinking in the art classroom. The poster was delivered to all 350 mainstream schools in Singapore to serve as a visual reminder to teachers and students of the thinking involved in the arts and to help develop a shared language for learning in the arts.

The shared language of Studio Thinking also can help align efforts across diverse communities. For instance, in Alameda County, California, Louise Music, then Coordinator of Arts for the county, led the Alliance for Arts Learning Leadership in adopting the Studio Thinking Framework as one of three countywide "analytic lenses" (the other two are *Teaching for Understanding* [Blythe et al., 1998; Wiske, 1998] and *Making Learning Visible* [Giudici et al., 2001]). The frameworks provide a shared conceptual language for teachers, students, administrators, parents, and the community; the language unites the educational philosophy and practices used throughout the 18-district county.

Using the Framework in Dance, Theater, and Music Education

With alterations to accommodate discipline-specific aims and contexts, the Studio Thinking Framework is being used to guide planning and teaching in other arts disciplines.

In music, for example, "Observe" becomes "Listen and Observe"; in theater, "Observe" is better thought of as "Attend" (as suggested by Judith Contrucci, former Coordinator of Visual and Performing Arts for the Cambridge, Massachusetts, public schools). And with respect to the Studio Structures for learning, musicians, dancers, and theater artists might add "Performance" or "Ensemble" as overarching learning structures (analogous to Exhibition), since collaborative group contexts are so central in teaching in those domains. These uses invite us to deepen our understanding of the habits as applied to the visual arts. As just one example, the ways in which dance and theater teachers highlight the expressive potential of the body makes us think more deeply about the role of the body in expression in visual art.

Embodied studio thinking in dance. David Alexander, advisor to the Boston Ballet's Center for Dance Education, carried out a 2-year study based on the framework (Alexander, 2010). The research team observed 34 intensive ballet classes taught by 11 different teachers, and they interviewed 46 students to understand whether the habits of mind we had described were also being taught in ballet. The students in these classes were involved in dance 8 to 9 hours per day for 5 weeks. The researchers concluded that young ballet students were being taught all eight habits of mind. While they found that 43% of the content of a class was devoted to craft, they also concluded that the teachers stressed all the other habits of mind in the service of developing craft. Students were encouraged to Envision (e.g., "Have you ever watched a cat or dog lick the floor? What they do with their tongue, that's what I want you to do with your foot") and Observe ("Notice how, with her raised leg engaged, the small inner muscles show up when it's done well") along with all the other habits of mind. When dance students were interviewed about the personal, intellectual, and social qualities needed to succeed in ballet, their responses were easily codable into the Studio Habits of Mind, with Engage and Persist, Envision, Reflect, and Observe being the ones most commonly mentioned.

When Mark Borchelt led the dance department at Interlochen Arts Academy in Michigan, he saw "immediate application to dance training" in the Studio Thinking Framework and contrasted that to Western theatrical dance training, which "is typically taught at a rote and ritualized level." He continued working with Studio Thinking at Utah Valley University until his retirement in 2021.

I have introduced the concepts in dance technique classes as well as dance composition and pedagogy classes with equal success. It is valuable that the dancers learn to evolve past being dependent on external motivation such as outperforming peers or garnering instructor approval, to find a stronger sense of self-motivation that encourages a deeper level of inquiry and curiosity. For example, following a discussion of the concepts of Envision and Express, students routinely find ways to manipulate the timing and phrasing of an exercise to create a more poignant expression of the movement. By thinking in terms of the Studio Structures, I have been able to organize my classes to more consciously shift between thinking and doing. The studio experience is more positive in tone and focused on unrealized potential rather than a fear of not meeting stated expectations.

Thinking in Theater Education. Thalia Goldstein, associate professor of applied developmental psychology at George Mason University, used a research approach guided by the Studio Thinking Framework to identify eight habits of mind taught through acting class in a National Endowment for the Arts–supported study (Goldstein, 2021; Goldstein & Thompson, 2019; Goldstein & Young, 2019). Some of the habits she identifies, such as Imagine & Envision or Reflect and Think Metacognitively, are close analogues to the habits of mind we found in visual art, while others are more closely tied to theater such as Think Collaboratively and Bodily Awareness and Control.

Evan Hastings, a theater teacher who works and consults internationally, talked to us about his use of the Studio Thinking at the high school level in schools in Alameda County, California, and with adolescents in the Buena Vista School at the Alameda County Juvenile Justice Center in Hayward, California. Evan asked students to select the habits they would like to focus on and assess themselves with this lens, prompting, "How will you know if you developed in this habit? What will it look like/feel like?" These reflections built over the semester, and he worked them into summative assessments and personal artist statements. In Evan's work with faculty and students at the Srishti School of Art, Design, and Technology, in Bangalore, India, he used playful, theatrical games to introduce and explore the habits with faculty and students in a sort of musical chairs game where people freeze into positions or create monologues that exemplify the habit they land upon. He has also used similar approaches in his work in New Zealand and across the Middle East. In all these settings, his invitations to interpret the framework in personal ways deepens the resonance of the framework and the quality of reflections.

Seeing Habits of Mind in Music. When the late Maestro Matthew Hazelwood (1954–2012) taught at the Interlochen Arts Academy in Michigan, he developed ways to teach the Studio Habits explicitly to students in his orchestra. In a beautiful example of teaching Envision as he conducted a rehearsal of Tchaikovsky's ballet, *Sleeping Beauty*, Matt stopped the group after they had played through a section, reached down, and put a pair of ballet toe shoes on his hands. With his hands in the shoes, he "danced" the rhythm of the music on the auditorium floor in a soft, delicate tapping. As he did so, he asked his students to Envision. "Remember, this is a dance. You are in the orchestra pit, and the dancers are on the stage just above you. Let's take it from B." The performance was transformed. The students moved from being tied to the notes in a rote and lifeless rendition to a light expressive flow. This demonstration is a good example of how a conductor can teach students to Envision in order to Express. As he taught, he also stressed Understand Art Worlds. While conducting, he continuously wove in historical anecdotes about the works the students were learning to perform. He told them about how the instruments, acoustics, and audiences differed in past eras so that they could play with a more authentic interpretation. After leaving Interlochen, Mateo (as he was called in Spanish) served as the conductor of the National Youth Orchestra of Colombia and the Music Adviser of Colombia's Batuta Youth Program. With Batuta, he used this Studio Thinking approach in over 100 music centers. Maestro Hazelwood died, tragically and unexpectedly, on May 31, 2012, and we have dedicated this book to him, as well as to Elliot Eisner (1933–2014), and Mihaly Csikszentmihalyi (1934–2021), all of whom have inspired our thinking and research.

The Studio Habits lenses can also reveal what may be missing. When Jill Hogan observed and coded 24 rehearsals of six public high school music ensemble classes (band, choir, and orchestra), she found evidence of eight habits of mind (Hogan & Winner, 2019). These did not always have the same names as our original ones, but they bear strong similarities: *engage and persist, evaluate, express, imagine, listen, notice, participate in community,* and *set goals and be prepared.* However, she did not observe two habits that she had hoped to find, and she named these *appreciate ambiguity* (more than one way to play a score, more than one meaning) and *use creativity.* The ensemble classes emphasized technique so much that she observed little room left for creative thinking and trying to solve musical problems in different ways. This situation contrasts with composition-based and general music classes, where students have some opportunity to make creative musical decisions. Noting that these two non-observed habits are ones that theorists assume are central to the arts, Hogan argues for changes in standard ensemble music curricula to ensure that these habits are taught and learned.

One benefit of using the framework across arts disciplines is that it shows how pedagogical patterns differ across art forms. For example, we learned by observing Mark Borchelt that dance classes tend to be structured with many repetitions of very short structures, such as a 1-minute Demonstration–Lecture, followed by a 2-minute Students-at-Work session and a 30-second Critique. Some music rehearsals at Interlochen were similarly structured, and because conductors demonstrate while students play, the Demonstration–Lecture and Students-at-Work structures often happen simultaneously in ensembles. Perhaps teachers of different art forms can learn more from one another when they have the framework as a common language. This is particularly important as new forms and fields evolve. For example, this shared language is needed in media arts where students take on multiple roles as musician, filmmaker, graphic designer, actor, and writer in individual and collaborative projects.

We share just these few examples to illustrate how Studio Thinking has been used across arts education (see Box 19.1).

Using the Framework in Preservice Teacher Education

Multiple art education programs in colleges and universities use the Studio Thinking Framework to help beginning teachers understand the purpose and rigor of arts education. At George Mason University, the framework is used to focus on thinking throughout the art education curriculum. In the first course for undergraduate BFA students considering becoming art educators, the Studio Thinking Framework is used to guide students' observations of arts classrooms, helping them make sense of what they see. The framework allows them to discern the structures of studio classes and the learning emphasized therein. As students advance in the program, they revisit Studio Thinking as they read and discuss research in art education, connect arts learning to broader theories of learning and development, plan curriculum and assessments, and do their capstone action research projects. Faculty have found that the framework helps shift preservice teachers' thinking from an emphasis on specific projects, media, and techniques to emphasizing what and how students learn through these projects. The framework has been used as a resource in preservice art teacher education at the Massachusetts College of Art and Design, at Pennsylvania State, and at Northern Illinois University, among others. Dave Donahue (former Associate Provost and Professor of Education at Mills College),

Box 19.1. A Sample of sites using the Studio Thinking Framework

South Berwyn School District 100 collaborated with the Chicago Teachers' Center at Northeastern Illinois University on a Department of Education Professional Development for Arts Educators grant from 2008–2011, ARTS Berwyn. Teachers throughout the District used the Studio Thinking Framework to assess and reflect across the disciplines. Over 91 arts-integrated units were analyzed with the Studio Thinking Framework.

The San Leandro Public Schools in San Leandro, California, used the Framework in elementary and middle schools. In 2010, Chris Lim, former superintendent of San Leandro, committed her eight elementary schools to a professional development project that paired classroom and art teachers in curriculum design, facilitated by Tana Johnson, then of the Alameda County Office of Education. The Studio Habits served as guides for unit goals and assessments, and students learned the language as a means to identify strengths and weaknesses through reflection and motivate sustained investment in learning. This program evolved into the Integrated Learning Specialist Program, a three-course certificate for arts- and non-arts teachers through the Alameda County Office of Education that used Studio Habits, Teaching for Understanding, and Making Learning Visible as foundations for curriculum planning. The program ran until 2020.

Shristi Manipal Institute of Art, Design, and Technology, Bangalore srishtimanipalinstitute.in/

This art college in India, has used Studio Thinking for faculty development since 2011. In summer 2020, around 40 faculty redesigned their courses by using the framework in a 2-week professional development course facilitated online by Lois Hetland. The faculty identified dispositional elements of each habit—skill, inclination, and alertness—in their own artistic practices and then revised their course learning goals, assignments, and assessments to emphasize previously under-addressed qualities of professional practice.

Brigham Young University (BYU) ARTS partnership, Provo, UT education.byu.edu/arts

An initiative housed in the Center for Improvement of Teacher Education and Schooling (CITES) in the McKay School of Education at Brigham Young University (BYU), the BYU arts partnership works to increase the quality and quantity of arts education in Utah public schools. Faculty use the Studio Thinking Framework to guide arts integration. They work with teachers to identify the Studio Structures in their teaching, and then help them expand the Students-at-Work, Critique, and Exhibition structures while reducing time dedicated to Demonstration–Lecture and Transition.

Singapore Teachers' Academy for the aRts (STAR), Singapore academyofsingaporeteachers.moe.edu.sg/star

Singapore Teachers' Academy for the aRts (STAR), Ministry of Education Singapore, has been inspired by the Studio Thinking Framework for over a decade. They see the framework as aligning with an inquiry-based approach to art education and providing a common language grounded in art for teachers to discuss student learning.

The Center of Creative Arts (COCA), St. Louis, MO www.cocastl.org

This multidisciplinary community arts center uses the framework for faculty development across visual arts, theater, dance, voice, and other offerings. The teaching artists use the habits to plan residencies with classroom teachers. COCA has worked with the framework regularly in faculty meetings as professional development for their teaching artists. The framework also supports observation of teaching artists during the center's programs, helping both faculty and administration recognize when the framework is used and how it could be used better.

KID smART, New Orleans, LA www.kidsmart.org

KID smART began using the framework in about 2010 with teaching artists, exploring Studio Habits as methods of assessment and looking at the framework across artistic disciplines. Studio Thinking has a prominent place in the KID smART logic model. Program outcomes are aligned with Studio Habits to foreground the artistic objectives of the work and support good teaching practice. When teaching artists are observed in the classroom, their development and facilitation of Studio Habits becomes a big part of the feedback conversation. Studio Habits give language to connections across the arts and academic and social–emotional learning. The framework has helped classroom teachers and school partners deepen what they are looking at and seeing in the arts. Including the Studio Habits on the organization's unit planning document guides both teaching artists and classroom teachers in continually thinking about and planning for the development of these habits.

Studio in a School, New York, NY www.studioinaschool.org

The Studio Habits framework was used to guide evaluation of a U.S. Department of Education Arts in Education Model Development and Dissemination grant at Studio in a School. Observers learned to assess classrooms and conduct work with reference to the Studio Habits and to examine these reflections over time.

The Marwen Center, Chicago, IL www.marwen.org

Marwen is a free, after-school community center that offers visual art courses, college planning, and career development programs to Chicago's underserved youth in grades 6–12, many of whom travel several hours daily on public transportation to take part. The Center offered professional development in Studio Thinking as a way to give teaching artists a common language to learn from one another across media and processes. They are currently focusing on the values of racial and social justice, youth voice, and collective action. In a recent email, Kate Adams, Manager of Teaching and Learning, affirmed that Marwen has "adored and utilized/discussed/explored the Habits of Mind over the years." This is one more example of how the Studio Habits work well with other initiatives, supporting artistic thinking even when other values take center stage.

Jennifer Stuart (art teacher at San Francisco Friends School), and Trena Noval (artist and action researcher featured in Chapter 17), also used the framework in preservice generalist teacher education.

Using the Framework in Museum and Gallery Education

India Clark, former Director of Gallery Education at Massachusetts College of Art and Design, used the framework to analyze college classes held in the gallery. She identified the Studio Habits and Studio Structures for learning being used and made recommendations to the college faculty for improving their gallery-based classes. India's analysis (Clark, 2011) revealed that the classes cultivated each Studio Habit of Mind and employed the Studio Structures.

The Studio Habits Framework is also being used in other museum education programs. One approach used at the National Gallery in Washington, DC, involves looking for the artist's mind in works. Can viewers see evidence that the artist Envisioned? Stretched and Explored? How, for example, do Mark Tansey's paintings (which make clever references to art history) show the artist's perspective on Understand Art Worlds? At the Columbus Museum of Art, Director of Education Cindy Meyers Foley has used Studio Thinking for over a decade with the museum's teaching artists. The framework helped the teaching artists break the boundaries between personal studio practice and teaching practice so that they work with students as collaborators and co-artists. Teaching artists often learn new skills alongside students, which blurs the distinctions between expert and novice, changes the dynamic of the lecture-demonstration format of gallery education, and fosters the development of independent, intrinsically

motivated, cultural producers. Most recently, the museum extended the framework to early childhood. The museum's early childhood specialist, Cat Lynch, adapted it to create a resource, Studio Habits for Young Children, which she uses as a planning tool for experiences for children 18 months to 5 years of age. She also uses it in working with student teachers at Wonder School and with students in other practicum courses with the Columbus State Community College Early Childhood Development and Education program. She and the student teachers use the framework to guide documentation of learning and emergent curriculum.

Influencing Art Education Policy

The Studio Thinking Framework has influenced visual arts education policy in the United States. For example, in 2008, at a professional development institute, state arts education managers, who shape arts education policy across the United States, read and discussed *Studio Thinking*. In 2009 the National Art Education Association, the world's largest professional visual arts education association and a leader in educational research, policy, and practice for art education, published *Learning in a Visual Age: The Critical Importance of Visual Arts Education* (revised 2016: www.arteducators .org/advocacy-policy/learning-in-a-visual-age). This report highlights Studio Thinking as defining what high-quality arts education provides. Studio Thinking was a resource text for the writing of the 2014 National Visual Arts Standards, which highlight the complex thought process involved in the arts (National Coalition for Core Arts Standards, www.arteducators.org/learn-tools /national-visual-arts-standards). The framework has been used as a tool to promote professional dialogue across local, district, state, and university contexts and across arts disciplines. In the politically charged atmosphere of accountability, tight budgets, and competing agendas, Studio Thinking can help explain and justify arts programs to parents, administrators, and groups who control resource allocation to schools.

STUDIO THINKING BEYOND THE ARTS

Studio Thinking also has been used productively in contexts outside of the arts. It has been used to guide arts integration with other disciplinary subjects and to help frame thinking in new technology contexts involving aspects of design and making. The studio approach provides a pedagogical frame that puts making and reflection at the center of learning, no matter what the discipline, and strengthens the quality of arts learning in interdisciplinary and integrative contexts.

Studio Thinking and Arts Integration

The Studio Thinking Framework has been a powerful resource for integrating arts into other subject areas for Brigham Young University's ARTS Partnership, which is housed in the Center for Improvement of Teacher Education and Schooling in the McKay School of Education. Cally Flox, Founding Director of the ARTS Partnership, and Heather Francis, Research and Creative Development Coordinator, both speak particularly to the value of the Studio Structures for arts educators in the performing arts as well as for non-arts educators working to integrate the arts in a meaningful way that improves student learning. They find that when generalist classroom teachers or teachers of subjects outside the arts, such as mathematics, organize their classes more like a studio, teachers reduce lecture time to focus on the application of skills and what students produce, which aligns with project-based learning standards in math and science while including artistic practice.

The Studio Habits of Mind offer additional insights for arts integration. Students usually respond with enthusiasm to arts experiences that are interspersed into instruction in non-arts domains. But often, the non-arts teachers do not know what constitutes a genuine arts experience as opposed to a trivial one. When using arts to invite interest in a non-arts topic, the Studio Habits of Mind can guide teachers to consider artistic values that the activities might foster. This is what upper elementary and middle school teachers did, led by Tana Johnson, then in the Alameda County Office of Education, in the San Leandro Unified School District in California. Elementary classroom teachers partnered with school specialists in visual arts to develop cross-disciplinary projects in reading, writing, and history, while middle school students worked similarly with arts and science integration. For example, in an artists' book curriculum, students explored and made a wide variety of book structures in art classes and then took them to their homerooms to add content, extending Understand Art Worlds into the reading curriculum. After looking at Lynda Barry's cartooning books, they moved into storytelling in comic format. Students used Envision and Express as they translated written texts into comic format.

Through a National Science Foundation research grant with Lynn Goldsmith at Education Development Center and other colleagues, Lois Hetland and Ellen Winner investigated whether skill in visual art envisioning transfers to envisioning in the discipline of geometry. They developed a measure of envisioning in art that included reducing an organic form to a basic geometrical structure, drawing a figure from a different view, drawing negative space, and imagining and then drawing cast shadows. Geometrical reasoning was measured using spatial geometry problems from standardized mathematics tests. They then tracked three groups of students (art, theater, and squash) on envisioning as they entered the 9th grade. The findings showed that the art group was better on both measures, suggesting that students who are good at envisioning in art are also good at envisioning in geometry. However, the findings do not demonstrate transfer. Why? Because the art group was better on both measures as they entered 9th grade. This problem would not have occurred had the researchers been able to randomly assign students to art vs. theater vs. squash, but this was simply not feasible. Still, the finding that high art envisioners are also high geometry envisioners shows us the breadth of the habit Envision.

Studio Thinking in STEAM (Science, Technology, Engineering, Arts and Math)

Studio Thinking has been useful for educators using new technologies for design projects in which art and design are connected with computer science and engineering. The framework provides a way to ensure that these interdisciplinary projects do not become so overwhelmed by technical concerns that the arts are treated superficially. Bequette and Bequette (2012) and Gettings (2016) both suggest that the kinds of dispositions we identify in the Studio Habits of Mind help illuminate overlap in ways of thinking in design and project-based STEAM (Science, Technology, Engineering, Arts and Math) learning. Kelly Gross, assistant professor of art and design education at Northern Illinois University, similarly sees the Studio Habits of Mind such as Observe as helpful in her work leading a STEAM program in Community Unified School District 200 in Illinois, noting, "Teaching students to observe closely and document accurately through drawing is a foundational skill of cross-disciplinary projects involving arts, engineering, and scientific principles."

Kim Sheridan has used Studio Thinking in research in digital technology-rich contexts for over a decade. For a National Science Foundation–funded project with Kevin Clark, Studio Thinking was an organizing frame for a design-based research study of a Saturday program in 3D modeling, animation, and game design for traditionally underserved youth in Washington, DC. The framework proved to be a valuable tool in making teaching and learning more open-ended, creative, and student-driven. The researchers combined the Studio Thinking Framework with a youth mentorship model in what they termed a *studio mentorship model*, where more experienced youth act as mentors in the classroom for beginning youth (Clark & Sheridan, 2010; Sheridan, 2011; Sheridan et al., 2013).

For instance, this framework helped a computer programming teacher move away from teaching precisely designed tasks through step-by-step instructions focused on skill with programming tools. Instead, he posed open-ended computer design problems while guiding youth mentors to assist students. A comparison of the class before and after implementation of the studio mentorship model was dramatic: The teacher talked less, student talk was more about their work, students completed more projects, and their resulting work was rated by the researchers as more complex and original, both in design and technical programming. All of these changes resulted after adopting the Studio Thinking approach (Sheridan et al., 2013).

Combining the Studio Thinking Framework with a mentorship model also led to greater agency in youth's conceptions of their own roles, potential, and responsibilities. Before the implementation of a studio approach, youth working in the program took on minor administrative roles. Afterwards, youth mentors began proposing and teaching their own class sessions. The program shifted from being taught by adult high school teachers to being entirely taught by youth. High school–aged youth identified new software to teach, developed strategies for teaching it, and presented their work at technology and education conferences (Sheridan et al., 2013). Just as we described in Chapter 16, the studio model helps build learner agency.

This focus on studios and agency extended into Sheridan's collaborative research with Erica Halverson, professor in curriculum and instruction at the University of Wisconsin-Madison. Their work focused on *makerspaces*,

multidisciplinary sites of hands-on making, where digital fabrication technologies such as 3D printers and laser cutters are often used alongside traditional arts and crafts such as woodworking, screen printing, and fiber arts (Halverson & Sheridan, 2014; Sheridan et al., 2014; Sheridan, 2017; Sheridan & Konopasky, 2016). They demonstrated that even in brief workshops, open-ended studio approaches to teaching support learning and agency more than just "make and take" approaches (i.e., step-by-step instructions for a specific project). Students in the studio used more "linguistic markers of agency" as they talked about their work and envisioned more ideas for future projects than students in the step-by-step approach (Konopasky & Sheridan, 2015). Similarly, in a study on STEM learning through making funded by the Institute of Museum and Library Services, the authors found that a studio-based codesign approach to engineering supported parents' and children's sense of agency in STEM (Konopasky & Sheridan, 2018; Sheridan et al., 2019). The importance of teaching for student agency is discussed in Chapter 16.

REINVENTING STUDIO THINKING

Looking across the contexts of application, we have been struck by the portability of the Studio Thinking Framework—how people carry the framework into their diverse contexts and find new ways to use it. Since the publication of our first edition in 2007, we have witnessed the framework being used in classes at all grade levels in visual arts—its use at the elementary level prompted the writing of *Studio Thinking from the Start* (Hogan et al., 2018). As we have described above, people use the framework to look at their work in interactive media, dance, theater, and music classes. We have seen it applied in schools, community arts settings, out-of-school programs, and museums. People have also adapted the framework to subject areas beyond the arts. We see how it provides grounding for work crossing disciplines and into ways of learning and working with new technologies. The framework has guided research and informed policy discussions.

As researchers, we are curious about why that is. Why would this work to uncover a "hidden curriculum," the why and how that underlie the practices of five teachers in two high schools from 20 years ago, be relevant to such diverse professionals now? We venture to suggest that this is because our framework describes but does not prescribe. Our research is grounded in a firm respect for the studio teaching tradition and a firm belief that students learn important ways of thinking from working in the arts. When researchers carefully examine the enacted practices of experienced professionals working in a tradition (in our case, the studio art teaching tradition), they of course find qualities that are particular to the place and moment, and they of course highlight aspects that are shaped by their viewpoints (in our case a psychological lens on thinking and learning), but they also uncover qualities that are central to and sustained by that tradition.

The psychological lens we brought to our description highlights the kinds of thinking artists develop and use and the ways studio art teaching works to develop this thinking. The Studio Thinking Framework provides a way of looking at a rich tradition of studio teaching in the arts and stimulates other curious professionals to use it to look at their own work. As they layer the framework with their many other pedagogical approaches, interests, and worldviews, they transform it.

Each time people use the framework to see their work in a new way, they also contribute back to the research, causing the framework to expand because it is viewed by new eyes in new contexts and practices. To use the Studio Thinking lenses, you do not need to follow a particular curriculum or pedagogical approach. Using the lenses only requires that you value studio teaching, consider thinking in art as meaningful, and view reflecting on practice as worthwhile. It is through this collective work that Studio Thinking is continually refined and reinvented as we all keep envisioning new ways of teaching and learning in the arts.

We hope that you, readers of this book, will be alert to any new ways that the Studio Thinking Framework supports your efforts to teach and learn, both within and beyond the classroom context. When you put the Framework to use, please let us hear from you!

Project Examples

School and Teacher	Project Name	Example Number
The Boston Arts Academy		
MÓNIKA ALDARONDO	Junior Shows	15.3
BETH BALLIRO	African Pottery	3.1, 11.2
	Imaginary Creatures	7.2, 9.1
	Inventing Colors	4.1, 6.1, 12.1
	Secret Ritual Vessels	13.2
	Sketching in Clay	10.1
KATHLEEN MARSH	Creating Hat and Vest	13.4
	Egg Drop	11.6
	A First Show	15.1
	Making Puppets	5.2
	Senior Show	15.4
	Self-Portraits in Colored Pencil	4.2, 9.3
GUY MICHEL TELEMAQUE	A Sophomore Show	15.2
	Using the Viewfinder	8.1
Walnut Hill School		
JASON GREEN	Centering on the Wheel	4.4, 13.1
	Ceramic Sets	11.3, 12.2
	Coil Sculpture	9.2, 11.5
	Repeating Units	10.2
	Tile Project	3.2, 5.1, 6.2
JIM WOODSIDE	Abstraction	13.3
	Contour Drawing	14.1
	Cubism	11.4
	End-of-Term Exhibitions	15.5
	Figures in Evocative Space	7.1, 11.1, 14.2
	Korean Students Show in Korea	15.7
	Light and Boxes	3.3, 4.3, 8.2
	A Senior Show	15.6

Conducting the Research

Research is only as trustworthy as the methods by which it is conducted. This appendix describes the methods we used to develop the Studio Thinking Framework to make transparent the empirical processes we employed in our research design.

SETTINGS AND PARTICIPANTS

Over the 2001–2002 school year, we filmed 38 classes in five classrooms at two high schools that focus on the arts, the Boston Arts Academy and the Walnut Hill School. Students at the Boston Arts Academy are proportionally representative of the demographic profile of the Boston area in socioeconomic status. Students at Walnut Hill are an international group including local suburban and urban students and students from across the United States and from abroad, with a concentration of Korean students. Students at Walnut Hill are mainly middle- or upper middle-class with some students receiving full scholarship. At both schools, students are admitted by portfolio review and/or on the basis of admissions tasks and interviews. Students who are admitted showed interest and promise in the visual arts, but few have highly developed levels of technical skills upon admission.

TEACHERS WHO CONTRIBUTED TO THE ORIGINAL RESEARCH

The five teachers who contributed to the original research are all practicing artists. The three teachers at the Boston Arts Academy are licensed by the State of Massachusetts, and all five have master's degrees in art or art education. We list each teacher below.

Beth Balliro, Boston Arts Academy, Painting and Ceramics

Beth Balliro, an exhibiting artist, began teaching at BAA when it opened in 1998. She is now a faculty member in the Art Education Department at the Massachusetts College of Art and Design.

Jason Green, Walnut Hill, Ceramics and Ceramic Sculpture

Jason Green, an exhibiting artist, began teaching at Walnut Hill in 1998 and is now on the faculty of Alfred University.

Kathleen Marsh, Boston Arts Academy, Sculpture and Drawing

Kathleen Marsh is a founding faculty member of BAA and a former Visual Arts Department Chair.

Guy Michel Telemaque, Boston Arts Academy, Photography and Design

Guy Michel Telemaque, an exhibiting artist, has taught at BAA since 2000 and continues in this position today.

Jim Woodside, Walnut Hill, Drawing

Jim Woodside, an exhibiting artist, has been a teacher and the Director of Visual Art at Walnut Hill since 1988 and continues in this position today.

DATA COLLECTION AND FIRST-LEVEL ANALYSIS

We documented classes that ranged from 1.5 to 3 hours in length: 22 classes at the Boston Arts Academy and 16 classes at Walnut Hill. Nine sessions were 3-hour, 9th-grade classes at the Boston Arts Academy; seven were 1.5-hour 9th-grade classes at the Boston Arts Academy; 16 were 3-hour mixed 9th- through 12th-grade introductory classes at Walnut Hill; and six were 3-hour 12th-grade classes at the Boston Arts Academy. This yielded a total of 103.5 hours of classroom observation. Data included videos with audio shot by our project videographer that focused on the teacher, field notes by a second researcher-observer, and memos written by the observing researcher immediately following each observation. Videos captured teachers talking to students but not conversations between students.

After each filming, we created video clips of events in the classroom that we wanted to learn more about, based on our review of the memo and on debriefing conversations between the videographer and observer. We wrote a standard interview protocol that we revised for each class to suit the circumstances, and we followed up with an audiotaped interview of the teacher about a week after the filming. During interviews one researcher viewed clips together with the teacher and probed what was going on. Additional data were collected in the form of photographs of student work and curriculum documents and/or program descriptions.

DATA ANALYSIS

Video and audio recordings of the interviews were transcribed. Analysis triangulated video and audio transcripts, videos, photos of student work and curriculum documents, and field notes and memos. Iteratively, we looked for patterns of interactions and uses of time and space, both within each teacher's classes and across all five teachers. This resulted in identification and then definition of the Studio Structures, which are based on characteristics observed across the teachers.

We then segmented transcripts of the documented classes into categories for each Studio Structure. Next, we reviewed the Students-at-Work segments of four classes we selected randomly as code-development cases, in order to develop categories of what we saw being taught. We looked for patterns in the transcripts and then developed *in vivo* concepts that described how each teacher talked about their intentions for student learning. Next, our research team collapsed the teachers' personal concepts into fewer categories, resulting in 11 codes for intended learning and a code we called "other." Through iterative comparisons across codes within the four code-development classes, our team of five researchers created a coding manual with examples from the transcripts that we used to guide the next phase of analysis.

At this point, we randomly selected and assigned about 35% of the remaining classes (12) to three members of our research team, two of whom coded each class. During this process, we continued to bring examples that confused us to our meetings to refine our codebook. When analysis of the 12 classes was complete, we tested the reliability across coders and found that it was strong (Cohen's Kappa between 0.7 and 0.9). We then randomly divided the remaining 22 classes among the three coders so that each coder analyzed seven or eight classes.

As we began discussing our preliminary findings with others in the field, we eliminated the "other" category and, in three cases, combined two codes (Technique and Studio Practice were combined into "Develop Craft"; Question and Explain and Evaluate were combined into "Reflect"; and Domain and Collaborate were combined into

"Understand Art Worlds: Domain and Communities"). The resulting eight categories of "what" art teachers intend to teach became the eight Studio Habits of Mind presented in the chapters in Part II.

UPDATES TO THE RESEARCH

Since the initial publication of the framework, we have updated the research in a number of ways. Some of this updating has been through our ongoing collaboration with partners and through the use of the Studio Thinking Framework in research projects detailed in Chapters 16 and 19. We have been working with this data and these ideas for two decades in varied ways that have informed our thinking in many ways. In what follows, we identify the specific additional activities we undertook to support the 2nd and 3rd editions of this book.

To support the development of the Studio Structure of Exhibition, we reviewed our initial data collection for accounts of exhibitions and then interviewed teachers from each school about their exhibition practices and documentation of specific examples of exhibitions, and observed student exhibitions. To support accounts of student learning in relation to teaching, we conducted dozens of portfolio interviews with students about their learning, including students we interviewed multiple times over 4 years.

For Part IV of the 3rd edition, we conducted 13 interviews to support our understanding of how Studio Thinking is being used in contemporary practice. The seven artist-teachers profiled in Chapter 17 were selected from a range of people we knew and those recommended to us as educators using Studio Thinking. We purposively selected participants who represented a range of geographical and pedagogical approaches and contexts. The three educators profiled in the assessment chapter were individuals we had collaborated with over time and who we knew had rich assessment practices. Through emails, interviews, reviews of documents and reflections on collaborations we gathered and documented examples of how Studio Thinking had been used in other settings that are represented in Chapter 19. After interviews were conducted, we sent all materials to the educators for them to iteratively review until our writing accurately represented their perspective.

Kim Sheridan's research underpinning Chapter 16 was supported by the National Endowment for the Arts (NEA) under Grant No. 1844329-38-C-18, a cooperative research agreement for the MasonARC research lab. Any opinions, findings, and conclusions or recommendations expressed in this material are those of the authors and do not necessarily reflect the views of the NEA. The data analysis process can be reviewed in Sheridan, Zhang, and Konopasky (2022).

References

Alexander, D. (2010, October). *Ballet dance and the develop-ment of eight habits of mind*. National Dance Education Organization annual conference, Tempe, AZ.

Alexander, D., & Cassell, Y. (2011, October). *Researching modern dance and the development of eight habits of mind*. National Dance Education Organization annual confer-ence, Minneapolis, MN.

Amabile, T. M. (1996). *Creativity in context*. Westview Press.

Baumeister, R. F., & Vohs, K. D. (2007). Self-regulation, ego depletion, and motivation. *Social and Personality Psychol-ogy Compass, 1*, 1–14.

Bequette, J. W., & Bequette, M. B. (2012). A place for art and de-sign education in the STEM conversation. *Art Education, 65*(2), 40–47. doi: 10.1080/00043125.2012.11519167

Blythe, T., & the researchers and teachers of the Teaching for Understanding Project. (1998). *Teaching for understand-ing guide*. Jossey-Bass.

Clark, I. N. (2011). Supporting artists in the gallery: The role of the museum educator at an art college [MALS thesis]. Skidmore College.

Clark, K., & Sheridan, K. (2010). Game design through men-toring and collaboration. *Journal of Educational Multime-dia and Hypermedia, 19*(2), 125–145.

Council of Arts Accrediting Associations. (2007). *Achieve-ment and quality: Higher education in the arts*. www.arts-accredit.org/wp-content/uploads/2016/04/Achievem entandQuality-2007SepDoc.pdf

Csikszentmihalyi, M. (1990). *Flow: The psychology of optimal ex-perience*. Harper and Row.

Douglas, K., & Jaquith, D. B. (2009). *Engaging learners through artmaking: Choice-based art education in the classroom*. Teachers College Press.

Dweck, C. S. (2000). *Self-theories: Their role in motivation, per-sonality, and development*. Psychology Press.

Efland, A. (1976). The school art style: A functional analysis. *Studies in Art Education, 17*(2), 37–44.

Efland, A. (1983). School art and its social origins. *Studies in Art Education, 24*(3), 149–157.

Eisner, E. (2002). *The arts and the creation of mind*. Yale Uni-versity Press.

Eisner, E. (2004). *What can education learn from the arts about the practice of education? International Journal of Educa-tion and the Arts, 5*(4), 1–13.

Ellis, A. (2003, June). *Valuing culture*. Paper presented at con-ference entitled Valuing Culture, National Theatre Studio, London. www.demos.co.uk/catalogue/valuingculturesp eeches/

Emirbayer, M., & Mische, A. (1998). What is agency? *Ameri-can Journal of Sociology, 103*(4), 962–1023.

Ericsson, K. A. (Ed.). (1996). *The road to excellence: The acqui-sition of expert performance in the arts and sciences, sports, and games*. Lawrence Erlbaum.

Ericsson, K. A., Nandagopal, K., & Roring, R. W. (2009). Toward a science of exceptional achievement: Attaining superior performance through deliberate practice. *Annals of New York Academy of Science, 1172*, 199–217.

Freedman, K., Heijnen, E., Kallio-Tavin, M., Kárpáti, A., & Papp, L. (2013). Visual Culture Learning Communities: How and what students come to know in informal art groups. *Studies in Art Education, 54*(2), 103–115. www .jstor.org/stable/24468178

Gettings, M. (2016). Putting it all together: STEAM, PBL, scientific method, and the Studio Habits of Mind. *Art Education, 69*(4), 10–11. doi: 10.1080/00043125.2016 .1176472

Getzels, J., & Csikszentmihalyi, M. (1976). *The creative vision: A longitudinal study of problem finding in art*. John Wiley & Sons.

Giudici, C., Rinaldi C., & Krechevsky, M. (Eds.) (2001). *Mak-ing learning visible: Children as individual and group learners*. Reggio Emilia, Italy: Reggio Children.

Goldstein, T. R. (2021, September). *Teaching body awareness and self understanding through acting classes in adolescence* [Paper presentation]. XXVI International Association for Empirical Aesthetics Virtual Conference, London, UK.

Goldstein, T. R., & Thompson, B. (2019, April). *The cognitive, social, and emotional skills taught in an adolescent theatre classroom* [Poster]. Society for Research in Child Develop-ment Biennial Meeting, Baltimore, MD.

Goldstein, T. R., & Young, D. (2019, August). *Theatrical thinking: A mixed methods study of teacher perceptions and actual classroom strategies* [Presentation]. American Psy-chological Association Annual Convention, Chicago, IL.

Gombrich, E. H. (2000). *Art and illusion*. Princeton Univer-sity Press. Orig. publ. 1960.

Goodman, N. (1968). *Languages of art: An approach to a theo-ry of symbols*. Bobbs-Merrill.

Groff, L. (2015, March 23). Interview with Christopher Chip-pendale. *Painting Perceptions*. https://paintingperceptions .com/interview-with-christopher-chippendale/

Gude, O. (2004). Postmodern principles: In search of a 21st century art education. *Art Education, 57*(1), 6–14.

Halverson, E. R., & Sheridan, K. (2014). The maker movement in education. *Harvard Educational Review, 84*(4), 495–504.

Hetland, L., Cajolet, S., & Music, L. (2010). Documentation in the visual arts: Embedding a common language from research. *Theory Into Practice, 49*(1), 55–63.

Hetland, L., Winner, E., Veenema, S., & Sheridan, K. (2007). *Studio thinking: The real benefits of visual arts education.* New York: Teachers College.

Hetland, L., Winner, E., Veenema, S., & Sheridan, K. (2013). *Studio thinking 2: The real benefits of visual arts education.* New York: Teachers College.

Hockney, D. (2001). *Secret knowledge: Rediscovering the lost techniques of the old masters.* London: Thames and Hudson, Ltd.

Hogan, J., Hetland, L., Jaquith, D. B., & Winner, E. (2018). *Studio thinking from the start: The K–8 art educator's handbook.* Teachers College Press.

Hogan, J., & Winner, E. (2019). Habits of mind as a framework for assessment in music education. In D. J. Elliott, M. Silverman, & G. McPherson (Eds.), *The Oxford handbook of philosophical and qualitative assessment in music education.* Oxford University.

Holland, D., Lachicotte, W., Skinner, D., & Cain, C. (1998). *Agency and identity in cultural worlds.* Harvard University Press.

Ito, M., Baumer, S., Bittanti, M., boyd, d., Cody, R., Stephenson, B. H., Horst, H. A., Lange, P. G., Mahendran, D., Martinez, K. Z., Pascoe, C. J., Perkel, D., Robinson, L, Sims, C., & Tripp, L. (2010). *Hanging out, messing around, and geeking out: Kids living and learning with new media.* MIT Press.

Jaquith, D. B., & Hathaway, N. E. (2012). *The learner-directed classroom: Developing creative thinking skills through art.* Teachers College Press.

Kent, C., & Steward, J. (2008). *Learning by heart: Teachings to free the creative spirit.* Allworth. [Orig. publ. 1992]

Konopasky, A.W., & Sheridan, K. M. (2015, April). *An experimental study comparing two educational approaches to making with simple circuits* [Paper presentation]. American Educational Research Association Annual Meeting, Chicago, IL.

Konopasky, A.W., & Sheridan, K. M. (2016). Towards a diagnostic toolkit for the language of agency. *Mind, Culture, and Activity, 23*(2), 108–123.

Lampert, M. (2003). *Teaching problems and the problems of teaching.* Yale University Press.

Lave, J., & Wenger, E. (1991). *Situated learning: Legitimate peripheral participation.* Cambridge University Press.

Lenhart, A., & Madden, M. (2005). *Teen content creators and consumers.* Pew Research Center. www.pewresearch.org/internet/2005/11/02/teen-content-creators-and-consumers/

Macur, J. (2012, August 1.) On rowing team, smallest body has the voice of authority. *The New York Times.* www.nytimes.com/2012/08/02/sports/olympics/voice-of-authority-directs-us-womens-rowing-team.html?src=me&ref=general

Marshall, J., & D'Adamo, K. (2011). Art practice as research in the classroom: A new paradigm in art education. *Art Education, 64*(5), 12–18. doi: 10.1080/00043125.2011.11519139

Marshall, J., & D'Adamo, K. (2018). Art studio as thinking lab: Fostering metacognition in art classrooms. *Art Education, 71*(6), 9–16.

Marshall, J., Stewart, C., & Thulson, A. (2021). *Teaching contemporary art with young people: Themes in art for K–12 classrooms.* Teachers College Press.

Nasir, N. S., & Cooks, J. (2009). Becoming a hurdler: How learning settings afford identities. *Anthropology & Education Quarterly, 40*(1), 41–61. doi: 10.1111/j.1548-1492.2009.01027.x

National Art Education Foundation. (2016). *Learning in a visual age: The critical importance of visual arts education* [Orig. publ. 2009]. www.arteducators.org/advocacy-policy/learning-in-a-visual-age

National Coalition for Core Arts Standards. (2014). *National visual arts standards.* Author.

Peppler, K. A. (2010). Media arts: Arts education for a digital age. *Teachers College Record, 112*(8), 2118–2153.

Perkins, D. N. (1986). Thinking frames. *Educational Leadership, 43*(8), 4–10.

Perkins, D. N. (1992). *Smart schools: From training memories to educating minds.* Free Press.

Perkins, D. N. (1994). *The intelligent eye: Learning to think by looking at art.* J. Paul Getty Museum.

Perkins, D. N. (2010). *Making learning whole: How seven principles of learning can transform education.* Jossey-Bass.

Perkins, D. N., & Salomon, G. (2012). Knowledge to go: A motivational and dispositional view of transfer. *Educational Psychologist, 47*(3), 248–258. https://doi.org/10.1080/00461520.2012.693354

Perkins, D. N., Jay, E., & Tishman, S. (1993). Beyond abilities: A dispositional theory of thinking. *Merrill-Palmer Quarterly, 39*(1), 1–21.

Pike, A. W. G., et al. (2012). U-Series dating of Paleolithic art in 11 caves in Spain. *Science, 336*, 1409.

Reeve, J. (2016). Autonomy-supportive teaching: What it is, how to do it. In J. C. K. Wang, W. C. Liu, & R. M. Ryan (Eds.), *Motivation in educational research: Translating theory into classroom practice* (pp. 129–152). Springer.

Ritchhart, R., & Perkins, D. N. (2005). Learning to think: The challenges of teaching thinking. In K. J. Holyoke & R. G. Morrison (Eds.), *The Cambridge handbook of thinking and reasoning* (pp. 775–802). Cambridge University Press.

Ryan, R. M., & Deci, E. L. (2000). Self-determination theory and the facilitation of intrinsic motivation, social development, and well-being. *American Psychologist, 55*(1), 68–78. doi: 10.1037/0003-066X.55.1.68

Sawyer, R. K. (2017). Teaching creativity in art and design studio classes: A systematic literature review. *Educational research review, 22*, 99–113.

Seidel, S., Tishman, S., Winner, E., Hetland, L., & Palmer, P. (2009). *The qualities of quality: Understanding excellence in arts education.* Project Zero, Harvard Graduate School of Education. www.wallacefoundation.org/knowledge-center/arts-education/arts-classroom-instruction/Documents/Understanding-Excellence-in-Arts-Education.pdf

Sheridan, K. M. (2011). Envision and Observe: Using the Studio Thinking Framework for learning and teaching in digital arts. *Mind, Brain, and Education, 5,* 19–26. doi: 10.1111/j.1751-228X.2011.01105.x

Sheridan, K. M. (2017). Studio Thinking in early childhood. In M. J. Narey (Ed.), *Multimodal perspectives of language, literacy, and learning in early childhood* (pp. 213–232). Springer International Publishing. doi: 10.1007/978-3-319-44297-6_11

Sheridan, K. M. (2020). Constructionism in Art Studios. In N. Holbert, M. Berland, and Y. Kafai (Eds.), *Designing constructionist futures: The art, theory, and practice of learning designs* (pp. 323–330). MIT Press.

Sheridan, K. M., Clark, K., & Williams, A. (2013). Designing games, designing roles: A study of youth agency in an informal education program. *Urban Education 48*(5), 734–758.

Sheridan, K. M., Daley, H., Byers, C. C., & Zhang, X. (2019). Making connections work: An initial analysis of the identity claims of parents and children in a hands-on making workshop. In *Proceedings of FabLearn 2019* (pp. 189–192).

Sheridan, K. M., & Gardner, H. (2012). Artistic development: Three essential spheres. In A. Shimamura & S. Palmer (Eds.), *Aesthetic science: Connecting minds, brains, and experience* (pp. 277–296). Oxford University Press.

Sheridan, K. M., Halverson, E. R., Litts, B., Brahms, L., Jacobs-Priebe, L., & Owens, T. (2014). Learning in the making: A comparative case study of three makerspaces. *Harvard Educational Review, 84*(4), 505–531.

Sheridan, K. M., & Konopasky, A. (2016). Designing for resourcefulness in a community-based makerspace. In K. Peppler, E. Halverson, & Y. B. Kafai (Eds.), *Makeology: Makerspaces as learning environments* (pp. 30–46). Routledge.

Sheridan, K. M., Zhang, X., & Konopasky, A. W. (2022). Strategic shifts: How studio teacher use direction and support to build learner agency in the figured world of visual Art. *Journal of the Learning Sciences,* 1–29. https://doi.org/10.1080/10508406.2021.1999817

Solso, R. L. (2001). Brain activities in an expert versus a novice artist: An fMRI study. *Leonardo, 34*(1), 31–34.

State Education Agency Directors of Arts Education. (2014). *National core arts standards.* Author.

Steadman, P. (2002). *Vermeer's camera.* Oxford, UK: Oxford University Press.

Stevenson, H. (1994). *The learning gap: Why our schools are failing and what we can learn from Japanese and Chinese education.* Simon & Schuster.

Stigler, J. W., & Hiebert, J. (1999). *The teaching gap: Best ideas from the world's teachers for improving education in the classroom.* Free Press.

Tabak, I., & Baumgartner, E. (2004). The teacher as partner: Exploring participant structures, symmetry, and identity work in scaffolding. *Cognition and Instruction, 22*(4), 393–429.

Tishman, S., Jay, E., & Perkins, D. N. (1993). Teaching thinking dispositions: From transmission to enculturation. *Theory Into Practice, 32,* 147–153.

Tishman, S., Perkins, D. N., & Jay, E. (1995). *The thinking classroom: Learning and teaching in a culture of thinking.* Allyn & Bacon.

Vygotsky, L. (1978). *Mind in society: The development of higher psychological processes.* Harvard University Press.

Vygotsky, L. (1984). *Thought and language.* MIT Press.

Winner, E., & Hetland, L. (Eds.). (2000). The arts and academic achievement: What the evidence shows. *Journal of Aesthetic Education, 34*(3–4), 3–307.

Winner, E., & Hetland, L. (2007, Sept. 2). Art for our sake. *Boston Globe,* pp. E1–2. Reprinted in *Arts Education Policy Review, 109*(5), 29–32 (2008, May/June); and in *National Arts Education Association News, 1* (2007).

Winner, E., & Simmons, S. (Eds.). (1992). *Arts PROPEL: A handbook for visual arts.* Project Zero at the Harvard Graduate School of Education and Educational Testing Service.

Wiske, M. S. (1998). *Teaching for understanding: Linking research with practice.* Jossey-Bass.

Index

Woodside, Jim (teacher); Abstraction Project, 106–109, 164; agency in the studio and, 127; classroom furniture arrangement, 13–14; Contour Drawing Project, 26, 112–113, 164; Critique, 15, 25, 56, 110, 111, 112–115; Cubism Project, 30, 87–90, 164; Demonstration-Lectures, 21–22, 60–62, 87–88, 98, 99; Develop Craft, 34–35, 39–40; End-of-Term Exhibitions, 120–121, 164; Engage and Persist, 8; Exhibition, 120–122; Express, 53–56; Figures in Evocative Space Project, 53–56, 85, 113–115, 127, 164; individualizing curriculum, 23; keeping a portfolio, 34–35; Korean Students Show in Korea, 121–122, 164; Light and Boxes Project, 21–22, 34–35, 60–64, 164; modeling by, 16, 21–22; Observe, 60–64; organization of space for materials, 13–14; peer interactions, 15; profile, 165; project list, 164; punctuated studio class shape, 26; Reflect, 34–35, 56, 63–64, 85, 88–90; A Senior Show, 121, 164; Students-at-Work sessions, 62–63, 88, 106–109; studio lighting, 14; Studio Practice, 34–35; teacher-student interactions and, 14; Understand Art Worlds, 84, 85, 94, 99; wall space and, 13–14

Young, D., 1, 157

Zhang, X., 123–124, 162, 166
Zones of proximal development (Vygotsky), 18

About the Authors

Kimberly M. Sheridan is an associate professor in Educational Psychology in the College of Education and Human Development and in Art Education in the College of Visual and Performing Arts at George Mason University. She is a codirector of MasonARC, the George Mason University Arts Research Center (https://masonarc.gmu.edu/), a National Endowment for the Arts–funded research lab. She received her doctorate in Human Development and Psychology from the Harvard University Graduate School of Education. Trained in the visual arts and developmental psychology, her research focuses on how contexts and technologies shape learning, with a particular focus on new media and arts learning. She uses design-based research methods to conceptualize and measure learner agency, and to understand how learning environments can be designed to support agency. She has published widely in scholarly journals and her research has been funded by the Fulbright Program, the National Endowment for the Arts, the National Science Foundation, the Institute of Museum and Library Services, and the Spencer Foundation.

Shirley Veenema brings the perspectives of a researcher at Project Zero from 1987 through 2007, an art teacher (elementary and high school), and an artist. Most recently, she taught art at Phillips Academy, Andover, Massachusetts. In addition to the arts, research projects have included portfolio assessment, technology, and schools using multiple intelligences theory. Originally focused on printmaking and media, much of her current work as an artist is in mixed media and artists' books. A recent handmade book (*Witches, Magic & Early New England*) tells a story that culminates in the Salem, Massachusetts, witch trials. The 5-part book, produced as part of the Digital Public Library of America Community Representative program to showcase what makers can do with the DPLA online collections, has interested educators looking for alternative ways of assessing student understanding.

Ellen Winner is Professor Emerita of Psychology and Neuroscience at Boston College and Senior Research Associate at Project Zero, Harvard Graduate School of Education. She served as President of APA's Division 10, Psychology and the Arts, in 1995–1996, and received the Rudolf Arnheim Award for Outstanding Research by a Senior Scholar in Psychology and the Arts from Division 10 in 2000. She is a fellow of APA Division 10 and of the International Association of Empirical Aesthetics. She is the author of numerous articles and books. Her most recent books are *How Art Works: A Psychological Exploration* (Oxford University Press, 2018) and *An Uneasy Guest in the Schoolhouse: Art Education From Colonial Times to a Promising Future* (Oxford University Press, 2021); the next will be *The Child as Visual Artist* (Cambridge University Press, 2022, as part of the Cambridge University Press Elements Series).

Lois Hetland, EdD, Professor Emerita at the Massachusetts College of Art and Design, trained in music and visual arts and then taught K–12 students for 17 years. She is coauthor of *Studio Thinking 2: The Real Benefits of Visual Arts Education* (2013) and *Studio Thinking from the Start: The K–8 Art Educator's Handbook* (2018). From 1992 to 2011, she worked with Project Zero, Harvard Graduate School of Education, where she conducted research (1992–2000), was Founding Director of The Project Zero Classroom Summer Institute (1996–2005), and was a Principal Investigator (2001–2011). She led research and professional development through USDOE-funded projects in Alameda County, CA (2003–2011); collaboratively conducted 10 meta-analytic reviews analyzing effects of arts learning on academic outcomes (1997–2000); and was Co-Principal Investigator on *Qualities of Quality: Understanding Excellence in Arts Education* (2005–2008). She also co-led the Studio Thinking Network, a monthly online conversation among U.S. and international educators who use the Studio Thinking Framework, from 2012–2014. Currently, she is Co-PI on an NSF-funded project integrating art with the science of extreme weather: *Cool Science: Art as a Vehicle for Intergenerational Learning*.